on
DIVERSITY

OTHER BOOKS BY RUSSELL JACOBY

Bloodlust: On the Roots of Violence from Cain and Abel to the Present (Free Press, 2011)

Picture Imperfect: Utopian thought for an Anti-Utopian Age (Columbia University Press, 2005)

The End of Utopia: Politics and Culture in the Age of Apathy (Basic Books, 1999)

Dogmatic Wisdom: How the Culture Wars Divert Education and Distract America (Doubleday, 1994)

The Last Intellectuals: American Culture in the Age of Academe (Basic Books, 1987; new edition by Basic Books, 2000)

The Repression of Psychoanalysis: Otto Fenichel and the Political Freudians (Basic Books, 1983)

Dialectic of Defeat: Contours of Western Marxism (Cambridge University Press, 1981)

Social Amnesia: A Critique of Contemporary Psychology (Beacon Press, 1975; Transaction Publishers, 1997)

on DIVERSITY

The Eclipse of the Individual in a Global Era

RUSSELL JACOBY

seven stories press
new york • london • oakland

A SEVEN STORIES PRESS FIRST EDITION

Seven Stories Press
140 Watts Street
New York, NY 10013
sevenstories.com

Library of Congress Cataloging in Publication Data has been applied for.

ISBN 978-1-60980-979-9 (hardcover)
ISBN 978-1-60980-980-5 (ebook)

Printed in the USA.

9 8 7 6 5 4 3 2 1

For Dice—not only different with an extra chromosome, but a heart of a heartless world

Contents

Acknowledgments

In my previous books I've been chagrined by the brevity of my acknowledgments: no lengthy roster of esteemed colleagues and devoted friends or rollcall of foundations, institutions and conferences that feted the author. Alas, my short list has barely changed over the decades. To Cristina Nehring, my passionate love, who attended the manuscript with her usual scrupulousness, my profound gratitude. To Paul Breines who gave me the benefit of his unvarnished comments, I owe much. I am indebted to Brian Morton, who egged me on and helped find me a publisher; and to William Hackman for his editorial acumen. I want to thank Eliott Eisenberg for his valuable reflections and references over the years; and I also want to salute two steadfast interlocutors: my sister, Wini Breines, and my loyal friend Whitney Green, who both probably disagree with much, if not everything, in these pages. I thank Dan Simon and Noah Kumin of Seven Stories for their support and professionalism, and Noah in particular for his editorial savviness. I take my hat off to Michael Tencer, my copyeditor. Finally, I am grateful to the UCLA Department of History for sustaining me for over two decades. The Eugen Weber Travel Fund enabled visits to European libraries and collections.

CHAPTER ONE

The Myth of Diversity

"I'm an individual—like everyone else!" I spotted this slogan on a cheap T-shirt on Venice Beach in Los Angeles. It captures the counterintuitive thrust of this book. In the age of mass marketing we boast of our individuality. In the age of globalization—the T-shirt was probably made in Pakistan or Vietnam—we announce our uniqueness. How can these coexist? How can we be both completely plugged in and completely separate? The diversity idea—or rhetoric or jargon—presents the same issues. It celebrates variety in a world that undermines it. Globalization knits the world together into one vast market. We become more alike—and simultaneously we proclaim our differences. Can both be true?

In recent decades the cult of diversity has swept the land. Virtually everybody practices it. Virtually everyone endorses it. Diversity spells decency and openness. Nowadays politicians, CEOs, and police chiefs call for diversity. In the universities, projects and programs pile up.[1] We have diversity initiatives, statements, requirements, training, and courses—even diversity officers, who monitor violations of diversity. We teach it, we advertise it, we praise it. To criticize diversity is to invite ostracism; you might as well climb on a desk and yell, "I am a racist and a fanatic!"[2]

The diversity enterprise has grown so vast it is difficult to know where it starts and where it ends. One thing is clear: Our obsession with diversity is relatively new. One marker might be the 1930s classic *Encyclopedia of the Social Sciences*, which was backed by virtually every scholarly organization and whose contributors included the leading lights of the academy. Its fifteen volumes include no entry for "diversity." Its comprehensive 150-page index has no reference to it.[3] Even a five-volume dictionary of the "history of ideas" from the 1970s has no entry for diversity.[4]

Now encyclopedias and handbooks exclusively devoted to diversity tumble off the presses. Diversity studies has become a minor industry. The editor of the new *Routledge International Handbook of Diversity Studies* celebrates the "outpouring of academic work surrounding diversity." The handbook has 41 contributors writing on subjects like "The Diversity of Milieu in Diversity Studies" and "Religious Differentiation and Diversity in Discourse and Practice."[5] An *Encyclopedia of Diversity in Education* runs four volumes and includes 700 entries.[6] A keyword search of diversity of a university library catalog kicks out almost 900 books published in a single year.[7]

Whence comes the creature? No one seems to know. Peter Wood, in his *Diversity: The Invention of a Concept*, writes that before the 1978 Supreme Court decision in *Regents of the University of California v. Bakke*, diversity was a "fairly marginal idea."[8] In Bakke, Justice Lewis Powell, writing the majority opinion, suggested that universities have a legitimate interest in seeking diversity, which might include racial diversity. In making this argument Powell leaned heavily on a two-page Harvard admissions document, which noted that the applications for admission to Harvard "greatly exceed" the available places; and that by test numbers, high school records, and recommendations, almost all were qualified for acceptance.

If only the top scorers were admitted, the admissions document claims, a monochromatic class would show up in Harvard Square. "For the past 30 years" the admissions committee has believed that the vitality of the educational experience would suffer without variety; "diversity adds an essential ingredient to the educational process." However, fifteen or twenty years ago "diversity meant students from California, New York, and Massachusetts; city dwellers and farm boys." This definition occasioned "very few ethnic or racial minorities" on the Harvard quad. "In recent years Harvard College has expanded the concept of diversity to include students from disadvantaged economic, racial and ethnic groups."[9] The formulation was brilliant. It avoided all red flags about racial quotas. It allowed admissions committees to discount scores and grades to admit someone in the name of diversity. It offered a broad idea of diversity that few could contest. It would have a fantastic run, which continues to this day.

Hatched in universities, diversity as a demand and as rhetoric has conquered the cultural world. Even the simplest roadmap of diversity would be endlessly complex. To begin, what is not a sign of diversity? Are race, poverty, and Asian Americanhood equally diverse? What about language spoken, religion, age, sexual orientation, income, and appearance? Or tallness? Left-handedness? And what about political allegiance? Some conservatives have turned the liberal diversity argument on its head. They have argued that college faculties dominated by left-leaning professors lack political diversity; and they have called for affirmative action for conservatives to achieve political parity.[10] Why not? Every year a new group pops up demanding representation in the name of diversity. One problem with the diversity jargon emerges: Diversity loses all meaning as it balloons. The term becomes so lax that everything and anything signifies diversity.

But a more central issue never aired by diversity champions or their critics needs to be broached. The world is not becoming more but less diverse. The eclipse of diversity and its consequences are the subjects of this book. The religion of diversity is a response to its decline; it is the new opiate of the people—or at least of the people's representatives. In a handleless world, it gives people a handle or an identity. Of course, this is not a new phenomenon. Many immigrants to the United States became more attached to their ethnic identity even as they assimilated. Decades ago the American historian Marcus Lee Hansen posited this as an almost universal process. The second-generation immigrant felt caught between an old and new world. But the more comfortable third generation advertises an old-world identity. "What the son wished to forget the grandson wishes to remember."[11] Yet the grandson—or granddaughter—has already surrendered the pith of old-world identity, which shrinks to symbols and buttons. "Kiss Me. I'm Italian."

The process that affected immigrants affects almost all today; and as people become less culturally different, they fetishize their differences. The real trend today is globalization, which signifies modernization, even American-style homogenization. We increasingly act, think, and consume like everyone else. The ironic slogan of "I'm an individual—like everyone else!" captures a truth. We differ in pose—and resemble each other in fact. We diverge in lifestyle and converge in life.

Evidently, we enter the domain of vast generalizations, but this applies to the exponents of diversity as well. To the critic, of course, belongs the task of challenging what many see as self-evident: that we live in an increasingly multicultural and diverse world. How can this be doubted? A million speeches, advertisements, and books proclaim it. Our eyes confirm it. Corporations broadcast it. "At Bank of America, we realize the power of our people and value our differences—in thought, style, sexual orientation, gender identity, culture, ethnicity and experience—recognizing that our diversity makes us a stronger company." Microsoft "capitalizes on the diversity of our people," which is our "increasingly global and diverse customer base" and our diverse employees, which it itemizes as Asians, Blacks, Disabled, Gay-Lesbian-Bisexual and Transgender, Hispanic/Latino, Parents, and Women. Professors join in: "The most certain prediction that we can make about almost any modern society is that it will be more diverse a generation from now than it is today," states the Harvard political scientist Robert D. Putnam.[12]

But what is this vaunted diversity? For starters, diversity talk today is group talk. By contrast, I concentrate in this book on the fate of the individual, not the group. No doubt, individual and group are inextricably related. People are not born alone; nor do they raise themselves. We are social beings. To have any meaning, however, the individual must be more than a group envoy; and for groups to differ in any significant way, they must be composed of individuals who differ from one group to another. But what if individuals are losing their singularity? How much do groups diverge if individuals that constitute them resemble each other? Moreover, how distinct are these groups if they share identical aims, which usually they do? Groups parade their diversity as they march in formation toward the same goal, American-style prosperity. Their ambitions may be warranted—why should any group be excluded from the benefits of success?—but signify that diversity is an ideology, not a reality. Each group wants to partake of the same good life with the same accoutrements.

For instance, Asian American actors want more roles in Hollywood films and American television.[13] Fine. But only in the loosest sense does this entail more diversity. Indeed, it is almost the reverse. The legitimate demand here—and of most outside groups clamoring for representation—is to join the mainstream and enjoy its benefits. Whatever the group and whatever the context—African Americans, Latinos, disabled people, women, immigrants—the issue is always their underrepresentation; and the implicit or explicit argument is that they perform equal to any other people.

Compare this common situation with the less typical one where groups stand outside the mainstream, and only want to stay outside. We do not hear complaints from the Amish or Hasidic Jews of underrepresentation. They wish to remain apart, rare exemplars of difference that seek to remain different. "The Amish are so different," writes Ira Wagler in his memoir, *Growing Up Amish*. The Amish reject cars, trucks, electricity, and telephones—and sometimes indoor plumbing. They speak a variant of German; and throughout his memoir, Wagler refers to outsiders as "the English." He observes of the Amish, "Mostly, they just prefer to be left alone."[14]

"We are different," writes Deborah Feldman in her recent memoir, *Unorthodox*, on leaving the Hasidic community of Brooklyn. That is the reason the Hasids, she believes, dress in such a conspicuous manner, "so both insiders and outsiders will remember the vast chasm that lies between our two worlds." That break is to be maintained, not blurred. Like the Amish, language plays a role in keeping the Hasids apart, since they speak Yiddish and distrust English. Feldman's grandmother warns her that English is "a slow poison." If she speaks or reads it too much, her "soul will be tarnished." The whole goal is to keep the main culture at arm's length. Feldman's teacher admonishes her that "assimilation was the reason for the Holocaust. We try to blend in, and God punishes us for betraying him."[15]

These stances are atypical but are illuminating for that very reason. The Amish and Hasids do not want to "blend in." They incarnate a diversity that gives a lie to its current form, whose adherents only desire to be let in, not left out. To be sure, most people do not want to dispatch their identities—religious, ethnic, sexual, or something else. But these identities devolve into labels and styles that are employed to open doors. The Asian American actors are saying, We are as talented as non–Asian American actors. We want the same roles. If successful, the representation of Asian American actors will increase in theater and cinema, which will "diversify." As praiseworthy as this is, diversity here means equality—different-looking people doing the same things as other people.

Much of this falls under the rubric of what is now called identity politics: your group defines your politics. Once we have seen your membership card, we know your basic orientation. Critics of identity politics have not been lacking but have been sidelined or overwhelmed. In many quarters identity politics is the main show. Diversity in these domains does not mean we have more unique individuals, but more contact between individuals-as-representatives of groups. But individual, not group, diversity is my concern. Diversity in its multiple incarnations turns hollow if the individuals are becoming not less, but more alike. And this is happening.

In a period of political regression, I do not want to be misunderstood about group diversity. All groups deserve representation. To end discrimination in any domain is exemplary. But to halt discrimination under the guise of diversity muddies the waters. The demand for equality or justice does not need cultural enhancements. Sometimes more is less. Nevertheless, I do not want the criticism I offer of diversity to be misconstrued. If the choice is between the KKK's white supremacy and Bank of America's diversity, I stand with the Bank of America; and sometimes this is the choice. When the US president failed to denounce a racist demonstration in Charlottesville, Virginia, leading American corporations took up the cause of diversity and equality. The president's American Manufacturing Council collapsed when its CEOs resigned in protest of the muffled stand of the White House. "Our country's strength stems from its diversity," stated the CEO of Merck Pharmaceuticals in his resignation. Nor was this an isolated case. Walmart objected to an Arkansas bill that would allow businesses to deny service to same-sex couples. "Every day, in our stores," Walmart declared in a statement, "we see firsthand the benefits diversity and inclusion have."[16]

However, the choice is not often between a virulent racism and an anodyne diversity; and even if it were, criticism of the latter should not cease. To abridge thinking in the name of the emergencies that today are permanent reduces it to slogans, perpetual cheerleading or naysaying. The notion that the current crises require a popular front in which liberals cannot criticize liberalism or leftists cannot criticize leftism partakes of a suspect tradition.[17] My object, in any event, is not to criticize the jargon of diversity for something worse, but for something better. To understand what renders diversity ideological is to understand what devitalizes it, an endeavor to realize, not junk it.

The relentless celebration of diversity today overwhelms any skeptics. To posit a decline of diversity seems obviously false. Yet evidence of this fall is everywhere. That it is not more noticed bespeaks both the allure of the diversity ideology and the damage of the intellectual division of labor. The appeal of the ideology taps into a venerable liberal ethos of fraternity that runs from the wildly successful 1955 "Family of Man" photographic exhibition and the equally successful 1985 charity song "We are the World" right into the present, where it is displayed in a thousand ads and promotion videos: the sense that we are all different but all together.[18] If anything, "the family of man" ethos resonates today more widely than ever. In the absence of a distinct program, progressives and leftists redouble their commitment to a variegated fraternity. It has become almost their sole calling card.

The damage caused by intellectual fragmentation is trickier to appraise; and, indeed, part of my project here is to retrieve a story that is known but has not registered with the diversity exponents. The decline of diversity as an empirical fact is well-established in several domains; it is a raison d'être for numerous scholars and associations. For instance, specialists, conferences, and entire fields have taken up the cause of declining biodiversity. This means a reduction of environmental diversity and with it the demise of many species. "I cannot imagine," writes Edward O. Wilson in *The Diversity of Life*, a problem of greater urgency for humanity than "the ongoing loss of biological diversity."[19]

"Biodiversity loss" has accelerated "massively" in recent decades, observe some experts. "Up to 30% of all mammal, bird and amphibian species will be threatened with extinction this century," they declare. "The loss of biodiversity" leads to greater risks of diseases and disturbances as individual species decline.[20] Other scholars draw a direct line between the decline of biodiversity and general health of mankind. "The global loss of biodiversity may lead—directly or indirectly, in the short or long term—to massive loss of health for humankind," state two specialists. They continue, "The alarm bells are ringing throughout the world among ecologists and also among eco-epidemiologists."[21]

Yet the bells that ring to alert us to the threat to biodiversity also ring to celebrate human diversity. Is it possible that humans diversify as the environment homogenizes? That even as the oceans become polluted, the land paved, forests razed, and species eliminated, human variety enlarges? "As industrial-scale farms flourish in the European Union," summarizes a *National Geographic* report, "its fields have grown quiet—robbed of the birds that once filled them with song." Single-crop fields and pesticides decimate the meadow pipits, whinchats, and skylarks. Not only songbirds but also insects decline.[22]

Does this industrial monoculture nourish human polyculture? To be sure, one might argue that no relationship exists between biodiversity and human diversity; and even as the former wanes, the latter waxes. To make this point, one could suggest a category mistake is at work: "diversity" in the environment and "diversity" in human culture refer to two distinct realms. That suggests a dwindling environmental variety has no impact on human diversity. This seems unlikely. The categories might be separate, but they overlap. After all, the whole point of ecology and eco-everything is the interrelationship of the human and natural domains. I return to this subject in the next chapter.

Diversity is a reality: that is obvious. The first sentences of the first chapter of Darwin's *Origin of Species* marvels at "the vast diversity of the plants and animals" across the ages and regions. But diversity is also an ideology; and like any ideology it can mislead and distort. The ideology can blind us to a reality that countermands diversity. Many domains might be examined, but I consider specifically language and clothing in Chapter Two, and childhood in Chapter Three. Each is central to how we live and who we are. They are indexes—and more than indexes—to the diminished diversity in our daily lives. While the importance of language and clothing jumps out, the significance of childhood may not. Yet the experiential platform of diversity is childhood. How we play and imagine informs our ability to experience the world as adults. What if the unplanned elements of childhood diminish? What if the activities of our children become more and more alike?

Diversity is not simply a political or ethnic category. The way we experience the world depends on our orientation to it. Diversity is subjective as well as objective. It relies on an experiential openness, which seems obvious, if difficult to define. What constitutes this openness? A mixture of spontaneity and creativity. Travel, for instance, hardly leads to new experience if the traveler cannot culturally leave home. This is not exactly a new notion. Ralph Waldo Emerson, who did a fair amount of traveling, criticized it as a "fool's paradise." "I have no churlish objection to the circumnavigation of the globe" for art or study, he wrote. But he wondered if travel led to individual growth. "I pack my trunk, embrace my friends, embark on the sea, and at last wake up in Naples; and there beside me is the stern fact, the sad self, unrelenting, identical, that I fled from."[23] A lighter version of this idea can be found in a recent *New Yorker* cartoon in which one woman recounts her travels—not Naples this time, but Tuscany. "Florence was fabulous!" she says to an acquaintance. "Wi-Fi to die for!"

Experiential openness is more than an individual quality or

virtue; it depends on who we are, how we were raised, what constituted our childhood; and this changes over time for society. I suggest that we are witnessing the closing of experiential diversity, itself based on the eclipse of childhood. To get at this, I turn to the Weimar critic Walter Benjamin, who was much interested in childhood, and wrote the autobiographical "Berlin Childhood around 1900." Benjamin elsewhere introduced the notion of the "impoverishment of experience." He wondered whether the dimensions of experience—he was writing in the 1930s—were flattening out. He wondered if we were losing the ability to experience and to recount our experience. The two conjoin. In "The Storyteller," Benjamin asked if storytelling declined because we lacked a certain patience or tranquility: "the art of storytelling is coming to an end." Fewer and fewer people can tell a story or want to hear one.

The storyteller for Benjamin belonged to a pre-industrial age. Rapid shifts subverted the storyteller and what might be called first-person experience: "experience has fallen in value." Newspapers and information overwhelm the narrator who has a quiet tale with a moral. People lived one way before World War I and lived another after. Automobiles, radios, telephones, and film entered everyday life. Society had been overturned. The individual cannot keep up and turns silent. "A generation that had gone to school on a horse-drawn streetcar now stood under the open sky in a countryside in which nothing remained unchanged but the clouds."[24]

To put it in terms I'm using here, the capability to experience diversity atrophies. Continuous assault on the individual, which begins in childhood, leads not to volubility, but the reverse. The individual contracts or withdraws. Without openness, diversity is a dead letter. This openness, the opposite of "the impoverishment of experience," rests on imagination and spontaneity that are themselves grounded in childhood—its rhythms, contours, and play. The universe of childhood is where diversity gets exercise, where it flexes its psychic muscles. Putting aside all the usual qualifications—not everywhere, not all kids—childhood is under siege. The structure of childhood has been dramatically shifting in the last decades. The space, the place, the typical activities of children have been transformed. Impulsive play in the outdoors dwindles as children hurry home to computers or organized activities. Playgrounds seem to be emptying out. Play is changing.

"I live in a neighborhood of several hundred families," writes Joe L. Frost in his essential *A History of Children's Play and Play Environments*. "It is close to a lovely park with a playground and a clear flowing stream." But he finds that children do not go there except on special occasions accompanied by adults. "In fact, they do not play outside. When they exit the school bus in mid-afternoon, they go directly into the house." He notes that in the dozen years he lived there, "I have seen as many as three children playing in the yards or streets only one time, and I have never seen an unattended child in the beautifully wooded neighborhood park."[25]

The consequences for health are many, but also for the ability to imagine and experience diversity. What happens when video entertainment that is designed by adults occupies the time and minds of the young? When the unorganized dimension of childhood fades? What are the implications of the hollowing out of the psychic and physical space of childhood?

To be sure, the threats to childhood are not new. Elegies for lost childhood mark the modern period. Perhaps the classic of the post–World War II years remains Robert Paul Smith's 1957

Where Did You Go? Out. What Did You Do? Nothing, which for the United States captured the moment when unstructured childhood devolved into activities organized by parents. Smith compared his own childhood of the 1920s with that of his offspring of the suburban 1950s and was stunned that his kids and their friends no longer could play by themselves. We kicked cans, he recalls of his childhood; we skipped and hopped and tied ropes. "We sat in boxes; we sat under porches; we sat on roofs; we sat on limbs of trees." In short, "we did a lot of nothing."[26] Those days were ending, as Smith saw it. Children no longer played by themselves or with each other.

Social thinkers joined in. Neil Postman's *The Disappearance of Childhood* dates from 1982. But the fact that the issue has been raised before hardly invalidates it. The refashioning of childhood pastimes, and indeed adult activities, might be accelerating. The warp and woof of experience does not stand outside of history; and as this experience shifts, so does the capacity to experience diversity.

The daily rhythms are altering, not just of infants, but of toddlers, children, pre-teens as well—and everyone else. People are plugged in—and left out. My students text in my classes when I'm ten feet away and stare them in the face. To gauge how experiential openness has contracted across time, choreograph two typically nervous gestures of adults: the once familiar reaching for a pack of cigarettes, pulling out one, lighting, inhaling, and looking up and around; and the now familiar reaching for a cell phone, tapping a code, reading messages, sending messages, reading messages—with head down.

The latter marks progress in health, in the decline of lung cancer, but perhaps regression in openness toward the world. And even the progress of health could be qualified—or, at least, the uptick in pedestrian deaths reveals how people are increasingly encased in themselves and closed off to the world. They walk into cars as they check their messages—or are run over as drivers check theirs. I sometimes greet people with a comment when on a stroll or bicycle. More and more I am met with blank looks. My compatriots hear nothing since they are plugged into earphones. The give-and-take flow of daily life constitutes the bedrock for experiential diversity. If we shut it out, we are left, as Emerson put it, with the unrelenting, identical "sad self."

And there is something else, which might seem a stretch, but addresses a critical issue: the relationship of play and democracy. Does spontaneous play nurture the individual's resources that sustain a liberal democracy? And conversely, does the waning of this play stunt talents essential for everyday citizenship? Several scholars connect play and democracy. When children play with each other they learn to resolve conflicts, if only to keep the activity going. "I quit!" ends the game. To mollify and accept opponents may be a vital lesson for a civil society.

"The opportunity to engage in unsupervised childhood play," writes a political economist, "acts as a school for learning . . . skills required to avoid and resolve the innumerable moments of conflict that fill our daily lives." In an article subtitled "The Importance of Unsupervised Childhood Play for Democracy and Liberalism," Steven Horwitz writes that "such play is central to democracy and the liberal order." The decline of unstructured play bleeds liberal society of something essential. People lose the ability to negotiate disagreements, an aptitude indispensable for civil interchanges. A "coarsening" of everyday life takes place.[27]

··•··

In Chapters Four and Five, I revisit a series of 19th-century thinkers who considered diversity under siege. They valued the individual as the irreducible ground of diversity but feared its eclipse. To use a term that gains currency after them, they worried that individuals were melding into "masses." It is easily forgotten that the great 19th-century liberals such as Alexis de Tocqueville and John Stuart Mill were also among the first critics of diversity. To be more precise, they prized diversity but dreaded its devitalization; they feared a looming uniformity would hollow out diversity, leaving it more a shell than substance. The epigraph to Mill's *On Liberty*, a quote from Wilhelm von Humboldt, accented diversity. It ran, "The grand, leading principle, towards which every argument unfolded in these pages directly converges, is the absolute and essential importance of human development in its richest diversity."

At the same time as Mill quoted Humboldt and celebrated individual development "in its richest diversity," he bemoaned its impoverishment. Mill's great words defending individual dissent from *On Liberty* are well-known: "If all mankind minus one were of one opinion, mankind would be no more justified in silencing that one person than he, if he had the power, would be justified in silencing mankind." But much less recalled is Mill's pivot later in *On Liberty* to the other threat, social uniformity, which he feared undermines individual diversity. For England at least, Mill did not see a danger to individual liberties from the state and its minions. Rather, constrictive social conditions impair robust individuality: this troubled Mill. For individual dissent to flourish, so must individual diversity. "There has been a time when the element of spontaneity and individuality were in excess," he wrote, but that time is past. "Society has now fairly got the better of individuality; and the danger which threatens human nature is not the excess, but the deficiency, of personal impulses and preferences." He called this process the "wearing down into uniformity all that is individual."[28]

These same notions imbue Tocqueville's work, a simultaneous commitment to individual diversity and fear of its future. Like Mill, Tocqueville agonized over the weakness of the individual. He registered again and again an incipient uniformity he found in the New World—and old Europe as well—that debilitates the individual. "Everything is threatening to become so much alike that the peculiar features of each individual will soon be lost in the common physiognomy."[29] This dispirited him about the future of democracy. If the individual has lost independence, then collectively individuals constitute not an informed electorate, but an uninformed mass.

Disparate figures on the left and right—and middle—have weighed in on the fate of the individual. Conflicting prognoses arise from conflicting definitions of the individual. Moreover, some political traditions contest that the individual should be honored at all. Communism of the Soviet ilk prized collectivism and disdained the individual. Soviet lexicons categorized "individualism" as a slur, a bourgeois ailment. For this reason, opposition to Soviet communism extolled the individual. "The surest defense against Evil is extreme individualism, originality of thinking, whimsicality, even—if you will—eccentricity," declared Joseph Brodsky, the poet who was expelled from the Soviet Union.[30] It seems hardly coincidental that another Soviet émigré, Alisa Rosenbaum, better known as Ayn Rand, made individualism a cult. If this makes sense amid authoritarian collectivism, which Marx long ago denounced as "barracks communism," does it make sense elsewhere, where individualism is extolled?

In accord with many 19th-century thinkers, Tocqueville distinguished individuality and individualism, which he viewed as opposites. He had no truck with individualism. For Tocqueville and his cohort, individualism connoted a corrosive ideology, sometimes associated with the French Revolution, sometimes with the modern economy; it signified abandoning larger society for narrow self-interest, which had previously been called egoism.[31] But Tocqueville and others did not surrender the idea of the individual. On the contrary. They held fast to the individual as something more than an isolated monad; they offered an idea of an individual embedded in wider networks. But what is this creature, the individual, or, more precisely, what should this fuller individual look like? Tocqueville never spelled it out.[32] I will follow him in that regard—except to indicate that we need a notion of the individual as more than a passive consumer, as more than a person whose only activity is to choose among items, apps, and goods. The accent in this book, however, is on the countervailing forces that subvert the individual; and the political dangers as the individual loses autonomy. Here, too, I follow Tocqueville, who had feared that a new age of democracy might usher in a new age of barbarism.

Today—again—we see the fragility of democracy, the ease with which it could slide into authoritarian populism. This possibility informs my inquiry. Although the terms were different, the 19th-century critics of diversity understood the peril. This is another reason to reconsider them. Their recognition of the threats separates them from today's diversity celebrants. If contemporary revelers recognize obstacles, they believe they know the source: reactionaries who resist diversity.

They are half right, but only half. Renewed movements across the globe do oppose diversity in name or substance. They pine for a nation of one race or religion. In Hungary the new populists call for ethnic and religious likeness. "I find it very important," declared the Hungarian prime minister, "that we should preserve our ethnic homogeneity."[33] But the issue in these pages is not the revanchist programs, which damn themselves, but the processes that render diversity a facade, not a reality, across the political spectrum. In no way am I drawing a direct line between a decline of diversity and rise of a populism or the re-emergence of the masses. I am indicating a subterranean relationship. Uniformity weakens the individual, which in turn weakens democracy. If individuals lose their singularity, they form a susceptible electorate.

This is not exactly news for Tocqueville scholars, or at least was not in the past. One of the pioneers of Tocqueville scholarship who knew something about fragile democracy framed his study of the Frenchman around diversity's demise. Jacob-Peter Mayer was a German Jewish refugee from Nazism who ended up in the United Kingdom. Among other things, he became a Tocqueville scholar, and editor of the modern French edition of his works. When he first started writing on Tocqueville in the late 1930s, the Frenchman had almost been forgotten. ("Up the present, even in the land of political biography *par excellence* [England] there is not a single book" on Tocqueville, Mayer declared.)

He broke the silence with his 1939 *Prophet of the Mass Age: A Study of Alexis de Tocqueville*.[34] The title suggested Mayer's emphasis. He noted in the preface that his book went to press "a few days" before Hitler's invasion of Poland, which began World War II. Mayer's concern lay with the preceding events, the popular support for fascism that brought Hitler to power. In alerting the world to "the rising of the masses," Tocqueville offers "a prophecy, a burden, and a warning." As a refugee from Germany, Mayer reminded his readers, "It was universal suffrage that led National Socialism to victory. The Weimar Republic was beaten by the ballot, even though force and terrorism later played a part."[35]

These events hardly enter my story here, although Mayer's words are worth pondering. He indicated that Tocqueville identified processes that devitalized the individual and abetted the rise of 20th-century fascism. Tocqueville was not alone in outlining the threats to the individual. By the end of the 19th century, doubts of the individual's backbone intensified. The vocabulary shifted. The talk was not of the beleaguered individual, but the crowd, the mob, and finally the masses, new phenomena that either betray or typify democracy. We meet the masses again in the 20th century. The diversity sceptics, whom I write about in Chapters Four and Five, anticipated these developments. We should heed them.

·•●•·

To argue that the jargon of diversity masks its decline hardly means we live in a world without differences. It does mean that cultural differences, despite the endless hoopla, do not expand, but diminish. It also means political differences contract. Once a left wing offered an alternative to the status quo, but now it compounds its worldwide defeats with self-delusion. Splintered, it promotes diversity as subversion, narcissism as rebellion. Radicals sponsor what has been derided as the "Oppression Olympics," which follow the rules of identity and symbolic politics. In the tournament, the categories run from *black* to *trans* to *fat*. Whoever can check the most labels wins. New brackets emerge regularly.

On campuses, shadowboxing has become a new sport for the politically-challenged. Befogged leftist scholars, who learned from their mentors that everything is text, can no longer distinguish a truncheon from a pencil or a rock from an insult. It's all the same. "Words can be like rape—they can destroy you," declares a Berkeley professor.[36] The logic of this position is clear; first speech, then teaching and writing, fall under suspicion. In a strange transmogrification, campus leftists who once championed free speech now oppose it. They seek to cancel speakers and censor articles they find upsetting.

"We support robust debate," declare the professors without conviction as they call for the university to stop a speech by a right-wing provocateur, who insults liberals, feminists, and minorities, "but we cannot abide by harassment, slander, defamation and hate speech." The administration had to remind its distressed faculty of something called the First Amendment.[37] But to no avail. The First Amendment no longer cuts it. "The Supreme Court is behind the times," opines Nancy Scheper-Hughes, an ahead-of-the-times Berkeley professor. "The First Amendment deserves to be re-looked at." Why? Because hate speech "can harm the central nervous system."

The incontrovertible evidence for this assertion can be found in the publications of Professor Scheper-Hughes and her colleagues, which, sadly, civil libertarians have not read. "The First Amendment," declaims this hip prof, "is ignorant of the vast research on these topics by medical anthropologists, clinical psychologists, and neurological scientists."[38] On Professor Scheper-Hughes's stomping grounds, the First Amendment has become not only a person but a rube ignorant of clinical studies on the injuries caused by free speech. Don't fret. Trained specialists tap vast research to re-hone the First Amendment for the 21st century. The First Amendment 2.0 allows free speech as calibrated by its effect on the central nervous system. Newly hired censors in the just-established All-University Politburo of Intelligence can't wait to begin their work—in fact they are already at their desks.[39]

Elsewhere, real politics shrinks to arguments as to whether the welfare state should be bigger or smaller. Within this framework, passionate and critical differences arise—about health care, environment, education, jobs, guns. These are decisive issues, but all unfold within the structure of the state and economy that virtually everyone accepts. In this sense, fortunately or unfortunately, the best political thinkers got it right, for which they have been roundly criticized. Over an arc of 30 years, from Daniel Bell in *The End of Ideology* to Francis Fukuyama in *The End of History and the Last Man*, they announced that liberal capitalism had triumphed with no alternatives in sight.

"The old passions are spent," announced Bell in the late 1950s after the Soviet invasion of Hungary, which chastened the last Soviet apologists. "The old politico-economic radicalism . . . has lost its meaning." The only possibilities are limited social reforms. Sweeping changes are off the agenda. "Politics offers little excitement," declared Bell.[40] At the end of the 1980s, in the wake of the dissolution of the Soviet Union and its allied regimes, Fukuyama reaffirmed the message: The end of the Soviet regimes signified the "death" of Marxism "as a living ideology of world historical significance." And, like Bell, he lamented the loss. Now we could only tinker with the welfare state. Politics had become boring. "The worldwide ideological struggle that called forth daring, courage, imagination and idealism" was over.[41]

Of course, this is not exactly true. Islamic radicalism has reawakened an ideological fervor. Yet Islamic fundamentalism has not offered any alternative to modernization, except to dismantle it. No matter its numerical strength, radical Islam appeals only to Islamic zealots. The name of the West African radical Islamists, "Boko Haram," or, as it is usually translated, "Western Education is Forbidden," requires little commentary. Is there any future without Western science or knowledge? The ability of Islamic regimes such as Iran or Saudi Arabia and, increasingly, Turkey, to balance religious traditions and Western modernity is still unclear; or, at least, the story is ongoing. In any event, this is not my concern here.

One type of difference increases but can hardly be apprehended by the idiom of diversity. Economic inequality and its consequences intensify, but here the vocabulary of diversity illuminates little. A half-fictional exchange between F. Scott Fitzgerald and Ernest Hemingway addresses the subject and cannot be bettered. To Fitzgerald's remark that "The rich are different from you and me," Hemingway supposedly responded, "Yes, they have more money." This gets it exactly—and can be inverted. "The poor differ from you and me." "Yes, they have less money."[42]

Poverty does not spell diversity, but exclusion. The unemployed, the underemployed, and the unemployable suffer from a lack of money—and everything that goes with it, including good housing, health, and education. A venerable belief posits outsiders as fundamentally different—and often superior. But outsiders may just be insiders without credit cards and nice cars. The poor differ from everyone else by a shortage of resources.

Of late, the accelerating economic inequalities across the world garner much attention—for good reason. But the usual categories of poverty, income, and wealth are revealing. They suggest that the system can be ameliorated without transforming it. For instance, Thomas Piketty's surprise bestseller *Capital in the Twenty-First Century* forcefully takes up economic inequality under rubrics such as "The Capital/Income Ratio" or "Inequality and Concentration."[43] But for him the old working or laboring class hardly exist; the talk is of economic inequalities, not classes. The entry in Piketty's index for "Labor" reads "*See* Capital–labor split." This makes sense because economic inequalities are what interest him, and nothing more. The solutions follow from the approach. To alleviate inequalities, Piketty proposes new tax schemes.[44]

His concerns reflect the distress of those today indignant at the obscene disparities of wealth. They want to flatten out the polarities. The goal is enviable, but diversity is not pertinent.[45] Again, it is more the opposite. The egalitarians seek to enlarge the mainstream. They ask, how we can get more people to escape poverty and join a decent middle class? There is nothing wrong with this aim, but let us be clear-eyed on what it means. The object is to incorporate more people into the establishment.

To the degree the impoverished outsiders are upset, they feel denied what is available to others. But this does not turn them into agents of history, as Japanese organizational theorist Kenichi Ohmae supposes. He blasts Fukuyama in his own *The End of the Nation State*: "Nothing could be further from the truth," he declares of Fukuyama's "the end of history." Ohmae highlights peoples across the globe who aggressively want to "participate *in* history" to gain "a decent life for themselves and a better life for their children." A generation ago they were "voiceless and invisible." Now they have "entered history with a vengeance."[46]

Yes, but under what banner or cause? No one doubts that the globe cries out with unhappy peoples—refugees, the impoverished, the dispossessed. The numbers are daunting. But they have no goal except, understandably, to escape misery and improve their lives. Do the desperate who flee Africa, the Middle East, or Central America have a political program? Even if numerous, they act as individuals, not as subjects of history with a subversive—or any—intent. They do not enter history "with a vengeance." They seek to slip into history without notice. They do not want to overturn but to get a turn.

One need not be a follower of Hegel to concur that history is a "slaughter bench" in which the happiness of states and individuals has been sacrificed, as he stated in his *Philosophy of History*. "Without rhetorical exaggeration, a simple, truthful account of the miseries" that nations and people suffer, he declared, gives rise "to the most hopeless sadness." Nor must one be a Hegelian to find resonance in the question he poses: "To what principle, to what final purpose, have these monstrous sacrifices been offered?"[47] But here we can diverge from the Berlin sage, who believed he glimpsed reason in history's machinations. He may have looked in the mirror, not through the window. It is less reason and more its absence that is visible in history today.

The point here is simple. Once upon a time a specter haunted the world, "the working class," which represented not inequality or poverty, but a different political system. I do not raise this in the name of lost causes, but simply to get a sense of the narrow political diversity of the world we now live in. Marx was hardly interested in inequality or poverty, and indeed frequently lampooned the demand for equality. The working class was not poorer than the peasants; that was never the crux. It was a class with "radical chains" that would refashion the world. The working class may have always been mythological, yet in principle it sought not a place at the table, but a new setting.[48]

Today the specter is a specter of itself and political diversity turns ghostly. Evidently political differences exist, but the register has narrowed. The hope that a Third World would be an alternative to advanced capitalism and state communism has long since died. Marxism has retreated to graduate seminars where professors serve gluten-free gibberish to aspiring professors. "Two arresting theoretical discourses of the twenty-first century" derive from Greek philosophy, begins a typical article, "The Vectors of the Biopolitical," by a Marxist poohbah. They are: "Michel Foucault's biopolitics, provocatively reformulated by Giorgio Agamben in terms of the relationship between sovereignty and the body, and the capabilities approach developed by Amartya Sen and Martha Nussbaum." This article, which opens a special issue of *New Left Review*, closes with this insight: "Reuniting the vectors potentially provides a means of articulating the politics of this conceptually expanded but biopolitically contracting field. In particular, it allows us to distinguish, in ways that Marx did not, the state of being equally social from that of being socially equal: the first is measured by convergence between vectors, the second by distributions effected by them."[49]

Other Marxists no longer even pretend to believe in an alternative to the existing society; they study the vocabulary of state power.[50] Outside the campuses a feeble liberalism confronts a rising authoritarianism, populism, and religious fanaticism. Everywhere industrial capital lays waste to the variety of the natural world and undercuts the individual. Meanwhile, the diversity cheerleaders schedule another celebration. "Don't wait to be hunted to hide," counseled Samuel Beckett nearly seventy years ago.[51] The advice still rings true.

CHAPTER TWO

"A Diversity Crisis!"

Sneakers, Species, and Speech

Identical twins can confuse strangers, even family members, but not themselves. This puts into a nutshell the subjective and objective dimensions of diversity. Each twin sees him or herself as unique, while others see replicas. Both hold true, but this hardly settles the matter. We all see ourselves as unique, but subjectivity cannot be the only measure. How does one determine individuality? Chromosomally we are the same species, but the difference between an Upper West Side liberal of New York City and a devout Hindu villager of India would be significant. Yet what happens if these two individuals begin viewing the same materials, doing the same things, and dressing more and more alike? This is happening. Does this indicate that the differences among us lessen?

"Most people around the world," writes the historian Niall Ferguson, "dress in much the same way: the same jeans, the same sneakers, the same T-shirts." He notes "there are just a very few places where people hold out against the giant sartorial blending machine." Consider the worldwide success of blue jeans, which originated at the firm of a German-Jewish American merchant, Levi Strauss, in San Francisco. Ferguson attributes the success of blue jeans to money and marketing.

Yet he admits it was more than just hype. The great answer to capitalism, Soviet communism, could not manufacture desirable trousers. "Perhaps the greatest mystery of the entire Cold War is why the Worker's Paradise could not manage to produce a decent pair of jeans."[1]

The domination of T-shirts, blue jeans, and athletic wear bespeaks the "giant sartorial blending machine." I will devote only the briefest attention to sartorial homogenization here; I offer it simply as an indicator of the larger processes that undermine diversity. Many study fashion and its shifts, but rarely with a wide-angled or global lens. Usually histories of clothes stick to one nation or region.[2] Conversely, histories of Europe or America rarely mention fashion and clothes—or only mention them fleetingly. The topic appears too slight for the serious scholar.[3]

The subject's lack of gravity was captured in Thomas Carlyle's satire *Sartor Resartus* (Taylor Retailored) from 1833. Carlyle's narrator-editor befriended the ponderous German Professor Teufelsdröckh. He received a book from the good professor with instructions to prepare an English edition. But our narrator had expected a book devoted to "higher philosophies," perhaps "a refutation of Hegel." Never once in their relationship had the professor discoursed on clothes.

To the narrator's amazement, an ungainly study, *Clothes, Their Origin and Influence* shows up. Teufelsdröckh expounds on the principle that "Man's earthly interests 'are all hooked and buttoned together, and held up, by Clothes.' He says in so many words, 'Society is founded upon Cloth.'" The proof is everywhere, notes our flustered narrator. "Lives there a man that can figure a naked Duke of Windlestraw addressing a naked House of Lords?" Imagination "will not forward the picture." To be sure, Teufelsdröckh's book is hardly perfect. Our narrator finds "most unsatisfactory" Teufelsdröckh's chapter on Aprons.[4]

Professor Teufelsdröckh may have been correct: society is stitched together with cloth, but his colleagues—past and present—have not been impressed. A curse of triviality still afflicts the subject, which can even be glimpsed in the recent and highly regarded *Empire of Cotton: A Global History* by Sven Beckert, a Harvard professor. Beckert declares that for 900 years (until 1900) cotton was "the world's most important manufacturing industry." To follow the path of cotton "will lead us to the origins of the modern world." Cotton was "the driving commodity behind the Industrial Revolution." But Beckert never says exactly that cotton and clothes virtually overlap. He remarks in the introduction that as you read about the ubiquity of cotton, "chances are you are wearing something woven from cotton . . . We wear it close to our skin. We sleep under it. We swaddle our newborns in it."[5]

Yet in his 600 pages Beckert never returns to this part of the story. He tells us about colonialism, slavery, the flying shuttle, Liverpool, the American Civil War, merchants, Uzbekistan, and more, but never takes up what drove the commodity that drove the industry that transformed the globe: people loved cotton. The English adored cotton clothes to the point that it gutted their own wool industry. To little avail, Parliament tried to limit cotton in favor of wool. It managed to pass legislation that required the dead to be wrapped in English wool, but had less success with the living. Its efforts to order female servants to wear wool hats failed. An historian called this "a rather vain attempt at sartorial compulsion," since female servants wanted fashionable cottons.[6] The fact is that people loved to wear cotton. Unlike wool and linen, it was light, soft, and dyeable; and unlike silk, it was also cheap and easy to clean. Indeed, people prized white cottons for underwear.[7]

Of course, it was not just "people." Cotton was not new to India or Egypt; it was new to denizens of Western Europe. They are the ones who wanted it and, as Stephen Yafa puts it in his book on cotton, "consumers couldn't get enough. In 1783 a London magazine reported that 'every servant girl has her cotton gown and her cotton stockings.'"[8] The Europeans fell for cotton cloth; and they had the wherewithal first to obtain raw bolls and second to fabricate cotton textiles in vast quantities. The cover of some editions of Eric Hobsbawm's classic history, *The Age of Capital: 1848–1975*, bears Edgar Degas's painting, "A Cotton Office in New Orleans," that shows members of the artist's extended family inspecting and appraising cotton.[9] Degas himself thought to sell the painting to a Manchester cotton magnate.[10] India had dominated cotton cloth exports for eight centuries—till the 1780s, when it was dethroned by the Europeans, who sold the textile back to the Indians.[11] Beckert asks the question that arises from this phenomenon: "Why was it that the part of the world that had the least to do with cotton—Europe—created and came to dominate the empire of cotton?"[12]

The topic here is related to Europe and North America's domination, not of cotton, but of clothes—the empire of clothes. The story has a thousand chapters and subchapters, but very roughly, Western dress with fits and starts entailed the spread of egalitarian and informal wear; and outside of the West, progress connoted adopting Western sartorial styles and surrendering local and national varieties. This needs at least one critical qualification. As an historian of fashion put it, "one of the most remarkable things" about fashion is that, from the 18th century, "the history of men's clothing has been quite different from the history of women's clothes."[13] In the West this divergence does not close till the 20th century, when working women, equal rights movements, and sports send to the attic corsets, voluminous skirts, and elaborate hats. Outside the West the divergence remains alive and well, especially in the Muslim world.

By the 18th century, simplicity and efficiency prevailed in men's clothing. Within a generation, men had abandoned "the velvets, brocades, satins, frills, and furbelows" for a "sober, increasingly uniform type of male clothing," observed Lee Simonson, a curator of a sartorial exhibition. The suit proved efficient, continued Simonson, with pockets for wallet, pencils, pens, notebook, and watch. "Doctor and lawyer, artist and scientist, professor and businessman are dressed virtually alike."[14] Some 19th-century observers saw the writing on the wall. The plain and simple garb not only spelled the end of visible differences between classes but the end of native dress throughout Europe. "It is sad," commented Friedrich Vischer, a 19th-century philosopher and aesthete. "Culture will mercilessly strip away all of the beautiful native costumes . . . nothing can be done about it." Railroads carry crowds and urban fashions everywhere. "Traditional Tyrolean dress is picturesque," he remarked, but is destined to disappear. Fashion responds to "rapid mobility" and movement, which is the "common element" of modern civilization. Urban transports lead to a "leveling effect" or an "egalitarian uniformity." It is horrible, Vischer lamented, but there is "no antidote."[15]

His pessimism seemed justified. By the end of the 19th century, ready-to-wear clothes, especially suits, established themselves across Europe and North America. The arrival of the "trusty blue serge suit" in the United States, noted another curator, "knew no class or economic group." It signified the "new Democracy of Male Dress."[16] It also signified progress. For this reason, outside the West wearing a suit became a "sign that one belongs to the modern Western world."[17]

This is not simply an outsider's view. From Russia in the 18th century to Japan in the 19th and Turkey in the 20th, the modernizers themselves wanted to adopt Western fashion as proof of progress or as a first step toward it. As soon as he returned from his European tour, Peter the Great wielded a razor to his court and cut off traditional beards so "as to conform to the guise of foreign nations," reported the Austrian representative.[18] Peter enacted a series of decrees that commanded officialdom to give up their long robes for German- or French-style waistcoats, breeches, boots, and hats. "All residents of Moscow," Peter ordered, "must wear German dress. Outerwear must consist of French or Saxon coats, sleeved vests, breeches, boots, shoes, and German hats. . . . From this day forward no one will be allowed to wear Russian dress, Caucasian caftans, sheepskin coats."[19] Despite detours and reversals, the same process would unfold in country after country.[20]

In the 1870s during the Meiji Restoration, when Japan sought to reform, government officials and court members were directed to adopt Western dress. "The most startling cosmetic change," notes Liza Dalby, an anthropologist of Japanese fashion, was "the abandonment of the custom of *ohaguro*, 'teeth-blackening.'" This practice of painting one's teeth with a fluid made by "mixing ferrous metal filings with an acidic liquid" might seem odd, Dalby continues, but it was considered attractive for centuries.[21] To mark the shift, in 1872 "the Empress appeared in public with natural eyebrows and gleaming white teeth 'à la Européenne' in order to discourage the custom of shaving eyebrows and staining teeth that were the mark of a married beauty in upper class Tokugawa society."[22]

In the same spirit, the new Turkish Republic aimed to promote Western dress by eliminating the common fez. This was the justification for the Hat Law of 1925. "Turkey has decided to join the family of civilized nations . . . thus the fez must be replaced by the hat, which is the symbol of civilization," declared a defender of the new law. To underline his support when he introduced the law, the Turkish leader Mustafa Kemal Atatürk dressed in Western clothes with a top hat. "I tell you as your own brother, as your friend, as your father, that the people of the Turkish Republic . . . must show they are civilized. . . . My friends, international dress is worthy and appropriate for our nation, and we will wear it."[23]

Similar stories transpire elsewhere. For instance, in the 1960s Tanzania launched an "Operation Dress-Up" campaign that encouraged the Maasai to give up their togas for trousers. In fact, the operation was also called "Maasai Progress Plan." Like many undertakings, it consisted of persuasion and force. A local newspaper crowed of success with at least one individual, and published "before" photos of a Maasai in robes and "after" photos of him in a suit. It reported that a Mr. Kilasia always used to wear "the traditional Maasai robes that make them wander around half-naked." But after coming to the capital, Dar es Salaam, and "hearing the invitation given by the Second Vice-President," who beseeched the Maasai to "wear modern clothes," Mr. Kilasia changed his ways. "He went to buy for himself a shirt, trousers, a belt and a tie."[24]

But did he keep wearing them? Sartorial Westernization is

hardly a one-way process. From India to Japan there were—and are—pushbacks in the name of tradition, religion, and anti-colonialism. Turkey in 2008 ended the ban on women wearing headscarves at universities, which had been established by Atatürk.[25] This was seen as a strike against Western secularization, but might be dubbed sartorial resistance, which is an ongoing story in many countries. A protest against Western attire permeated the entire Indian independence movement. Gandhi insisted that nationalists and anti-colonialists give up Western fashions and imported cottons in favor of local hand-spun cotton—khadi—that was in fact less comfortable and more expensive. Gandhi also pioneered a special cotton hat, which became known as the Gandhi cap.

Photos from the early 20th century showed two Gandhis—very much like the pictures of the Maasai before and after, but reversed. In the first, Gandhi is wearing Western dress with a dark suit, collared shirt, and shoes. In the latter he is wearing a white, loose, draped khadi. "The telltale markers of colonial taste and domination—Western coats, hats, and shoes," write Lisa Trivedi, an historian of modern Indian dress, "have been replaced both in style and in material." Gandhi convinced many to follow his lead, and khadi became a symbol of the Indian nationalist movement.

Yet in the long run this sartorial resistance seems to have failed. By the time of national independence, foreign fabrics had already returned, which distressed Gandhi; and 70 years after independence, home-spun cotton fashions have receded to the margins. The role they played in Indian politics exists no longer, except sometimes the Gandhi cap. Common (and cheap) Western garb that preceded Gandhi succeeds him. According to Trivedi, apart from its historical resonance, khadi today is associated with traditional folk art. At the same time, it "serves as a kind of 'authentic chic' for a cosmopolitan Indian community that moves between London, New York, Sydney, and Hong Kong."[26] An anthropologist of Indian dress calls the recent period "ethnic chic" when a wealthy elite dresses as poor villagers as poor villagers dress as regular Westerners. In this way, the elite "can differentiate themselves from the increasing mass of the sari-wearing, denim jeans-wearing middle classes."[27]

The sartorial trend across the globe seems obvious. Gatherings of young people in China or Morocco or Spain nowadays look very similar: the same cotton shirts, jeans, and athletic footwear. (Again, the qualification: not women, especially for the Muslim world, where hijabs are common.) The distinct garb, for instance, of a working class has long since faded away, as have the accoutrements of the wealthy. Both the worker's caps and top hats are gone. The sartorial markers of poverty and wealth no longer jump out. In a crowd of students on a college campus, at least in the United States, to pick out in a glance the trust-fund kids from the food-stamp kids would be difficult.

Eric Hobsbawm, the Marxist historian, remarks in his autobiography that the real impact of the 1960s may be cultural, even sartorial, not political. He recalls that he had always taught that the great London dock strike of 1889, a standard reference point for labor historians, may be overrated; it proved less significant than the adoption by industrial workers in the 1890s of the peaked cap as a "recognizable" class badge. This demonstrated a class solidarity with lasting impact. But lasting does not last. The worker's cap and other class insignia faded away by the end of the twentieth century. "It may be argued that the really significant index of the history of the second half of the twentieth century is not ideology or student occupations, but the forward march of blue jeans."[28] In this matter, the Marxist historian Hobsbawm and the conservative historian Ferguson agree.

The charge that blue jeans and cotton shirts is just surface, not substance, cannot be dismissed. The plaint that the similarity of fashion hides dissimilar economic realities has its truth. This was first a charge of the Right, and later of the Left. "It is the curse of this nation that the labourer and the mechanic will ape the lord," grumbled an 18th-century Brit. "The different ranks of people are too much confounded."[29] He was not alone in his unhappiness. "It is hard matter," complained Daniel Defoe, the prolific author of *Robinson Crusoe*, "to know the mistress from the maid by their dress." Frank Trentmann, who cites Defoe in his history of consumption, *Empire of Things*, elaborates that "the clothing revolution ran roughshod over an inherited system of sartorial distinctions that had mapped dress to rank."[30]

More than two centuries after Defoe, a socialist offered the same observation. Michael Harrington, in his 1962 book on poverty, *The Other America*, protested that "clothes made the poor invisible." He lamented that "it is much easier in the United States to be decently dressed than it is to be decently housed, fed, or doctored." Mass production has been successful with clothes. As a result, "even people with terribly depressed incomes can look prosperous." Harrington concludes that "America has the best-dressed poverty the world has ever known."[31] The homogeny of fashion masks the heterogeneity of lives.

The point stands—up to a point. Economic divergence does not in itself denote cultural or intellectual diversity, as I brought up in Chapter One. The poor might simply lack money and whatever it enables—good housing, health, and employment; and this might be true of the very poor outside the industrialized nations. They may dress as average Joes, but do not command the clean water and indoor plumbing of average Joes. Their situation does not indicate that they incarnate diversity or even aspire to a different life than that of the better compensated. Our appearances do not float untethered to essences. Who we are also shows in the surface; it is not simply locked in a secret vault. Our daily lives—clothes, gestures, language—displays our choices and desires. This is hardly a novel or profound idea, and is well-captured by Erving Goffman's classic, *The Presentation of Self in Everyday Life*.[32] The poor person who manages to dress like a rich person wants to be a rich person. Fair enough. Let us not pretend otherwise.

··•··

For humanists, the diversity of languages has often been a starting point of reflection. The classic 19th-century work on language by the scholar Wilhelm von Humboldt (not to be confused with his more famous brother, the naturalist Alexander) bears *diversity* in its inelegant title, *On the Diversity of Human Language Construction* (1836). Before and after Humboldt, the multiplicity of languages puzzled scholars. What distinguishes separate languages? What ties the universality of speech to the "variability of language"? On one hand, the universality suggests languages are intrinsic to mankind. The creation of language is "an innate necessity of humanity," declared Humboldt. The universality implies "the structural character of languages might be discovered even among apparently unrelated languages and language groups."[33] On this basis, Noam Chomsky cites Humboldt in support of his theory of a universal structure to language.

On the other hand, languages are individual, specific, and regional. No one speaks a universal language, but everyone speaks. For Humboldt the "peculiarity" of each language "is of immeasurable extent and of unfathomable depth." How can one understand this? "The organization of the lexical structure and word order in Sanskrit, Greek, and Latin is very similar and in many respects identical." Nevertheless, their differences penetrate deep into their make-up. Humboldt wanted to capture the individuality of the languages, not just their similarity.[34] He loved languages. "I am enormously attracted by the wonderful, mysterious inner connection of all languages," he wrote in a letter, "but above all by the pure enjoyment of entering into a new system of thought and feeling with every new language."[35] The Basque language fascinated him, but it seemed unrelated to other European languages. How and where did Basque originate and what is its connection to other languages? How is it different? These are typical questions for those who study languages. As one linguist put it, "Linguists by profession and by inclination are attracted to the multiple varieties of speech and language that have grown up in the world."[36]

Languages can serve to illuminate the knotty issue of gauging human diversity. They are universal, but their trajectories reflect specific histories. The world's inhabitants speak more than 6000 languages, "an astounding array of linguistic diversity," as some scholars recently put it. The array is arrayed unequally. The island of New Guinea supports more than 900 languages, while Russia, which is twenty times larger, is home to about 100.[37] To apprehend the dazzling diversity of languages, linguists have fallen into several camps; some stress the universal structure of all languages, others the particularities and the ways languages are acquired.

The multiplicity of languages has often been viewed as a blight, not a gift. To follow Genesis in the King James Version, once "the whole earth was of one language and one speech." But for building a tower in Babel that would reach to the heavens, the Lord punished humanity. The Lord set out to "confuse their language, that they will not understand one another's speech." This proved effective. Mankind ceased building the tower and scattered. Martin Luther identified the division of languages as "the seedbed of all evils" because it led to political and economic confusion.[38]

Through the ages, dreamers imagined that a universal language would bring peace to the world. Umberto Eco, in his *Search for the Perfect Language*, reviewed a dozen of these efforts across the centuries—and refers to a vast scholarship that examines scores more. The vision stayed alive right through the end of the 19th century, when a young medical student, Ludovik Zamenhof, who identified himself as Doktoro Esperanto (Dr. Hopeful), invented a new language, Esperanto, to heal the world's ills. Two biographers have dubbed Zamenhof "the man who defied Babel."[39] Personal reasons inspired Zamenhof, like many before him, to found a common tongue; he was raised in a town that incarnated the Babel of languages, Białystok, now part of Poland. "I was taught that all men were brothers," Zamenhof recalled. But "in Białystok, the population consisted of four diverse elements: Russians, Poles, Germans and Jews; each spoke a different language and was hostile to the other elements."[40] Zamenhof, who was also some sort of Zionist, died in 1917 and was spared the lethal hostility of "other elements" later in the century.

"The story of the search for the perfect language," noted Eco in his account, "is the story of a dream and of a series of failures."[41] Yet Eco's statement from the early 1990s might today have to be revised. A universal language may be in offing, but less as a dream than a troubling reality. Low-slung offices outfitted with computers and mobile phones offer universal communication that renders obsolete the Tower of Babel. Contemporary humanists no longer seek a universal language to heal the world's ills, but the opposite. They do not worry about too many languages, but too few. They fear that one language, usually English, will be a universal language that will quash other tongues. Evidence is on their side. Across the globe, languages disappear as English dominates. The issue in this chapter is not simply the dwindling of the world's languages, but the extent that language diversity indexes diversity in general. Does the decline of language diversity—the emergence of a global language—reflect a widespread decline of diversity?

For years, scholars have sought to calculate the extent of linguistic diversity and its connection to social and economic realities. This was the goal more than a half-century ago of a classic piece, "The Measurement of Linguistic Diversity," by the Columbia University linguist Joseph H. Greenberg.[42] The decline of linguistic diversity did not interest Greenberg, but he did suggest that, as communication and economies improve in any region, one language might come to dominate. This remark would be echoed by others. As linguists studied the world's languages, they increasingly noticed their field was shrinking—or at least the number and variety of languages were declining. Over time, the plenitude of spoken languages has sharply dropped. "Obviously we must do some serious rethinking of our priorities," declared one linguist some years ago, "lest linguistics go down in history as the only science that presided obliviously over the disappearance of 90% of the very field to which it is dedicated."[43]

These were not just passing observations, but have become the cri de cœur of organizations, conferences, and scholars that have devoted themselves to endangered languages. A scholarly collection on the subject opens by observing that of the 6000 languages in the world, 90% may well disappear. "What are we linguists doing to prevent this catastrophic destruction of the linguistic world?"[44] This volume, *Language Death and Language Maintenance*, contains studies with titles like "An Endangered Language: The Gùrdùn Language of the Southern Bauchi Area, Nigeria" and "Language Endangerment in Indonesia: The Incipient Obsolescence and Acute Death of Teun, Nila and Serua (Central and Southwest Maluku)." UNESCO has launched an endangered languages project, publishing an *Atlas of the World's Languages in Danger* that seeks to raise awareness of the "need to safeguard the world's linguistic diversity." It categorizes languages from "safe" to "critically endangered" and "extinct." Critically endangered means "the youngest speakers are grandparents." It estimates some 3000 languages are "endangered" and 250 have become extinct since 1950.[45]

"Language death is real," declares one of the pessimists, David Crystal, a British linguist.[46] "Languages are dying at an alarming rate all over the world," declares another linguist.[47] Many languages are spoken by small populations and are endangered, if not lost. For instance, a linguist, Bruce Connell, documented Kasabe, a language of Cameroon. But on a return visit, he discovered that the language had vanished when its last speaker died. "On 4 November 1995, Kasabe existed; on 5 November, it did not."[48] Other linguists, even more upset over vanishing languages, talk of "language genocide." The unlovely title of one of these call to arms runs "The Stakes: Linguistic Diversity, Linguistic Human Rights and Mother-Tongue-Based Multilingual Education—or Linguistic Genocide, Crimes Against Humanity and an Even Faster Destruction of Biodiversity and Our Planet."[49] Biologists raise an alarm about the loss of biological diversity, notes another linguist, but the loss of linguistic diversity is far worse. "Why are we linguists so much quieter about it than biologists?"[50]

These scholars are not shy about foregrounding the connection between diversity losses in language and the natural environment. On the contrary. A few groups and organizations have devoted themselves to exactly this topic; they have drawn a direct line between linguistic diversity and biodiversity. Both are menaced. Luisa Maffi, an anthropologist and one of the principals in this domain, has explained that just as biologists and ecologists were broaching ideas of diminished biocultural diversity, linguists were mulling on diminished language diversity.

"Only more recently," she states, "the idea has begun to emerge that, along with cultural diversity . . . linguistic diversity should also be seen as inextricably linked to biodiversity." All these diversities face threats.[51] In response to these threats, Maffi co-founded an organization, Terralingua, that is devoted to preserving cultural and biological diversity. Uniformity in both the environment and culture undermines humanity's well-being. "'Monocultures of the mind' have the same end results as monocultures in nature: they make our planet more fragile and vulnerable."[52] We are facing, according to one adherent, a "diversity crisis."[53]

"A diversity crisis"! To step out of the usual offices that issue proclamations about tomorrow's wondrous diversity is to stumble upon an alternate universe. Here we are not told that teeming diversity will mark the future, but the opposite; the future will witness less variety. Although "the diversification of languages, cultures, and species" originates separately, conclude some researchers, "similar forces currently appear to be driving biological extinctions and cultural/linguistic homogenization." In both cases a Western industrialized economy brings about "habitat loss" or decline in diversity of animal species and human languages.[54] With a drop of diversity comes heightened risk of communicable diseases—for plants, animals, and people. "Homogeneity means vulnerability," declares Edward O. Wilson in *The Diversity of Life*.[55]

Here we are not urged to take out the banners to celebrate diversity—or to damn the reactionaries who oppose it—but are informed of the irreparable loss of diversity taking place in the here and now and the danger that entails. But these reports do not reach the diversity celebrants. Why? Perhaps the intellectual division of labor plays a role. The diversity enthusiasts talk to each other and supporters; they form a dense world of interlocking directorates. They also do not want anyone to rain on their parade. The diversity doomsters—a much smaller crew than the diversity boosters—have their own groups and conferences.

The biologists and kindred scientists who address diversity decline well understand that they are looking at manmade shifts; and they employ an idiom that overlaps with the vocabulary of this book about accelerating uniformity. Indeed, they have introduced a term, "biotic homogenization," that speaks to increased species likeness in environments that once existed as separate and distinct domains. Biological homogenization signifies the invasion of non-native species and extinction of native species that undercut diversity. A recent collection on the subject, *Biotic Homogenization*, opens by declaring that "biological homogenization" is the "dominant process" that shapes the globe. Local environments get eradicated. "This process is affecting all aspects of our world: language, economies, and ecosystems alike. The ultimate outcome is the loss of uniqueness and the growth of uniformity." Indeed, the editors of this book appreciate they are challenging the cult of diversity: They call "diversity" the watchword of the present era. "With every important conceptual idea there is a flipside, an apostate that lends insight into a difficult problem. 'Biological Homogeneity' is that apostate to diversity."[56]

The researchers who study the homogenizing process, however, usually stay away from political and cultural dimensions—for some obvious reasons. The social foundations of diversity decline are evident, but also outside their expertise. They are biologists or botanists, not sociologists. Moreover, the larger social realities resist hard numbers, the bread and butter of scientists. "We submit," these scientists declare, "that quantifying how the process of invasion and extinction contributes to rates of biotic homogenization . . . should be at the foreground of future research."[57]

Numerous studies tackle homogenization that afflicts flowers, fish, and animals. For instance, one investigates "Homogenization in Grassland of Switzerland";[58] another "Homogenization of the Aquatic Fauna of Tennessee";[59] a third "Homogenization in Ungulates" across the globe, meaning "hoofed animals" for us non-biologists. Its authors cautiously point out that the "underlying proximate causes of homogenization" are not well understood, but they hazard that it is related to urbanization, landscape alteration, and climate change.[60]

To be sure, some biologists foreground the economic dimension of the homogenization process. In a piece entitled "Biodiversity versus Biomonotony," a South African botanist explains that he opens his class on biological invasives "with a slide showing a big McDonald's sign glaringly (to me) out of place against the grand old buildings on Wenceslas Square in Prague, Czech Republic." He then goes on to discuss biological invasions "one of the most obviously negative side-effects of globalization."[61] Other scientists make a plea for their colleagues to raise the alarm about diversity decline; and they underscore the parallel of biological and cultural homogenization: "Conservation biologists must recognize the urgency of educating policy makers and the public about the homogenization process," they declare in "The Human Dimensions of Biotic Homogenization."

Again, the terms here are virtually identical to those employed in the non-biological domain. Both "the increasing global uniformity in biological life" and the "process of cultural homogenization" undermine diversity. "Biotic homogenization elicits serious concern among conservationists as a major threat to regional individuality." In the same way, cultural homogenization such as suburbanization threatens "the uniqueness of small towns whose diversity is a national treasure."[62]

These reports on declining diversity can easily be multiplied. Any periodical search of scientific literature on "homogenization," meaning a loss of biological diversity, will yield hundreds of articles on plants and animals. These findings do not cloud the vision of the diversity boosters in corporate or campus America. They live in their own world. One of the authors of "The Human Dimensions of Biotic Homogenization" teaches in a Department of Aquatic and Fishery Sciences and a Center of Limnology, which refers to the study of inland waters. When was the last time a diversity devotee rang the Department of Aquatic and Fishery Sciences to chat with a fish expert?

To be sure, to draw a direct line between dwindling species and languages seems simplistic. What, for instance, can it mean that for North America "linguistic diversity shows a moderate degree of positive correlation with tree species diversity"?[63] Some arguments of language decline are overheated, misleading, or tangential. After all, a language is not exactly like a species of fish. A few scholars have challenged the biological metaphor and its implications: "The most basic problem," notes a critic, is that "language is not organic"—and it does not live, flourish, or die like an animal species. The metaphor can also simplify what "saving" a language entails. "We have passed regulations forbidding some sorts of hunting and fishing, and allowing stocks to recover," observes John Edwards, a Canadian psychologist, in his book *Language and Identity*, but how does one do this for a language?[64]

James W. Underhill, a Scottish scholar, has raised salient objections to this new field of ecolinguistics that dwells on the eroding treasures of linguistic diversity. He notes that the classical linguists like Humboldt pored over texts in Latin, Greek, Sanskrit, Basque, and Kawi to divine each language's specific essence. But the new linguists often hardly know the languages they are championing. The old linguists—really philologists—cherished individual languages and their idiosyncrasies. The current linguists partake of another intellectual world. This observation seconds that of George Steiner in his *After Babel.* He remarks that the language schools of earlier 20th-century Prague and Moscow possessed living links to contemporary poets and writers. Linguists like Roman Jakobson moved in avant-garde literary circles. Contemporary linguists rub shoulders only with other linguists at professional conferences. The "modern analytic linguists are no friends to language." In their search for elementary and universal patterns, Steiner detected an "unmistakable displeasure" at the "anarchic prodigality" of languages.[65]

To follow Underhill, the modern linguists with their scientific ideal isolate elements of the linguistic system; they know bits and parts. They have become "blind to individuals and deaf to their speech." They "embrace and cherish all languages indiscriminately," which makes "their love of languages of a rather lukewarm (if not insipid) affair." A prime case for Underhill is David Crystal, cited above, one of the foremost alarmists of language death. But "Crystal has no intention of going out to learn the languages he intends to save. . . . [In Crystal's view] diversity would seem to require merely that a wide variety of languages simply exist."[66]

This point suggests that the diversity celebrants and alarmists converge in one regard. They share what might be dubbed a consumer notion of diversity: more is better. The camps diverge in their appraisal of the current situation, but both subscribe to the same model. This presents culture as an empty vessel that can be filled by language or religion or food. Like cereal boxes in a supermarket aisle, all varieties happily coexist. The boosters are pleased so many brands are in stock and want more; the gloomsters are chastened so few brands are in stock and want more. A saccharine multiculturalism, the source of much diversity nonsense, underlies both camps. This envisions a world where all cultures mix harmoniously; and each contributes something precious to humanity. "The entire world needs a diversity of ethnolinguistic entities for its own salvation," writes one of the believers, "for its greater creativity, for the more certain solution of human problems, for the constant rehumanization of humanity in the face of materialism . . . for arriving at a higher state of human functioning."[67]

To the Hallmark vision of the world, the alarmists add exoticism. In this scenario, all beleaguered languages and peoples harbor precious knowledge. As Underhill notes, to the doomsayers "the more exotic the language, the better."[68] And the more vulnerable a culture, the more valuable it is. "Much of the knowledge about how to maintain biodiversity," claims one of the alarmists, "is encoded in the small languages of Indigenous/tribal and local peoples." If we get rid of these peoples, "we kill the prerequisites for maintaining biodiversity."[69]

No one sane favors killing off peoples or cultures, but some obvious truths should be remembered. Small is not always beautiful. The losers in history are not superior because they lost. Defeat does not inexorably lead to wisdom. Not all cultures are benign. Not all are worth saving. At least not all cultural practices can be cherished. Some are vicious, racist, and misogynist. Foot binding? Honor killings? Genital mutilation? Segregation? Castes? Cultural diversity, one critic notes, is more than "cuisine and costume." It is not simply "chomping chorizo in Chula Vista and gagging on lutefisk in Lake Wobegon." It also can be ugly and suppressive. "I didn't like my culture," writes H.E. Baber in her critique of multiculturalism, *The Multicultural Mystique*.[70] An affable diversity can blanket a caustic reality.

"True pluralism belongs to the concept of a future society," writes Frankfurt School critic Max Horkheimer.[71] But cultural diversity is currently what the doctor prescribes for left-leaning politicos who have overdosed on reality. We prefer saving beleaguered cultures to addressing economic inequalities. The former is sexy and tragic, the latter old-fashioned and boring. Compare on any campus the number of public lectures on identity and culture to that on poverty and wages; it runs probably ten to one—or zero. Walter Benn Michaels makes some of these points in his *Trouble with Diversity*, which denounces the fetish of culture. He relays an observer's dire description of the state of Mati Ke, an Australian aboriginal language, reduced to a population of just one brother and sister. The situation is even worse than it appears, since Mati Ke culture prohibits brother and sister from conversing after puberty. Nevertheless, scholars urge that it is an indigenous culture worth saving. We have, notes Michaels, "an increasingly passionate commitment to culture" and at the same time a "greater indifference to inequality." He marvels that "this is what the commitment to diversity is all about, since a world of people who are different from us looks a lot more appealing that a world of people who are poorer than us."[72]

Languages should not be conflated with cultures, but they raise related issues. Is linguistic diversity always beneficial? Are all languages valuable? Cameroon has about 279, the Democratic Republic of Congo 217, Nigeria 527. Indeed, two economists have challenged the cult of linguistic diversity. They have asked a loaded question: when are numerous languages too numerous? In *How Many Languages Do We Need? The Economics of Linguistic Diversity*, Victor Ginsburgh and Shlomo Weber mull over the costs of extreme linguistic diversity. They suggest that excessive linguistic variety leads to problems; or, at least, they stress that linguistic diversity comes at a price. They refer to studies that compare growth in Africa and Asia, such as that in Tanzania and Japan, through the lens of language diversity; the studies conclude that ethnolinguistic diversity has had a devastating impact on Africa. The book's authors—a native Swahili speaker and native Russian speaker—cautiously conclude that inordinate linguistic diversity "weakens institutions, slows the path to their improvement, and causes political instability."[73]

For the developed world, however, the problem is not excessive linguistic diversity, but the opposite, dwindling diversity. Here the biological metaphors are appropriate: invasive species undermine native idioms and bring about linguistic homogenization. The implications of dwindling linguistic diversity are endless—and affect not only small languages but major ones like French and Japanese, all of which get sidelined by English. "What will become of all the national languages that are not English?" asks the Japanese novelist Minae Mizumura in *The Fall of Language in the Age of English*, a book that became a bestseller in Japan. She regrets that the growing power of English undermines other languages, no matter how important they are.

The facts are hard to dispute. Not so long ago, French ranked first in prestige among Western languages. European aristocrats spoke French as either a second or even first language. Frederick the Great, the 18th-century Prussian king, famously preferred French everything—language, thinkers, and musicians—over German. He called the German language a "semi-barbarian" idiom that was impossible for an author of genius to employ. He himself spoke and wrote in French.[74] Under his watch the royal academy of sciences went from German to French. The *Königliche Akademie der Wissenschaften* became the *Académie royale des sciences et belles-lettres*.[75]

In 1784 the academy held an essay contest on why French had become and would remain the universal language.[76] The winning essays spoke to the moment, but even as supporters championed French, its standing was ebbing—ebbing, but hardly out. In the 1920s the League of Nations could still command that passports "should be drawn up in at least two languages, i.e. in the national language and in French." The member countries offered no objection to this language requirement.[77] In the 1950s Mizumura recalls that as a child she sent a postcard to her father in the United States and was instructed to write "Par Avion" on it. Why? Because of an international agreement to use French on international mail. But that time has passed. Today pilots and air traffic controllers involved in international flights are mandated to know English, not French.

The French have long complained about the dominance of English and have sought—usually with little success—to impose restrictions on English. Even the effort of the *Académie française* to exhort the French themselves to use "un courriel" for the English "email" has failed. Signs throughout Paris advertise "happy hours" or "brunch." In a revealing slight, English–French dictionaries give the French translation of "weekend" as "weekend," not "fin de semaine." Recently a hundred French writers signed an open letter demanding the Ministry of Culture halt the intrusion of English. A Paris book festival that used the category "Young Adult" along with other English (and half-English) terms sparked their protest. "In the streets, on the web . . . everywhere, in fact, English tends to replace French, little by little. . . . But even at a book fair in France?" With the relentless encroachment of English, the letter writers raised the specter of "global linguistic uniformity."[78]

Mizumura, who speaks French, considers the fate of the language in a chapter subtitled "The Fall of French." The French are becoming like the Japanese, she believes, known only in translation. She noticed a difference between Japanese students who went to study in the United States and those who went to France. Those in the United States had gone to gain a specialty, engineering or banking, and learned English along the way. Those in France had gone with the goal of sitting in cafés, smoking Gauloises, and speaking like a native. "In retrospect, that the French language no longer functioned as a means to learn something else portended its dark future."[79]

The future belongs to English, according to Mizumura. All other languages are damned to second-rate status. "What was once a national language may be reduced to nothing more than a local language . . . that no discriminating person takes seriously." She fears this is even happening with Japan's younger novelists, who want to appear in English. Mizumura asks us to consider a future in which "the best-educated" and "the brightest minds" only express themselves in English, while other languages become quaint. "What a narrow, pitiful, and horrid world that would be!"[80]

In different registers such laments are voiced throughout the world, the fear that not simply small languages but major ones will lose their vitality as English sucks out the air. "Educated Arabs are drifting away from their own language," notes the *New Yorker*'s Egyptian correspondent, Peter Hessler. Middle- or upper-class children in Cairo are "educated primarily in English or French, at private schools." Hessler quotes a Cairo professor who states that many of his upper-class students can barely use written Arabic and wonders about the political impact. "They will make public policy about a country they don't know."[81]

Mizumura closes her heartfelt defense of Japanese (and other non-English tongues) by asking for a little humility from English speakers. Indeed, she eloquently criticizes the late Benedict Anderson's *Imagined Communities: Reflections on the Origin and Spread of Nationalism*, an oft-cited volume on the formation of the nation-state and the rise of the vernacular. For Anderson, the modern state and printing press sustain each other. With the emergence of the printing press, the state and the vernacular become coterminous. In France, Germany, Netherlands, Italy, Spain, Portugal—and the list goes on—national languages link people horizontally into national communities. As convincing as this story is, Mizumura offers a telling criticism: "As a nonnative speaker of English, I cannot help sensing a strange lacuna in the book. . . . English is treated as merely one of many national languages." Anderson completely ignores the dominance of English today—and he does so through three editions of the book over 25 years. He misses that English unseats other tongues to become the universal language today. "Why does he fail to mention this?"

Mizumura hazards that the reason is because Anderson, despite having been personally multilingual, shared "the general blindness of those whose mother tongue is English." He was unaware that, when writing in English, he writes in the privileged or the universal language. For the same reason, she challenges his glib support of multilingualism, "a typical position taken by European intellectuals." It is glib not because of the ideal of multilingualism, which Mizumura herself shares, but because of its shallowness in not recognizing the crushing dominance of English. She suggests the European Union is an example of this. While officially multilingual with 24 languages, English dominates as "a de facto common language." One of those official languages is Gaelic, the language of Ireland, where Anderson retained his citizenship. While the Irish government heavily supports Gaelic, few know it or use it.

No one pretends it will displace English. The Irish policy on Gaelic, observes Mizumura, "is akin to someone who lives in a sumptuous palace putting up a shack with a thatched roof on the grounds in order to enjoy a bit of rustic life."[82]

What has made English the dominant language? If Anderson, a leftist academic, avoids the subject, Mizumura, the non-political novelist, hardly fills the gap. She notes that the supremacy of English has come about only "through a series of historical coincidences." "In this age of global communication some language or other was bound to become a universal language used in every corner of the world." It just happened to be English. She calls it "an accidental universal language."[83]

This is surely true—but it's not the whole truth. Intrinsically, nothing in English ensured its ascendance. But "a series of historical coincidences" cover a lot of grounds. The modern economy triumphed first in an English-speaking country, Great Britain, a fact which many grasped. "What I have to examine in this work," Karl Marx wrote in the preface to *Capital*, is "the capitalist mode of production." "Until now," he noted, its "*locus classicus* has been England. This is the reason why England is used as the main illustration."[84] Ten thousand scholars puzzle over the question: Why did Western Europe in general and England in particular give rise to the Industrial Revolution? Referring to the most advanced district of China—the Yangzi Delta area—Kenneth Pomeranz asks in his book on this topic, *The Great Divergence*, "Why wasn't the Yangzi Delta England?"[85]

The answers run from the idea that it lacked wage labor to a lack of science, technology, colonialism, wars, Protestantism, the Enlightenment, and more. In an ambitious foray into this question, Deirdre McCloskey argues that neither power nor domination, but a new rhetoric about equality that valued markets and improvement, led to Western wealth. In *Bourgeois Equality: How Ideas, Not Capital or Institutions, Enriched the World*, McCloskey cites Samuel Johnson's credo as illustrative. Johnson declared, "No man but a blockhead ever wrote, except for money," a principle that blesses the market. In the same spirit Johnson endorsed progress: "The age is running mad after innovation; all the business of the world is to be done in a new way; men are to be hanged in a new way."[86]

The dominance of English is as accidental as the dominance of capitalism, which is to say, not at all. A former English-speaking colony of Great Britain—the United States—forced Japan to join world commerce, not the reverse. Or as the author of *English as a Global Language* declares, the dominance of English is based on England's imperialism and America's economic power.[87] The issue is not to score points against Mizumura for neglecting larger economic realities. Her concern is with the fate of Japanese and other non-European languages that are not English. The issue is to situate shrinking linguistic diversity within global realities that undermine diversity in general.

No one has an answer to dwindling linguistic diversity in the United States or in most major developed countries. It seems inescapable. My grandmother spoke Yiddish. Her daughter barely did. I don't at all. Mizumura herself ends up recommending something she has already debunked: "Acquiring a foreign language should be a universal requirement of compulsory education."[88] Yet at least this moves diversity from the theme parks to everyday life; it seeks to render languages part and parcel of daily interactions, instead of exhibits in the museum of endangered cultures. Indeed, it is striking that the linguists and anthropologists who lament language loss do not address the decline of foreign language study in the United

States or foreign language proficiency in developed countries. This does not interest them. Go through their books, catalogs, and websites and you will find information about the fate of indigenous languages among peoples of Papua New Guinea or Cameroon, and sometimes among Native Americans, but nothing about foreign languages in major population centers. For this reason, they can be charged with exoticism; they love preserving languages as long as they are elsewhere. Of course, exoticism has many benefits. To travel to an Indonesian island to document a language beats a trip to Cleveland to assess high school French instruction.

The subject of declining American foreign language proficiency has been studied and regretted, but typically by professional teaching associations with no resonance beyond those circles. This is another instance where reports of diversity loss make no impression on larger discussions. The story of American foreign language instruction has always been bad—and has gotten worse. Today Americans study foreign languages less than ever.[89] The numbers are dismal. Foreign language skills regress; language programs are being eliminated in both K–12 and higher education. A few colleges have closed their language departments; many have reduced them.[90] National programs and standards have dropped foreign language goals. Across the board, science and technology rank far above foreign languages. One national plan criticized language education as "elitist."[91]

Once educated Americans knew foreign languages, including German, which was considered (*pace* Frederick the Great) the language of science. When Sigmund Freud came to Clark University in 1909 to celebrate its anniversary, he lectured in German, with everyone from William James, the philosopher, to Emma Goldman, the anarchist, in attendance. Neither the participants nor reporters mentioned that Freud spoke in German.[92] Why? It called for no notice because knowledge of German was assumed for the audience. Today in the United States, for a visitor to a major campus event to lecture in a language other than English would be inconceivable.

Language skill seems relevant to diversity. Why amid the diversity celebration are languages not mentioned? Would it put a damper on the party to insist that if one is half-serious about diverse cultures then one must be serious about language acquisition? It is surely fair to ask, What is cultural diversity without diverse languages? Evidently one can order, and enjoy, Thai food in English, but can one gain access to a larger Thai culture without the command of the Thai language? The old and thorny issue of culture and translations will not be pursued here, but the failure to address foreign language proficiency puts into question the gravity of diversity talk. The enthusiasts want diversity on the cheap—and they get it.

Sneakers, species, and speech seem like unrelated entries under "S" in an encyclopedia. Yet an inner relationship exists between them. What has been called by ecologists a "rampant homogenization of the earth's ecosystems" affects not only animals and plants but also fashion and language.[93] Invasive species such as zebra mussels wreck native habitats. At the same time, the world dresses more and more alike and speaks fewer languages. These are different facets of globalization. To indicate the widespread threat to ecological and cultural diversity does not mean we should just accept it; nor does it mean we should sanctify every language or cultural practice. It requires tacking between defeatism and exoticism. "The critical path alone is still open."[94]

CHAPTER THREE

Playing with Diversity

In 1960 an obscure employee of an obscure French office, the Institute of Colonial Fruits and Citruses, published a weighty tome that had nothing to do with lemons or mangoes. In *Centuries of Childhood* (more literally translated as *The Child and Family Life in the Old Regime*), M. Philippe Ariès, the state official, declared that modern society invented childhood. The author claimed that medieval Europe did not recognize children as unique beings; rather it treated them as miniature adults—and even dressed them as little adults. Evidently children always existed, but he believed that the focus on, if not celebration of, children was relatively new. As soon as possible, medieval society launched children into an adult world; it lacked awareness of childhood as a singular phenomenon. Only modern society recognized childhood as a special stage between infants and adults. "A new concept of childhood" appeared that stressed its "sweetness, simplicity, and drollery." Not at first, but eventually Ariès's book found an audience and set the terms of a discussion. For Ariès, the modern era established childhood.[1]

Ariès's argument has been met with skepticism. But skepticism does not spell rebuttal. The Frenchman has been subject to withering criticism, especially by historians, who charge he knew little about the past. A full-scale takedown by a medieval historian concludes that Ariès's views have been influential—"especially among those who are not medieval historians."[2] Nicholas Orme, the medieval historian, declared in *Medieval Children* that Ariès misread or ignored the evidence. Children were everywhere in medieval Europe. To affirm the reality of children, the cover of Orme's *Medieval Children* consists of a detail of Pieter Bruegel's painting *Children's Games* (1560) that depicts more than 200 children occupied with 75 toys and games. Bruegel did not exist for Ariès.[3] Orme demonstrates the continuity of the concept of childhood over the centuries. Others weighed in, correcting, challenging, amending Ariès. Yet for all the huffing and puffing, Ariès's house has not been blown down.

What is that house made of? The issue in this book is diversity and its eclipse. Yet diversity consists of more than the usual topics of politics, culture, and identity; and more than groups and options. Its platform rests on experience, how people see, feel, and approach the world. This subjective component of diversity does not emerge out of thin air; history and society, especially childhood, permeate the subjective innards of diversity. Some familiar truths need recalling. We are products of our childhood, more or less. Its rhythms and timbre inform who we are. What shapes childhood shapes us. The ability to experience the world in all its diversity emerges from our childhood, which suggests that what defines childhood defines that facility. If childhood contracts, our capacity to embrace diversity contracts as well. We are less able to meet the world, to step out of the narrow self.

To pursue these ideas, a series of questions emerge: What is and what has happened to childhood? Have childhood activities changed? We are assessing not simply the emergence of childhood but its transformation. Have the activities of children become less diverse, and more uniform? Less imaginative and more prefabricated? Are children becoming more insular, more self-enclosed? And if so, what is the impact of this shift on experience itself—on the faculty to experience diversity in the world? Again, diversity is not just a matter of the choices available; it is also subjective, how we meet the world. That is the topic of this chapter, the subjective preconditions for diversity as they coalesce in childhood.

Has childhood changed? Ariès in fact may have overstated his argument inasmuch as the appreciation of childhood always existed—among the elite, who had the wherewithal to enjoy children. How else can one explain, for instance, the letter of Plutarch, the Roman essayist, to his wife on the death of their young daughter? "There is a special savor in our affection for children of that age . . . Our daughter was the sweetest thing to fondle, to watch, and to hear."[4] Indeed, information about the existence of children tilts heavily towards the well-born, which the historian Orme admits: "The surviving evidence is biased towards the wealthy." For instance, "The best documented family of medieval England is the royal family."[5] This is not surprising, but can one generalize from such limited sources? The issue may not be the recognition of childhood by the few, but the situation for the many. When does childhood become not exceptional, but common?

This shift may not have happened till the later 18th century, and perhaps can be called the democratization of childhood. Only in the modern period does childhood become a reality for a broad population. In previous centuries the realities of poverty and work strangled childhood. A person sped from infancy to adulthood. For instance, childhood finds no place in Daniel Defoe's 1726 *Complete English Tradesman*, which offered advice on raising a successful apprentice. Since apprenticeship begins with "very young" boys, he counsels that the first few years should be devoted to "submission" to master and "dutiful attendance" to the shop. "After they have entered the fifth or sixth year," Defoe believes "then is the time to put them upon useful preparations for the work."[6]

The reasons that the idea of childhood emerged are not obscure. Improved nutrition and sanitation that lowered the infant mortality rate, compulsory schooling, and limits on child labor (and apprenticeship) opened a space between infancy and adulthood. More children survived, and fewer moved directly into adulthood; they could be children first. A cultural attitude that appreciated, even idolized, childhood took shape and found adherents throughout society.

The fascination, perhaps fetishization, of children, dates to at least Rousseau, who remains a good benchmark. "Childhood is unknown," he stated in *Emile* in 1762. "The wisest men . . . are always seeking the man in the child without thinking of what he is before being a man."[7] To compress sharply this history, the adoration of children intensified over the following century. By 1900, a Swedish feminist published a book titled *The Century of the Child*. Ellen Key, this Swedish reformer, cited a drama that appeared a few years earlier. In that 1896 piece a protagonist stated that "this century has been the woman's century," but "the next century will be the century of the child." Key concurred. "The time will come in which the child will be looked upon as holy."[8] The prediction proved accurate.

The preoccupation with childhood has been maintained, but its parameters have been contested. In 1982, some two decades after Ariès, a less obscure professor at a less obscure institution announced the modern era had disestablished childhood. In *The Disappearance of Childhood*, Neil Postman of New York University posited that the onset of television had led to the demise of childhood as a unique period. He turned Ariès upside down. If in the medieval era children were miniature adults, who had in turn become "children" only in the modern period, today the reverse has occurred. Children, says Postman, have become little adults again. In the way they dress, act, and play, children seem like adults. "Eleven-year-old girls wear high heels." For Postman, as "childhood diminishes, the symbolic markers of childhood diminish with it."[9] He announced the eclipse of childhood.

Like Ariès, Postman touched a chord. If he did not start a debate, many followed in his wake and reported the decline of childhood in contemporary society. We remain situated between Ariès and Postman. We celebrate childhood; we fear its demise. Childhood as a stage in life, of course, cannot vanish, but has its content altered? Have children's activities changed?

These are elusive subjects, and fittingly an elusive thinker might help illuminate them. Walter Benjamin, the Weimar critic, thought long about the connection between childhood and experience. Any leap into Benjamin's ideas on childhood and its salience must be qualified by the statement: not all children are in question. Benjamin himself came from a prosperous Berlin family. The Western middle class is here the focus. Nevertheless, this class is not exactly a minor outfit; its modes and manners imprint much of the world. Doting on children, for instance, does not qualify as an arcane ritual of a fringe group. Such practices or foibles spread with the spreading middle class. Viviana Zelizer, in her book on the "priceless child," reports that the "urban middle class" shifted from viewing children as economic crutches to blessed progeny by the end of the 19th century. She cites a father from 1904 as illustrative of the new ethos that comes to permeate the middle class: "We work for our children, plan for them, spend money on them, buy life insurance for their protection."[10] The issue here, however, is not so much the advent of the priceless child, but his or her fate in contemporary society.

··●··

At the Café de Versailles across from the Paris-Montparnasse train station, two refugees from Nazism met weekly in 1936: Walter Benjamin and a Swiss theologian, Fritz Lieb. For all their differences, they enjoyed an uncommon closeness. Benjamin judged Lieb "one of the best people I have gotten to know here."[11] Lieb, a leftist much interested in Russia, esteemed Benjamin and asked him to contribute an article to a periodical he was editing. Benjamin, always desperate for paid writing commissions, accepted although he was not enthusiastic about the assignment, an essay on the little-known 19th-century Russian novelist Nikolai Leskov. Benjamin thought he would use the occasion to expand on an observation he had already made about the demise of the storyteller in modern society.

In several pieces during those years—published and unpublished—Benjamin pondered this topic. For Benjamin, the storyteller partook of a vanishing oral tradition. Yarns retold by the old to the young no longer existed. "Why is storytelling on the decline?" Benjamin asked. "Who still meets people who really know how to tell a story?" "Who can still call on a proverb when he needs one?" "And who will even attempt to deal with young people by giving them the benefit of their experience?"[12] Why has this decline in storytelling occurred? In the essay "Experience and Poverty," Benjamin noted that the World War I generation returned from combat surprisingly silent, "not richer but poorer in communicable experience." Nor was it just the war; sweeping technological shifts had undermined the ability to relate and hear stories, yielding a new "poverty of human experience."[13]

The essay "The Storyteller," which Benjamin wrote for Lieb's journal, offered the fullest version of these ideas. Benjamin again noted that fewer people know how to tell a story. "More and more often, there is an embarrassment all around when the wish to hear a story is expressed." The texture of daily experience that once sustained storytelling has been altered. "Every morning brings us news from across the globe, yet we are poor in noteworthy stories." Relentless information undermines the storyteller, who relies on quiet and relaxation. When these conditions are not met, the story cannot be told. After all, the storyteller is "repeating stories" and requires a receptive, even bored audience. Benjamin hazards that the audience diminishes because "the state of relaxation" is becoming "rarer and rarer." He accents boredom as a prerequisite for the storyteller. "I realized that people who are not bored cannot tell stories," he wrote elsewhere. "But there is no longer any place for boredom in our lives."[14] His most lyrical formulation ran:

> If sleep is the apogee of physical relaxation, boredom is the apogee of mental relaxation. Boredom is the dream bird that hatches the egg of experience. A rustling in the leaves drives him away. His nesting places . . . are already extinct in the cities and are declining in the

> country as well. With this the gift for listening is lost and the community of listeners disappears.[15]

To attempt to put a date to the decline of storytelling might seem laughable. It is not a discrete object that can be tracked, but a leaf—or a dream bird—subject to wind and weather. Even the impact of World War I might be exaggerated by Benjamin. Was it the war, or the happenings before the war, that altered the tempo of life?[16] Moreover, Benjamin's observation might be dismissed as a refugee's lament for an irretrievable life.

Yet this would be unfair. We live in an era in which to locate someone on a grid of history or ethnicity ends instead of begins a discussion. All people live in particular times. No one floats outside of history. But this truism does not condemn culture to a specific time and space. If so, we would not read Shakespeare or Dostoevsky—or listen to Beethoven or look at Correggio. The universal emerges from the particular; it is not poisoned by it. In any event, Benjamin's thoughts have surfaced again and again—in different times and circumstances.

Forty-four years after the appearance of Benjamin's essay, near the juncture of Texas State Highway 79 and Texas State Highway 25, and some five thousand miles from the café where "The Storyteller" was commissioned, another writer contemplated the fate of the storyteller. One day in 1980 Larry McMurtry, novelist, screenwriter, and Pulitzer Prize–winner, set himself up in the Dairy Queen of his hometown, Archer City, Texas, and prepared for a morning of reading and observing. He had with him a Walter Benjamin collection, edited by Benjamin's cousin-in-law Hannah Arendt. The volume, *Illuminations*, included the essay "The Storyteller." McMurtry sat in the Dairy Queen, sipped his Dr Pepper, and went through Benjamin's essay. He mulled over the argument. Years later, in 1999, McMurtry published his memoirs titled *Walter Benjamin at the Dairy Queen*.[17]

The circumstances of Benjamin, a German-Jewish refugee subsisting in Paris as war threatened Europe, and McMurtry, a successful American novelist and screenwriter residing in the North Texas town—population under two thousand—in which he was raised, could not be more different. They lived in separate universes: that was obvious. "The Storyteller" had been published in 1936, the year of McMurtry's birth and five years before electricity had reached his rural Texas hometown. "Remember," reflects McMurtry, "that Walter Benjamin, in 'The Storyteller,' was writing at sunset. In four years he would be dead." He notes, "I was a boy of four, with not yet even a radio to listen to" when Benjamin killed himself in 1940.

Yet this American man of letters asked the same question and witnessed the same phenomenon. He read "The Storyteller" and concluded "Walter Benjamin was undoubtedly right." Storytellers were "nearly extinct, like whooping cranes." The day of the storyteller was over, which means that something about how we experience and how we narrate has been altered. "It was startling to sit in that Dairy Queen, reading the words of a cosmopolitan European, a man of Berlin, Moscow, Paris, and realize that what he was describing with a clear sad eye was more or less exactly what had happened in my own small dusty county in my lifetime."[18]

McMurtry observed that he was born "into a world of rural storytellers." "What had become of them?" He ponders the experience of his grandparents, pioneers who came to an almost empty Texas. "My grandfather died not long after Walter Benjamin—very little that was European clung to my grandfather, whereas almost nothing that wasn't European touched Walter Benjamin. . . . He saw one sunset, my grandfather another—in his case it was the sunset of the American frontier." Yet resemblances emerged. What sort of stories could be told, McMurtry wondered, in rural Texas, a place where little happened? Mainly stories about local lives. These were discussed "on the porch after supper, a dribble of family history usually involving accidents, injuries, bad choices, good choices, mistakes made with horses, misjudgments of neighbors, and the like."[19]

Such storytelling depended on a slow cadence of life activities such as tamping and smoking a pipe. McMurtry recalls his grandfather always whittling, reaching for some wood to carve a toothpick. "The decline of whittling, which is the slow paring away of a stick, usually for no other purpose than to occupy the hands, has clearly deprived storytellers of many willing listeners—most of the old men who filled the spit-and-whittle benches outside the rural courthouses of my youth regaled themselves as they whittled with story after story."[20] This remark tallies with that of Benjamin, who linked the decline of storytelling to the fact that "people have ceased to weave and spin, tinker and scrape."[21]

In 1980, more than forty years after Benjamin's reflections on the decline of storytelling, McMurtry confirmed them.* He

---

* A vast scholarship surrounds Benjamin's work. Every Benjamin essay, including "The Storyteller," each book and unpublished manuscript, gets picked over and commented upon. Scholarly monographs tumble off university presses. An academic press issues a series called "Walter Benjamin Studies." A university library lists almost three hundred books containing Walter Benjamin in the title or subtitle published just in the last five years. An International Walter Benjamin Society holds regular conferences with scores of lectures such as "The Image as Abbreviation: Walter Benjamin on Mallarmé's Poetic Monadology" or "The Concept of Gesture in Walter Benjamin: Between Political Criticism and Theology."

Yet in this academic flood, a reference to, much less a discussion of, *Walter Benjamin at the Dairy Queen* barely exists. Why? The book is not exactly hidden. It was published by a leading American press. It contains Walter Benjamin in the title. Any online search will kick it out. In the book, McMurtry ponders not only "The Storyteller" but also Benjamin's larger work.

was addressing a different world, but what was true for Western Europe early in the century would be true for rural Texas later. "When I left for college," writes McMurtry, "I had never seen a television program. . . . The range of seductions offered by the media now were unavailable to me."[22]

The issue at hand is the knot that ties together the experience of diversity, childhood, and now storytelling. The demise of storytelling bespeaks the eclipse of an unhurried life. Of course, this shows in adults. The Austrian writer Stefan Zweig, who came from the same milieu and generation as Benjamin, recalled that he never saw his successful father or his friends rushing about. They walked with measured gait through life. "I cannot remember ever seeing him [his father] run up or down a staircase, or indeed do anything in visible haste."[23] The increased pace affects all, but especially children and their capacity for diversity.

Benjamin never neatly put together all the strands of storytelling and children. He wrote often about childhood—and even did children's radio shows. Benjamin's most popular work is probably "Berlin Childhood around 1900," a series of vignettes of growing up in Berlin. He lovingly summons up his city, his grandmother's apartment and the courtyards. He also recalls the clang of modern life, the fright of the telephone that still hung as "an outcast" in the back hall next to the gas meter, "where its ringing served to multiply the terrors of the Berlin

---

The explanation for this silence is simple. Larry McMurtry wrote about Walter Benjamin, but he did not cite any Benjamin scholarship, an unpardonable offense. He just read and reflected upon Benjamin. McMurtry is a well-known novelist and screenwriter, but he cannot hold a candle to the lowest assistant professor at the humblest college for this reason: If you quote him, he will not quote you in return. In other words, he does not trade in the coin of the academic world: mutual citations, fulsome tributes, and fawning acknowledgments. For the Walter Benjamin industry, founded on the writings of a self-proclaimed Marxist, the value of Larry McMurtry is zero.[24]

household."[25] But one more element must be examined that both Benjamin and McMurtry singled out to illuminate how children's activities get recast.

··•··

For Benjamin and McMurtry, the basis for the storyteller was slow and unfocused activity—or non-activity: boredom. "Boredom is the dream bird that hatches the egg of experience." McMurtry uses this sentence from Benjamin's "The Storyteller" as the epigraph for his book. McMurtry wonders, what has happened to boredom, and the curiosity that it feeds? "It may be true," he notes, that Western society suffers from boredom, but now it is "apt to lie deep in the psyche," muffled by 24-hour news feeds. "Real curiosity now gets little chance to develop—it's smothered with information before it can draw a natural breath."[26]

Benjamin might be considered a specialist in boredom. He once asked, What is the "dialectical antithesis to boredom?"[27] He never answered. In any event, the issue is not just boredom, but the activities and imagination that boredom might sustain. Does boredom have a history? Does its form change over time? Strange to say, boredom too has its specialists, who contrive an exact method, the Multidimensional State Boredom Scale, for an inexact topic.[28] Others gather in international conferences—yes, international conferences on boredom!—where they lecture to each other about boredom.[29] Its history does not get much attention, although some scholars have sought to trace the genesis of boredom and distinguish it from kindred conditions such as melancholy or sloth. *A Philosophy of Boredom* and *Boredom: A Lively History* are two of many recent books.[30] A few historians view boredom as little more than an eternal ailment of life, a new name for "acedia," the torpor that bedeviled monks.

Boredom as a general phenomenon belongs to the modern age. Benjamin believed that boredom began to be "experienced in epidemic proportions" in the 1840s.[31] "It is the 'privilege' of modern man," writes Lars Svendsen, a Norwegian philosopher, in his book on boredom. "Before Romanticism it seems to have been a marginal phenomenon, reserved for monks and the nobility."[32] Kierkegaard and Chekhov can serve as two markers for when boredom besets a population. In *Either/Or*, Kierkegaard declares that he begins with the principle that "all men are boring." Moreover, boredom, "the root of all evil," is spreading. "What wonder, then, that the world is regressing, that evil is gaining ground more and more, since boredom is on the increase."[33] Chekhov's plays would confirm Kierkegaard's point. Boredom overwhelms his characters. "Life is boring, it's stupid, it stinks," proclaims the doctor in *Uncle Vanya*.[34]

The onset of boredom cannot be dated. Perhaps this much can be hazarded: at a certain point, boredom becomes a general affliction. Moreover, in the modern period, boredom largely shifts from an objective to a subjective characteristic.[35] In a Horace satire, boredom comes from without; it is a person, a bore or a pest, who annoys the poet.[36] In the modern period, the pest migrates inward. Once someone was a bore; now boredom is a state that afflicts the individual. "I'm bored!" says the child.

For the United States, Robert Paul Smith's 1957 memoir *Where Did You Go? Out. What Did You Do? Nothing* remains a good touchstone for twining together this chapter's last two strands, boredom and play. "I didn't know the word [boredom]," Smith writes of his own youth in the 1920s. We were bored as kids, but we didn't know it. "We never thought that a day was anything but a whole lot of nothing interrupted occasionally by something." But nowadays, Smith observed, we worry if our kids are not occupied—and they have lost the ability to do nothing.[37] They no longer know how to play by themselves. Now they have organized sports like Little League.

The shape of boredom shapes play. We have been led from the eclipse of traditional boredom to the eclipse of storytelling and now to the rhythms of how children play. Children can no longer do nothing, to follow Smith. The preconditions for experiencing diversity remains the issue; and this requires an assessment of children's play, and how it sustains a capacity for diversity.

To address play and its evolution brings us to Johan Huizinga, a Dutch historian best known for *The Waning of the Middle Ages*. Play and its fate long fascinated him. On a trip to the United States in 1926 he remarked that organized sports were replacing unstructured play. "Play is culture." It is art and rite and dance. But modern sports subject play to "uniformity in the service of the machinery of rules." The loss, for Huizinga, is "palpable."[38] Several decades later Huizinga returned to this subject. His *Homo Ludens*—Man the Player—subtitled "A Study of the Play-Element in Culture," has become a classic. He considered play essential to culture and tried to characterize it. He defined its first two features as freedom and pretense. Play could not be compelled; and it necessitated "stepping out of 'real' life into a temporary sphere of activity. . . . Every child knows perfectly well that he is 'only pretending,' or that it was 'only for fun.'"[39]

At the end of his study Huizinga mooted the issue of how much the play spirit is "still alive in our own day." He again regretted the "increasing systematization and regimentation" of sports. Professional sports lack the spontaneity and carelessness of real play. "Really to play, a man must play like a child." He denounced what he called "false play," where adolescents with badges march in parades. Huizinga was writing in 1938 as Nazism advanced. Several years earlier he had sounded an alarm. "We are living in a demented world. And we know it," ran the first two sentences of that warning, *In the Shadow of Tomorrow*.[40] Now in *Homo Ludens* Huizinga alluded to Nazi mass spectacles. The goose-steppers are not playing. He denounced parading as adolescent puerilism, which should be distinguished from playfulness. "A child playing is not puerile."[41]

Homo Ludens did not inaugurate the study of play but sparked renewed interest in the domain.[42] Today the study of play has become a cause and an academic field with journals, conferences, and scholarly controversies. Rochester, New York, boasts the Strong National Museum of Play, which publishes the *American Journal of Play*. Few doubt the importance of play for children.[43] Yet it remains a fuzzy subject. The issue here is how play and its recasting affect the way children encounter the world.

Popular attention to how and where children play dates from the end of the 19th century, when it was bolstered by folklorists, who usually saw themselves as documenting practices about to vanish. A sense of loss infused the study of children's games. Already William Wells Newell, in his 1883 *Games and Songs of American Children*, which cataloged children's pastimes, regretted "the threatened disappearance of these childish traditions." The old games and songs, he believed, were not marked by mechanical repetition: "The mind and heart were active, the spirit of the language appropriated, and a vein of deep though childish poetry nourished sentiment and imagination." Newell, who was the founder of the American Folklore Society, observed that children themselves composed the games, and adds, presciently, "The loss cannot be made good by the deliberate invention of older minds. Children's amusement, directed and controlled by grown people, would be neither childish nor amusing."[44]

In fact, children's play does fall under the sway of adults. With all due qualification, the play of children has altered, especially over the last 70 years. Between 1945 and 2015 the quantity and type of play has shifted. The evidence is both anecdotal and sociological. Children play less—less with each other, less outdoors, and less with things of their own making. The spontaneity and self-direction of play may have flourished in the immediate past. Howard P. Chudacoff, in his *Children at Play: An American History*, titles one chapter "The Golden Age of Unstructured Play, 1900–1950."[45] New forms of play undercut the subjective dimension of diversity; that is, the psychic space that enables a child to encounter the world on its own dwindles. As adult-run activities, organized sports, and computer games occupy this space, the capacity for diversity shrinks. To be sure, the restructuring of play after 1950 is not only due to television and computers.

The history of play cannot be neatly sliced into decades, even half-centuries. Chudacoff notes that the period of "unstructured play" saw the emergence of the American toy industry, with teddy bears, Erector Sets, Monopoly, Kewpie dolls, Tinkertoys, yo-yos, jacks, Lincoln Logs, and model trains. Yet these toys call up an era both not-so-distant and irrevocably past. What girl today plays jacks? What boy today plays with model trains or Erector Sets? These toys belong to a period in which children seemed to have more time, patience, or concentration. The A.C. Gilbert Company that patented and began marketing the Erector Set in 1913 became the largest American toy company. It sold some 30 million Erector Sets. But its decline, evident in the 1950s, ended with bankruptcy in the late 1960s. The company mirrors the trajectory of play in America—and more than play, since it once constituted a large New Haven manufacturer. Today offices and studios occupy its old factory.[46]

Henry Petroski, the Duke University engineer and writer, recalls spending long hours with construction sets and model trains. "Like many of my war-baby contemporaries . . . I played with Erector sets," which presented "considerable challenge" inasmuch as they came with no plans. "With a screwdriver and wrench" and with "only a picture in our mind's eye of some great bridge or tower of our own devising," children were expected to assemble the pieces and build.[47] Numerous scientists recall similar childhoods. "At home I spent much of the time by myself in a large front room which was my private world," recalls the late Harry Kroto, who shared the Nobel Prize in Chemistry in 1996. "As time went by it filled up with junk and in particular I had a Meccano set [the European version of the Erector Set] with which I 'played' endlessly." The set required dexterity. Indeed, Kroto calls the extinction of the Erector Set by Lego "a major disaster." Kids love Lego "partly because it is so simple and partly because it is seductively colored."[48]

Lego itself reflects a shift in the modes of play. Founded in Denmark in the 1930s, the company became successful in the late 1950s after it switched from wood to interlocking plastic bricks. In its new phase Lego marketed just a handful of bricks and sets, all interchangeable. These sets, according to one study, sustained "spontaneous" play because "the bricks were still fairly generic and would allow for the creation of many personal ideas." Moreover, the sets lacked detailed manuals, which also contributed to self-directed play. But Lego shifted track in the 1990s. Lego's own marketing department concluded that its sets looked "boring and old fashioned" compared to electronic toys. The company accelerated its product "differentiation," which entailed the introduction of more specialized and flashier sets. By 2004, Lego was stamping out twelve thousand different pieces, many of which could only be fit together in one way. The sets de-emphasized self-directed or imaginative construction. "More often than not," explains a Dutch scholar, the new sets "were tied to other media products such as films, television, comics or computer games."[49]

The reason for the demise of the Erector Set and the rise of Lego is up for grabs. The next generation lost interest—boys in Erector and chemistry sets, girls in jacks and jump rope. Not only Lego but also television and then video games showed up. One account cautiously explains the demise of the A.C. Gilbert Company by the fact that the Erector Set "takes patience and planning, attributes more suited to children of another era."[50] In any event, the 1950s can be considered a transition period, signposted by a new five-day-a-week variety television show, *The Mickey Mouse Club*, which began in 1955. The Mattel toy company largely sponsored *The Mickey Mouse Club*.

The point is: both the stuff and rhythms of play have been transformed over the last decades. Not only jacks, marbles, and paper dolls have entered the domain of the archaic, but also unorganized outdoor play seems endangered. Urban street games such as stickball, stoop ball, and jumping rope have much diminished, if not disappeared. In the 1930s a thousand-page manuscript by two New York City researchers documented hundreds of street games and their variations. Fifty years later two folklorists followed up and concluded the urbanscape had much altered.

With the earlier compendium as a benchmark, Amanda Dargan and Steven Zeitlin declare in their 1990 *City Play* "we did not find anywhere near the number or variety of games played out of doors."[51] Numerous diarists and autobiographers confirm the same situation. Stuart Brown, in his book *Play*, returns to his old Chicago neighborhood and finds little spontaneous play on the sidewalks and streets. His last trip back "revealed no empty lots, no pick-up games, a lot of adult-supervised youth sports," he writes.[52] The *New York Post* asked in 2010, "What happened to New York's storied street games?" Versions of these games reach back centuries. "The strategic sliding of bottle caps across a city street known as Skelly, the heroic dodging and weaving of Ringoleavio, the fast-moving batting of Boxball—these and other classic streets games are all but extinct in New York."[53]

Brian Sutton-Smith, in his careful study of play in New Zealand, finds the same trend already in 1950: "There is much less variety in 1950 than in 1900." Many games such as knucklebones, stagknife, and marbles have disappeared. He notes children themselves ran these games without the adult-awards of organized sports. He worries about their decline and makes a point that informs this chapter: Play "produces diversity and increases creativity." It makes people "more flexible." But play can be "extinguished."[54]

Classic pastimes of children required few or no possessions. They operated outside the market economy; or, at least, they called for limited materials and purchases. Many games used only a rope, stick, or ball. "The streets were the ideal playgrounds," recalls a New York memoirist of playing stickball in the 1930s. "No uniforms were required." Manhole covers and sewer grating served as bases. "For bats we obtained old broom handles, sawed off at the proper length. . . . And the ball? Our favorite ball was the rubber 'Spalding.'"[55] The classic pink ball of stickball sold for 25 cents in the 1950s. Jump rope cost about the same. Hide-and-seek was free. From a business perspective, these games were disasters.

Contemporary children's games differ in kind and cost. For starters, adults design them, a simple fact true of even the most creative computer games. Moreover, from organized sports, which necessitate uniforms and specialized equipment, to video and computer games, which require hardware, the games are not cheap. Video games often sucker children into spending money by updating versions or through links to merchandise. Newspapers regularly run stories of children who have unwittingly purchased upgrades or spent imaginary money that turned out to be real.[56] Today the market saturates children's activities. In Aldous Huxley's 1932 dystopic *Brave New World*, the Director of Hatcheries and Conditioning shows visitors around headquarters. They come across children playing outside with a large apparatus. The Director muses that in the past children played with just a ball and a stick. "Imagine the folly of allowing people to play elaborate games which do nothing whatever to increase consumption." Nowadays, he remarks with satisfaction, the authorities would not approve new games unless they maintain purchases.[57]

The authorities have been largely successful. This has happened in part by moving children's activities indoors, where they unfold in front of television and computer screens. As one aging gamester bemoaned in the documentary *New York Street Games*, a superhero with magic powers easily vanquishes a stick and ball.[58] The decamping from outside to inside cannot be simply attributed to iPads and seductive videos, but to worsened automobile traffic that rendered streets more dangerous; suburbanization that shifted children out of the cities to bigger homes with indoor space—and fewer kids outside; and accelerating fear of unattended youth. The last covers a lot of ground, but since the 1950s with its crisis of juvenile delinquency, captured in films like James Dean's 1955 *Rebel Without a Cause*, paranoia has struck American parents. "Not even the Communist conspiracy," intoned a US senator in 1954, "could devise a more effective way to demoralize, disrupt, confuse, and destroy our future citizens than apathy on the part of adult Americans to the scourge known as Juvenile Delinquency."[59]

The idiom has changed over the decades, but not the anxiety. In recent years obsession over grades, scores, and achievement has redoubled the general stress over drugs and delinquency. The pressures lead parents and schools to reduce free time, which seems dangerous as well as useless. Over a twenty-year period, children's time in organized sports has leaped 50 percent. Nowadays the earliest grades limit recess and expand directed activities.[60] "Even in preschool, play is under assault," writes Hara Estroff Marano in *A Nation of Wimps*. "Desks and work sheets are increasingly replacing blocks and make-believe." A tutoring industry devoted to two- to six-year-olds has emerged.[61] A sign of the times: a primary school eliminates the annual kindergarten play. Why? "Professional decisions" led the school to cancel the play so that the tots could spend time more usefully—on their careers. In accord with the "demands of the twenty-first century," the school informed the parents, "we are responsible for preparing children for college and careers with valuable lifelong skills."[62] Hence no more rehearsals for the little ones. The 21st century needs budding financial wizards, not kindergarten matinee stars.

The disquiet of parents has even been reflected in dull playgrounds, which may also have nudged children indoors. Not only the psychic space but the physical space that allows diverse experiences contracts. Several causes coalesce to render playgrounds bland, but parental fear and litigation rank high. A social reforming ethos always informed playground construction. Early reformers wanted to save play from the crowded cities, where they believed it suffocated. This notion drove Henry Curtis, a founder of the 1906 Playground Association of America. "The American city," he declared, "which has mixed up Jews and Greeks and Italians and Slavs in a single community," had no common life and no support for play. "Play has not been encouraged."[63] An advertisement for a playground slide from the 1920s touted "Better the playground and trained leaders than reformatories and uniformed guards." But these old playgrounds boasted 30-foot slides, as well as colossal seesaws and towers.[64] Today such structures get nixed by the town's lawyer.

Safety concerns and lawsuits have refigured playgrounds. One outfit, the National Program for Playground Safety at the University of Northern Iowa, announces on its website that more than 200,000 children are injured on playgrounds each year; and it provides report cards, as well as kits, and training to evaluate playground safety. By enrolling in their courses, a concerned parent can graduate to become a Certified Early Childhood Outdoor Play Inspector.[65] The number given for those hurt on playgrounds is dubious; at least the clear majority of bruises appear to be minor, mainly hand and wrist injuries. However, many parents are convinced that playgrounds are dangerous—and sue for damages.[66] While the number of children declined 7 percent in New York City between 2005 and 2013, claims for playground injuries rose 53 percent.[67]

Playground design, like landscape architecture with which it is allied, bears witness to fashion and political trends. Some towns do buck trends to construct imaginative playgrounds, but increasingly one playground resembles another; most have adopted colorful tubular plastics or the so-called "post-and-platform" system, a connected series of tubes, low platforms, and slides.[68] Sandboxes, monkey-bars, seesaws, and high slides have largely disappeared. "Fear of litigation," reported the *New York Times* in 2011, "led New York City officials to remove seesaws, merry-go-rounds and the ropes that young Tarzans used to swing from one platform to another."[69]

One art historian believes that "concerns about safety, combined with panic about liability and insurance" have led to the "homogenization of playground design." In her *American Playgrounds*, Susan Solomon writes that the McDonald's model of play space—brightly-colored, oversized, easy-to-maintain, safe plastic modules—has become the norm. These playgrounds offer little possibility for experimenting or creativity. Children "follow the restricted options offered by a post-and-platform ensemble: wait, go up, go across, go down, start all over again."[70] Michael Gotkin, a landscape designer, observes that "a brief" moment existed when artists, architects, and parents collaborated on rethinking playgrounds, but that is gone. "You don't really design playgrounds now. You order them out of a catalogue."[71]

Even Darell Hammond, a playground enthusiast and founder of a nonprofit organization that builds them, regrets the trend.

He believes that children suffer from what he calls "play deficit." In recent decades "kids have lost between 9 and 12 hours of free play each week." Over the same period the time children expend on computers and smartphones has jumped. Cause and effect get jumbled. Do playgrounds lose out because they have become bland? Sparked by legal suits, schools and towns eliminate playgrounds or render them dull. Hammond complains that some playgrounds are "too safe," with guardrails and components close to the ground. "It's as if," he writes, we are "building playgrounds for adults . . . when we should be building playgrounds with the intent to provide an environment of play, fun and risk."[72]

As one playground denizen reports, "It is no longer easy to find a playground that has an element of surprise, no matter how far you travel. Kids can find the same slides at the same heights and angles as the ones in their own neighborhood, with many of the same accessories."[73] Saccharine playgrounds are only one part of the story, the writer Hanna Rosin continues. "It's hard to absorb," she observes, "how much childhood norms have shifted in just one generation. Actions that would have been considered paranoid in the '70s—walking third-graders to school, forbidding your kid to play ball in the street, going down the slide with your child in your lap—are now routine. In fact, they are markers of good, responsible parenting."[74] It is also hard to absorb how the basic activities of children have shifted in one generation. A *New Yorker* cartoon has a child in his room glued to a computer tablet, who responds to an admonishing parent, "Go out and play? What is this, 1962?"

On a tangential but revealing note, far fewer children today bicycle or walk to school—even when it is a mile or less from home—than in the recent past. "Overwhelmingly," a study concludes, children arrive at school in their parent's car, "a significant reversal from four decades ago." In 1969 almost 88 percent of American students between the ages of five and fourteen walked or bicycled to school. In 2009, the numbers had dropped to 38 percent.[75] The same trends surface elsewhere. A study of British youths found that the number of eight- and nine-year-olds that traveled to school by themselves plummeted over twenty years from more than 80 percent to less than 20 percent.[76] Apart from issues of health and obesity, this might have little significance. Yet traveling by car with a parent, and increasingly with a tablet or phone, might delimit fantasy, if not openness to the world.

Studies confirm that children's free time has declined, swallowed by organized activities and computers. The figures bandied about suggest that from seven to twelve hours a week of free time has evaporated. "Although seven and one-half hours in a week," researchers note, "may not seem significant, it represents more than an entire school day."[77] By any calculation today young people spend a gargantuan amount of time on social media and other smartphone or computers activities. Children "devote more time to media than to any other single activity apart from sleep."[78] Even the youngest children plug into iPad and video games—at the expense of play. One researcher concludes that "children today do not play as often as children in the past." She confirms "the notion that today's children lead a more passive, inactive life indoors than the previous generation."[79]

Like much of social science research, correlations and causes easily conflate. One result of the eclipse of play, especially outdoors, may be the rise of childhood obesity.[80] Another, less obvious and more contested consequence may be the spread of attention deficient disorders. This has been argued by the late neuroscientist Jaak Panksepp, who believed in the biological necessity of play. "The explosion" of attention disorder diagnoses, he wrote, "may largely reflect the fact that more and more of our children no longer have adequate spaces and opportunities to express this natural biological need—to play with each other in vigorous rough-and-tumble ways, each and every day."[81]

Along kindred lines, but with larger claims, Boston College psychologist Peter Gray attributes to "play deprivation" the increased rates of depression, anxiety, and other psychopathologies of young people, including suicide, which has quadrupled among youth under age 15 since 1950. Like Panksepp, he finds that outside play is crucial for mental health. Such play is not only egalitarian and voluntary but hones social skills. "To keep the game going—whether it is a rough-and-tumble play fight, a sociodramatic fantasy game, or a pickup game of baseball—it is essential to keep the other players happy, or at least happy enough that they will not quit. Rules must be negotiated."[82] Gray registers a rise of narcissism and a fall in empathy as free play shrinks. With the decline of play, the psychic resources of children decline.[83]

From a slightly different angle Sherry Turkle concurs in her *Reclaiming Conversation*; she observes that as face-to-face interaction sinks, so do "the foundations for emotional stability and social fluency." Children become agitated, withdrawn, and depressed.[84] A bus driver in the documentary *New York Street Games* comments on the difficulty of transporting children nowadays, who squabble more than in the past. He explains the clashes by the fact that children no longer have much unsupervised play and with it the experience of getting along with others. The observation seconds the idea advanced in Chapter

One, above: democracy and play sustain each other. The blue-collar driver and the white-collar scholar agree that democratic talents thin as free play wanes.

··•··

The boredom of rainy Sunday afternoons that led children to paper dolls and Erector Sets evokes scenes that seem as dated as horse-drawn buggies and gas-lit streets. Now children have something faster and easier, video games or movies on a tablet. The underlying psychic energy seems composed of nervousness or anxiety. Boredom has been vanquished. Of course, nervousness is not confined to children, but has become a general social phenomenon. Nor is it new. But is it linked to the eclipse of diversity? Stefan Zweig, the Austrian-Jewish writer, thought so.

Like Huizinga, he traveled to the United States; and like Huizinga and other well-educated Europeans, he found the New World wanting. In 1925 he published a piece that distilled his experience. Its title, "The Monotonization of the World," indicates the thrust, a lament over dwindling diversity. For Zweig, the traveler cannot avoid the impression that "everything is become more uniform." It is "the most urgent, the most critical phenomenon of our time." Along with the observers cited in the previous chapter, Zweig comments that the distinctive traits of countries are vanishing: "The characteristic habits of individual peoples are being worn away, native dress giving way to uniforms, customs becoming international." Zweig fears the "complete end of individuality." People are dressing the same and doing the same things. "Faces become increasingly similar through the influence of the same passions, bodies more similar to each other through the practice of the same sports, minds more similar for sharing the same interests."[85] Zweig announced the end of diversity.

Some ten years before Benjamin's "The Storyteller," Zweig also identified a new type of boredom. The old kind came "from calmness, from sitting on the park bench playing dominoes and smoking a pipe." It allowed for reflection, storytelling and individuality. The new type is "restless, nervous, and aggressive. . . . It has lost its playfulness"; it scurries about looking for new sensations and activities. Zweig also knew the origin of the new boredom: the United States. The old variety of boredom was European, the new American. Europe has imported a "dreadful, quite specific" American boredom. Historians of the future will have no doubt. America has colonized Europe. America is "the source of that terrible wave of uniformity" that gives everyone the same skin, fashions, books, conversation—and the same boredom.

The demonization of America put Zweig in good company. At least since the last decade of the 19th century, critics began to bemoan Americanization—or on rare occasions to celebrate it. The British journalist W.T. Stead published a book in 1901, *Americanization of the World*, to reassure his countrymen that whatever the achievements of the United States, they accrue to Britain, its originator. He focused on the economic superiority of the United States and wanted to avoid "recriminations, caviling, and bitterness" in what he dubbed "the Americanization of the World."[86]

Much more typical were the attacks on America and how it threatened old Europe. The French writer Georges Duhamel's 1930 account of his travels were published as *America the Menace*. "I belong to a community of peasants who for centuries have lovingly cultivated fifty different varieties of plum, and who find in each a taste deliciously unlike that of any of the others." Such an array had no place in the United States, where quantity and uniformity were prized. "What strikes the European traveler," declares Duhamel, is the progressive "effacement of the individual." He saw the future, consumerism and fast cars hustling through a homogeneous landscape.

He took a trip with a wealthy couple; the husband was a businessman. What better symbol of America could there be, he asked, "than this madly rushing machine, turned loose at full speed between two pasteboard landscapes, steered by a charming woman with manicured nails and beautiful legs, who smoked a cigarette while traveling between fifty and sixty miles an hour, while her husband, seated on the cushions of the rear seat, with set jaw scribbled figures on the back of an envelope"?[87]

This stuff—and the references can easily be multiplied—is easy to dismiss as the plaints of elitist Europeans, which in fact they largely were. Even as a young adolescent, Stefan Zweig inhaled high culture and pursued the poets of the day. He lived in an ethereal world of art, literature, and music. It is indicative that Zweig not only never learned to drive, he never learned to bicycle. When he arrived in Manhattan Zweig asked the hotel concierge for directions to the first on his to-do list—a visit to the grave of Walt Whitman. The fellow never heard of the poet, much less could he direct Zweig to the site.[88]

Nevertheless, the snobbism, no matter how distasteful, can be ignored for the larger issue. Americanization became a shorthand for advanced capitalism, something not confined to the New World. Sociologists such as Max Weber and Georg Simmel saw this clearly. Simmel's 1903 essay "The Metropolis and Mental Life" situated the "atrophy of individual culture" within the modern commercial city that prized "punctuality, calculability and exactness." The money economy hollows out "the core of things, their peculiarities, their specific values and their uniqueness and incomparability." Simmel feared "the vast overwhelming organization of things and forces" was swamping the individual.[89] There was nothing here about Americanization, but about life in an industrial society, and the accelerating shocks that beset the urban dweller.

The intensifying anxiety of modern life by 1900 had not only become a common observation, it retained an American angle. George Miller Beard, an American doctor, popularized the idea of neurasthenia or nervous exhaustion; and in 1881 published a book called *American Nervousness*. He asked forthrightly, "Why not English, French, German, or Irish nervousness?" For Beard Americans were the most nervous, because they led the way in modernization, but other countries too were affected: "The nervousness of America is extending over Europe, which, in certain countries, at least, is becoming rapidly Americanized."[90] Even those who were sympathetic to Beard, and they included Freud, doubted the American particularity. Freud quoted the comment of a Swiss psychiatrist, Ludwig Binswanger, that Beard's claim of discovering a nervous disease specific to the United States was "of course erroneous." However, Binswanger had continued, the fact that "an *American* physician" first described this disorder points to its close relationship to modern industrial society.[91]

American Nervousness offered a compendium of astute and off-the-wall observations. For more than one hundred pages Beard argued passionately against the "old superstition" that too much mental activity undermined health. To the contrary, Beard analyzed statistics on occupations and longevity and concluded that the "brain-working classes," which he identified as "clergymen, lawyers, physicians, merchants, scientists, and men of letters," lived longer than "muscle-working classes." Beard died at age 43.[92]

Yet Beard perceived that modern industrial society exacted a price on the psyche. Electric lights, steam power, printing, railroad travel, and noise all contributed to American nervousness. Beard even noted that American presidential electoral politics exacerbated nervousness. After months of "infinite wranglings and controversies," half the population wakes up after an election with "concentrated agony" to face "the long-drawn-out disappointments of the coming years." For Beard "modern nervousness is the cry" of the individual "struggling" with advanced society.[93]

While this was hardly his focus, Beard noticed the effect on children, who suffer from ill-conceived education riven with "inflammatory competition" and endless tasks, lectures, recitations. No wonder American children are "so nervous." Beard compared this to a classical education: "The education of the Athenian boy consisted in play and games and songs, and repetitions of poems, and physical feats in the open air." His education was more like a "long vacation" than the stress of the American lad.[94]

The vacation of childhood with unstructured time and space has largely vanished. Today speed and instant-everything slay the boredom of childhood. With what results? "What I'm wondering," writes Larry McMurtry, almost exactly a century after Beard, is "the level of curiosity" that exists today. For Walter Benjamin curiosity was "nurtured to some extent by boredom."[95] This is the bird that hatches the "egg of experience." With the usual qualification that generalizations are not valid for all children, the link between play and experience frays; at the same time, the demise of quiet boredom impedes unfettered curiosity. To experience diversity depends on the ability to step out of the self and to imagine—and embrace—the world. The subjective capacity cannot flourish without the psychic space that environmental clutter sabotages. Today the dream bird and the whooping crane are endangered. We need, writes Tim Wu in *The Attention Merchants*, a reclamation project to recover the most vital human resource: our "mental space."[96]

"When I leave home to walk to school / Dad always says to me, / 'Marco, keep your eyelids up / And see what you can see.'"[97] So opens the classic 1937 children's book *And to Think That I Saw It on Mulberry Street* by Dr. Seuss. Marco imagines many things as he walks home from school. But what does today's student commuter see or imagine? *And to Think That I Saw It on Mulberry Street* was loosely based on Theodor Seuss Geisel's own childhood in Springfield, Massachusetts. Could it be rewritten for today's generation? Marco is no longer walking to school; and with phone or tablet in hand, his eyelids are down. Today Marco sees nothing on Mulberry Street.

CHAPTER FOUR

Diversity and its Vicissitudes

Across the Centuries

"The diversity of the breeds is something astonishing." This is Darwin in the first chapter of *On the Origin of Species*. He is characterizing domestic pigeons as he seeks to unravel the "mystery of mysteries," or the origin of divergent species. "I have, after deliberation, taken up domestic pigeons. I have kept every breed which I could purchase or obtain." He went to pigeon shows. He hung out with pigeon fanciers. "I sat one evening in a gin-palace in the Borough amongst a set of Pigeon-fanciers," he wrote to a friend, as he collected information.[1] What he finds about pigeons amazes him. He considers the English carrier, the short-faced tumbler, the runt, the barb, the pouter, and the fantail and revels in their differences. He examines beaks and heads. The English carrier is "remarkable" for the "wonderful development of the carunculated skin about the head," which is accompanied by "greatly elongated eyelids" and "large external orifices to the nostrils." He compares this head to that of the short-faced tumbler with a beak "almost like that of a finch."[2]

The chapter is called "Variation under Domestication." Darwin was a master of detailing slight variations. Such is the work of thinking, pondering differences and their significance.

The old saw that you can't compare apples and oranges is wrong. You can and do. After all, they are both fruits. They differ but they are also related. Yet sometimes small variations reveal more than large ones. Darwin's work turns on small variations.

The diversity of pigeons is astonishing, but so is the diversity of all of nature, which would not be news to Darwin. "Consider," writes the botanist Hope Jahren in her recent scientific memoir *Lab Girl*, that more than a hundred thousand leaves grow on a single oak tree and "no two of them are exactly the same. . . . Every oak leaf on Earth is . . . unique."[3] The idea of exuberant diversity of nature is as old as the hills, as it were, and can be found already among Greek thinkers. To be sure, the favored term was not diversity, but variety, which overlaps with it, but has a longer history and reach.

In *Variety: The Life of a Roman Concept*, William Fitzgerald, a classicist, follows the trajectory of variety among the Romans. He notes that in recent years the "semantic power" of "variety" has "migrated" to "diversity." The Latin motto for the European Union, for instance, is *In varietate concordia*, but the English translation runs "United in Diversity."[4] Several millennia prior to the EU phrase, the variety of nature puzzled the Greek Stoics. How can one explain the plenitude of nature? Perhaps the first thinker who expressed the idea of an exuberant and variegated nature was the Stoic Chrysippus (279–206 BCE). He declared (according to Plutarch) that nature "rejoices" in variety and produces many creatures "for the sake of beauty." Nature takes "delight in richness of colors and shapes." Chrysippus added what Plutarch called a "strange observation," but which does not seem strange. For the Stoic, the peacock's tail proves that nature delights in variety. "The peacock was created on account of its tail, on account of the beauty of the tail."[5]

The idea of a diverse and fecund nature can be followed through the ages. It played out in the notion of the "plurality of worlds," which also has classical antecedents. "An infinite number of worlds exists in the universe, some of which worlds are like and some of which are unlike our own," declared the Greek philosopher Epicurus.[6] The fecundity of nature served as the argument. Nature covers everything. Why would it stop with the visible? This also becomes the logic of Epicurus's follower, Lucretius. He refers to the fact that "seeds innumerable in number and unfathomable in sum are flying about" to suggest the existence of other worlds.[7]

In the modern era, voyages to the New World and Copernican cosmology redoubled the question of multiple worlds. If the Earth were no longer center of the universe, the prospect of other worlds seemed possible.[8] The idea found its most elegant expression in the popular 17th-century dialogue *Conversations on the Plurality of Worlds* by the French publicist Bernard Le Bovier de Fontenelle. A philosopher and a marquise discuss the implications of Copernicus for the prospect of life elsewhere, especially on the moon. "I love the Moon," the marquise aptly says, "for staying with us when all the other planets abandoned us." The issue is whether life exists on the moon and beyond, and if so, what sort. The philosopher sidesteps theological hazards and argues that the fecundity of nature would hardly stop at the moon. The marquise is convinced but "perplexed by the diversity" of the inhabitants of the cosmos. I see, she says, that since Nature is "an enemy of repetition," it makes everyone in the universe unique. "But how can one picture all that?" The philosopher has an answer. "The diversity which Nature must have placed among all the worlds" is like the diversity of faces in this world. "All faces in general are made on the same model." But each is different. "What secret must Nature have possessed to vary in so many ways so simple a thing as a face?"[9]

As in nature, so in life; at least this would be argued by humanists such as Erasmus in the 16th century. If nature loves diversity, so do people. In his book on rhetoric Erasmus advises youth that good style requires variety. Nothing is more offensive or tedious than repetition, declared Erasmus. Without variation, one sounds like a cuckoo and "croaks out the same words repeatedly." To escape this "monotony," take a cue from nature. "Nature herself especially rejoices in variety; in such a great throng of things she has left nothing anywhere not painted with some wonderful artifice of variety."

The mind as well needs variety, which writing must supply. "If all things continually present themselves to the mind without variation, it will at once turn away in disgust." This is the object of studying rhetoric, to be able to write and speak in different modes. Erasmus takes as a model the Greek wrestler Milo of Croton, who apparently boasted a repertoire of moves. "It will be well" to emulate him, "making at first two variations, then three, then more and more."

Erasmus gives an example of prose diversity with multiple versions of a simple sentence. "As an experiment," he wants to see how many variations can be formulated for the statement: "Your letter has delighted me very much." This sentence might not seem to offer many possibilities, but in a tour de force Erasmus wrings from it over a hundred and fifty variants that go on for pages. These start from "What you wrote has given me incredible pleasure" and "Your epistle has cheered me exceedingly," then move on to "How should I tell you what joy titillated the spirit of your Erasmus when he received your letter," "When I looked at your letter an extraordinary multitude of joys seized my mind," and "No dainty so caresses the palate as your letter charms my spirit."[10]

For theologically minded thinkers, and this means all up to the recent past, not simply the plurality of worlds and words, but the plurality of human actions presented an issue. The 18th-century German philosopher Gottfried Leibniz, satirized by Voltaire in *Candide*, joined those who sought to reconcile an omnipotent God with the plurality of behavior. Why would an all-seeing divinity not populate the world with virtue of one stripe? Because variety provides more benefits than its absence, answered Leibniz, a truth valid for nature and mankind. "Nature has need of animals, plants, inanimate bodies"; it requires more than one type. So too with people. "Wisdom must vary," stated Leibniz. The example of Midas confirms Leibniz: "Midas proved to be less rich when he had only gold." Diversity beats uniformity. In a rare passage of eloquence, Leibnitz declares, "To multiply one and the same thing only would be superfluity, and poverty too. To have a thousand well-bound Vergils in one's library, always to sing the airs from the opera of Cadmus and Hermione, to break all the china in order only to have cups of gold, to have only diamond buttons, to eat nothing but partridges, to drink only Hungarian or Shiraz wine—would one call that reason?"[11]

··•··

To survey the celebration of diversity in the modern period can be misleading. A thousand authors can be cited who rejoice in human and natural variety; and those references can be extended till yesterday—or till today. Yet the vector of modern thought pointed in the opposite direction; it led to establishing regular and uniform laws for nature and society. The laws of motion and gravity associated with Newton and Galileo stamp modern thinking; they posited patterns of universal validity or what has been called "the mathematization" of nature.[12] To grasp the "book" of the universe, stated Galileo, one must understand its language and letters. "It is written in the language of mathematics, and its characters are triangles, circles, and other geometric figures."[13]

The impact of such thought cannot be overstated. The *philosophes* of the Enlightenment saw themselves as working in tandem with the Newtons and Galileos. Voltaire celebrated Newton as almost God. After his return from England he published a book to introduce Newton to the French. The allegorical frontispiece of that book shows a heavenly shaft of light passing through Newton, bouncing off Voltaire's lover (Madame du Châtelet, who translated Newton) before finding Voltaire at his writing desk. *Philosophes* like Voltaire applied to society invariable laws that had already been established for motion and gravity.

Conceptually the universal and the particular do not stand in contradiction. On the contrary. Fontenelle's example of human faces offered a good example. All have faces but each differs. Diversity and uniformity coexist. Darwin both marveled at the variability of species and sought the law that explained it. *On the Origin of Species* closes on an almost poetic note that ties the diverse and the uniform together. "It is interesting to contemplate an entangled bank, clothed with many plants of many kinds, with birds singing on the bushes, with various insects flitting about, and with worms crawling through the damp earth," stated Darwin in the final paragraph to his chef d'oeuvre, "and to reflect that these elaborately constructed forms, so different from each other . . . have all been produced by laws acting around us."[14]

Though Darwin loved orchids with a "passion," and his son recalled his father's "great delight in the beauty of flowers," he studied flowers to understand how they reproduced and evolved.[15] Likewise, though Galileo devoted his life to studying the natural world, he derided the notion that mere aesthetic appreciation led to an understanding of nature. "A little poetic flower" does not constitute knowledge, he wrote. "Nature takes no delight in poetry."[16] Darwin and Galileo set forth laws of evolution and motion. While reconciling the universal and the particular belongs to the oldest philosophical project, in the modern era the discovery of lawful universals and their application dominate. Galileo's *Discourses Concerning Two New Sciences* takes place in a Venetian arsenal and included an appendix on the paths of cannon projectiles. As one historian of science put it, "the routinization and management of gunpowder artillery" served as the crucible for the scientific revolution.[17] But it is not simply warfare. The employment of uniform laws in society defines the modern period. The thinkers of the 18th and 19th centuries who emphasized diversity were swimming upstream.

The object here is to consider a few thinkers of this countertrend. They championed diversity and its *locus classicus*—the individual—in a world they believed undercut both. Unlike today's diversity boosters, the Humboldts, Tocquevilles, and Mills apprehended the social forces of uniformity; they were not ideologues. They prized diversity and feared its eclipse. They looked at the world with eyes wide open.

The venerable historian Arthur O. Lovejoy is a good starting point to appreciate these counter-thinkers. He noted that a belief in simplification and uniformity marked the Enlightenment. For the French *philosophes*, universal laws imprinted mankind and nature. However, the commitment to uniformity generated a countermovement, an accent on difference, itself a reworking of an idea of plentitude. "There have, in the entire history of thought, been few changes in standards of value more profound and more momentous," stated Lovejoy in *Great Chain of Being*, than when in the late 18th century the belief arose "that diversity itself is of the essence of excellence." This countermovement took many forms such as "the revulsion against simplicity; the distrust of universal formulas in politics; the aesthetic antipathy to standardization; . . . [and] the cultivation of individual, national, and racial peculiarities." Lovejoy declared that, for better or worse, "the discovery of the intrinsic worth of diversity" has marked the modern period.[18]

To make his argument about the rediscovery of diversity, Lovejoy drew upon the German Romantics of the late 18th and early 19th centuries. He turned to Friedrich Schleiermacher, a liberal theologian and philosopher, who fit Lovejoy's bill inasmuch as he championed sentiment and variety against cold uniformity. Schleiermacher is not exactly a household name, but he looms large in liberal Protestant theology. His first book, which brought him fame, *On Religion*, bore the subtitle *Speeches to Its Cultured Despisers*.

Schleiermacher addressed himself to educated circles that disdained religion. The "cultured despisers" failed to understand the varieties of religion. Schleiermacher hammered away at the systematizers, those who reduce religion to a uniform construct. Indeed, he expressed sympathy for the polytheism of ancient Rome that was open to "divine abundance" and that aimed to overcome "narrowness and one-sidedness." The systematizers crush all differences under a "bald uniformity."

The "dogmatizing love of system," he wrote, "excludes all difference." It turns Christianity into a "dead letter." The systematizers set up a rule "so rigid that it condemns everything of another shade." For Schleiermacher individual touch, not uniform regulations, defines religion. With a pizzazz not associated with German philosophers, Schleiermacher pronounces, "This moment is a kiss, an embrace. Without it religion is but a spinning of formulas."[19]

Lovejoy did not draw upon Wilhelm von Humboldt, whom we met in Chapter Two, above, though he could bolster Lovejoy's argument with a crucial element. Humboldt not only praised diversity but highlighted its fate and that of the individual in an age of uniformity. With Humboldt a shift takes place in that diversity becomes more than an idea, a rhetorical goal, or fact of nature; it subsists in society—or doesn't. That is the issue. To Humboldt, modern society saps diversity; the individual begins to suffer from enervation. The specter of a pallid diversity and wan individuals troubled numerous critics in the 19th century such as John Stuart Mill and Alexis de Tocqueville, as we will see. For these observers, not only is the world homogenizing, singularity ebbs from its citizens.

Humboldt left his imprint in many domains, including as the co-founder of the University of Berlin. But a book of his youth, never published during his lifetime, proved his most influential contribution. *The Limits of State Action* tackled diversity and the individual as political issues. Humboldt wrote it in the early 1790s. He was in his mid-twenties and had just visited revolutionary Paris, but the book did not appear till 1851, when published by his brother Alexander fifteen years after Wilhelm's death. Scholars argue over how much the French Revolution influenced this work. Humboldt seemed impressed by the revolutionary ethos and doubtful of the consequences. He saluted "the oppositional energy of the individual and his sense of freedom," but feared what people would do with freedom.[20] In Paris, he of course visited Rousseau's grave, a lodestone for Romantics.[21]

The English translation of *The Limits* caught the eye of John Stuart Mill, who became enamored of the book. Mill used a sentence from it as an epigraph for his own classic, *On Liberty*. "The grand, leading principle, towards which every argument unfolded in these pages directly converges," ran the sentence that Mill cited, "is the absolute and essential importance of human development in its richest diversity." Note the priority of "diversity." It will become Mill's polar star.

Humboldt's book explored the role of the state, which he wanted to circumscribe as a threat to the individual. For this reason, the book became a favorite of conservatives. A conservative publishing house has put out the most recent edition in English. But the place of the state does not exhaust the book. Mill caught its intellectual heart. For Humboldt any analysis of government must rest on the criterion as to what aids or hinders the development of the individual. "The true end of Man," he wrote in the first sentence of the main text, "is the highest and most harmonious development of his powers to a complete and consistent whole."[22] The unfolding of these powers did not solely depend on a limited state, however.

Humboldt posited two conditions for individual development. This is where things get intriguing for tracking diversity and its vicissitudes. Though freedom is "the first and indispensable condition" for individual development, Humboldt suggests another condition in the second sentence of his text: "There is besides another essential [condition]—intimately connected with freedom, it is true—a variety of situations" ["Mannigfaltigkeit der Situationen"]. This is not a throwaway phrase. Humboldt propounds that to unfurl potential, the individual requires variety in habitat.

To follow Humboldt, individual diversity necessitates living diversity—diversity in real situations. Humboldt underlined the point by indicating what happens if monotonous conditions reign. With no variety, the free development of individuals suffers. "Even the most free and self-reliant of men is hindered in his development, when set in a monotonous situation." For Humboldt, freedom and diversity complement each other. Indeed, "these two conditions, of freedom and variety of situation," he stated, may be regarded "as one and the same."[23]

Humboldt was famously a less than clear thinker, but he was clear enough here—and he returned to the issue several times. Individual growth required variety, which sustains energy and creativity. Again, Humboldt was in his early twenties when he expressed these thoughts, fresh from living in revolutionary Paris. In his letters and notes scholars find evidence that Humboldt was searching for his own path and valued diversity in personal relations with women, which might explain how he appreciated a "variety of situations."[24] For Humboldt, individual development needed something he called "Sinnlichkeit," an amalgam of energy, force, sensuality, and instinct.[25] The "whole greatness of mankind," he believed, depended on original and vigorous individuals. Whatever facilitated individual energy he judged a plus; whatever diluted it, a negative. Diverse situations nourished this energy. But a problem arose.

Humboldt believed that variety was dwindling in modern society, which took a toll on the individual. As the world becomes less diverse, people become less energetic, less individualized, less multidimensional. Humboldt supposed that the ancients possessed "greater and more original energy and individuality" because they faced a more variegated environment than modern peoples. Uniformity weakened both environmental diversity and the individual. "Every later epoch—and how rapidly must this decline now proceed!—is necessarily inferior in variety to that which it succeeded: in variety of nature—the vast forests have been cleared, the morasses dried up and so on; in variety of human life, by ever-increasing intercommunication and agglomeration."[26]

These observations join an old dispute, the so-called quarrel of the ancients and moderns, but give it a twist. The partisans of the ancients believed that the achievements of Greece and Rome towered over that of their successors; nature, creativity, and variety blossomed in classical times and faded afterwards.[27] Nature aged and diversity dimmed. Of course, dissenters always popped up. In his return to Renaissance Florence after exile, the humanist Leon Battista Alberti was stunned by the city's artistic achievements. He used to grieve over the superiority of the classics, he declared. "I believed what I had heard many people affirm, namely that Nature had grown old and tired and was no longer producing giants in body or mind." But at last he saw in Florence genius equal to any of the past. His contemporaries, he felt, "should not be slighted in favor of anyone famous in antiquity in these arts."[28]

Fontenelle weighed in and put the issue concisely. If the ancients had "more wit or capacity" than the moderns, the cause must have been a "larger and more beautiful" nature. The discord boils down to "whether the trees were larger in those times than they are today. If they were, then Plato, Homer, and Demosthenes cannot be equaled in our time." But Fontenelle did not accept the argument. Trees today are as grand as the trees of Greece; moreover, we moderns possess better philosophy than the Greeks. Descartes gave us a "new method of reasoning" that surpasses the cloudiness of Aristotle.[29]

The ongoing argument circled around the vigor of nature, society, and diversity. Humboldt and his successors left much of the old quarrel behind, yet they preserved one precept, a belief that diversity and energy attenuate. This was central to Humboldt—and became the crux to Mill and Tocqueville: a creeping uniformity that enfeebled the individual.[30] The theme ran through *The Limits of State Action*, where Humboldt raised the specter of a government that replaces "variety and character" with "national uniformity."[31]

In his discussion of uniformity Humboldt referred to Rousseau's *Emile*, published in 1762. Rousseau had taken up the topic when he evaluated the merits of wide travel for "young people." It was "not sufficient to roam through various countries," he noted. One needs "eyes" and the ability to "turn them toward the object one wants to know." Like Humboldt, he deemed the Greeks and Romans superior to his contemporaries. "The ancients traveled little," declared Rousseau, but "they observed one another better than we observe our contemporaries." Herodotus and Tacitus surpass "all our modern historians" in their depictions of other countries. Those who study the ancient authors know the Greeks, the Romans, or the Persians "better than any people of our day knows its neighbors."

But Rousseau raised something else that Humboldt pursued. The ancients not only possessed superior talent of observation, but their domain also offered a more variegated world to observe. Across Europe diversity waned. The differences between peoples, which "previously struck the observer at first glance," declines, noted Rousseau. Formerly "each nation remained more closed in upon itself." With "little far-flung commerce" and "less communication, less travel, fewer common or contrary interests, and few political and civil relations among peoples," each nation developed separately. In words that Humboldt seemed to borrow, Rousseau stated that nowadays, with "the forests leveled, the marshes dried up, and the land more uniformly—although worse—cultivated," differences between countries decline. "There is now a hundred times more contact between Europe and Asia than there formerly was between Gaul and Spain. Europe alone used to be more diverse than the whole world is today."[32] Or, as he wrote elsewhere, "Say what you like, there is no such thing nowadays as Frenchmen, Germans, Spaniards, or even Englishmen—only Europeans. All have the same tastes, the same passions, the same customs."[33]

For Lovejoy, the rediscovery of diversity expressed one of the mind's "constant propensities" that "for some reason" became "particularly potent at this time."[34] He offered no explanation for the renewal beyond the regular oscillations of thought. Social conditions that fueled an appreciation of diversity did not interest him. But material circumstances illuminate why "for some reason" diversity became "particularly potent" in the mid-18th century. A new commercial society was in the making; it brought in its wake not only more travel and trade among peoples, as Rousseau noticed, but a push for uniform standards—and a protest against it.[35] Expanded markets needed uniformity in measure, coin, and laws. But some figures of the Enlightenment resisted. Diversity gained adherents as society turned less variegated. Montesquieu, who traveled about Europe for nine years, is a classic example.

Montesquieu's 1748 *Spirit of the Laws* contemplated "the

infinite diversity of laws and manners." While Montesquieu inspired many political liberals, and is often derided for his abstractness, a devotion to differences and their fragility marks his book. He wanted laws to be rooted in the particular situation of nations—not derived from universal principles.[36] Nor did he want laws to override local customs. Indeed, he condemned Peter the Great's edicts on native dress: "The law which obliged Muscovites to cut off their beards, and to shorten their clothes . . . were instances of tyranny."[37] Montesquieu objected to the seductiveness of "the ideas of uniformity" that attract "little souls," who find therein a "kind of perfection." These small souls want to institute "the same authorized weights, the same measures in trade, the same laws in the state, the same religion in all its parts." Montesquieu challenged the uniformity obsession. "And does not a greatness of genius consist rather in distinguishing between those cases in which uniformity is requisite, and those in which there is a necessity for differences?"[38]

That is the rub: at what point does uniformity become oppressive? When does "a necessity for differences" outweigh a necessity of uniformity? We see at the end of the 18th century calls for uniformity, both as a philosophical and economic project, the latter a condition of a new market economy; and we see a protest against it in the name of diversity and individuality. For the "uniformitarians"—to use Lovejoy's term—philosophical and economic imperatives fed each other.

Montesquieu alludes to those seeking uniformity in "authorized weights." The campaign for uniformity of measurement illustrates the problem inasmuch as local codes of size and coin, which varied from region to region, bedeviled the 18th century. The French scientist Pierre-Simon Laplace believed that ending diversity in measurement would lead to advances in daily life. He complained of "the prodigious numbers of measures in use . . . their whimsical divisions, inconvenient for calculation, and the difficulty of knowing and comparing them."[39] Those who supported expanded trade usually supported uniform measurements. The evangelists of uniformity moved from money, weights, and measures to time, language, and beyond. Uniformity became not simply a program, but a cause.

Arthur Young, a British agriculturalist, toured France before the Revolution and complained of the maddening scales that differed everywhere. England and Ireland are bad enough, he noted, but "in France the infinite perplexity of the measures exceeds all comprehension." He observed that they "differ not only in every province, but in every district, and almost in every town." Moreover, "these tormenting variations" encompass both weight and length.[40] Historians confirm Young's observation. On the eve of the Revolution, France possessed more than a thousand units of measurement, with several hundred thousand local variations.[41]

In the name of trade and good government, 18th-century politicians regularly pressed for uniform measurements. In his first address to the United States Congress, George Washington called on it to attend to "an object of great importance," establishing "Uniformity in the Currency, Weights and Measures." His secretary of state submitted to Congress in 1790 a *Plan for Establishing Uniformity in Coinage, Weights, and Measures of the United States*. That secretary, Thomas Jefferson, became a principal devoted to a system of standard lengths, weights, and currency. A new currency should be based on tens, he believed, with a dollar divided into a hundred parts. The decimalization of the currency proved successful, but Jefferson had less success with the rest of the program. His efforts to adopt decimals for weights and measures came to "naught," remarks an historian.[42]

Today the United States stands almost alone in the world in its resistance to the metric system. "Our system is so confused we don't even know what to call it," grouses John Bemelmans Marciano in *Whatever Happened to the Metric System?*[43]

But France embraced decimals with a vengeance, an example of uniformity gone amuck. Very roughly, in tandem with the zeal of the French Revolutionaries, the French upped their decimalization. They began with weights and measures, adopting meters and grams—and kilometers and kilograms. But as the revolution escalated, so did the decimalization frenzy. The revolutionaries devised a new calendar, and apart from renaming the months, they established the ten-day week. Gilbert Romme, a French mathematician charged with proposing a new calendar, explained that only in a revolutionary period could the old "diversity, incoherence and inexactness" be overcome. Note the terms: diversity equals incoherence. The new plan followed the rigor of nature rather than the superstitions of the past.[44] The ten-day week proved less than popular, if only because it entailed working for nine straight days rather than six.[45]

At the most extreme phase, the revolutionary government sought to apply decimals to time. The revolutionary National Convention decreed that, to complete the "system of decimalization," the "day will be divided into ten parts, each part of which will have ten parts," which will continue to the smallest unit.[46] To Romme, all this made perfect sense. The decimal second equaled "the pulse rate of the average-sized healthy man, marching at a military pace."[47] However, to much of France this was perfectly inane. An historian observes, "People rebelled against the 10-hour days, 100-minute hours, and 100-second minutes." Not only Sundays vanished but also the ten-hour day required new decimal clocks. "The horologists of France shouted the loudest in opposition, since this ill-conceived plan rendered obsolete every watch and clock ever produced."[48] Yet decimal time had its supporters. When it was the turn of Saint-Just, a devoted fan of the guillotine—itself an example of standardization of capital punishment—to experience the machine firsthand, he carried a decimal timepiece.[49]

The uniformity cult of the period can be glimpsed not only in ten-hour clocks but also in language. If language inspired humanists like Humboldt to prize diversity, it also reflected then and today opposing realities, forces of uniformity. Alongside the intellectual mission to found a universal language, discussed in Chapter Two, above, arose the imperative to consolidate languages, in effect to establish one national tongue. These were less philosophical endeavors than projects driven by economic, state, and sometimes revolutionary principles.

In the name of security and prosperity, the modern states monopolize language, which means reducing or eliminating competing tongues. Much of this story is not pretty, but the standard tale of oppression distorts the record. To enter mainstream society sometimes meant acquiring the dominant language and leaving another. This does not always happen with force. Many immigrants to the United States, for instance, gave up their native tongues without regret. In general, however, a language gains supremacy by economic or political power. Populations with minor languages are cowed to relinquish theirs. "A language is a dialect with a navy and army," goes a trenchant maxim. Who first uttered it is up for debate. Little doubt exists, however, that the adage popped up following a lecture on the future of Yiddish, which is apposite.[50] Yiddish lacked an army and has virtually disappeared.

Calls for language uniformity in the name of progress and

reason surfaced in the French Revolution. Yiddish tangentially figures in the French story and exemplifies the tangle of progress, uniformity, and domination. For those of the revolutionary persuasion, uniformity smacked of reason and progress. During the Revolution, Abbé Grégoire, a radical priest, pushed for a "Frenchification" of France that entailed the elimination of local dialects and languages. Not coincidentally, he championed the equality of Jews and blacks—and campaigned for the application of science to business and life.[51] He was a founder of the "Société des amis des Noirs," which advocated for the abolition of the slave trade and slavery. He was also a founder of the Bureau des Longitudes that sought to improve navigation with superior measurements. This Bureau has been dubbed "one the great centers of enlightened science."[52] For a man of reason, the commitments to human equality, longitudinal precision, and linguistic standardization overlapped.[53]

The Jews must be compelled to study French, asserted Abbé Grégoire, and to give up Yiddish. "That Tudesco-Hebraico-Rabbinical jargon which is used by the German Jews, which is intelligible only to them, and which tends greatly to increase their ignorance, or veil their deception, will doubtlessly one day be extirpated." The ill of local languages did not only afflict Jews, however. For Abbé Grégoire, too many Frenchmen did not speak French and remained trapped in dialects. Perhaps eight million Frenchmen "can scarcely utter a few mangled words, or disjointed phrases of our language." The state should address this problem. Governments, the good abbé declared, "do not know, or are not sufficiently convinced, of how much importance the abolishing of gibberish is to the spread of enlightenment."[54]

With the revolution Abbé Grégoire assumed some power,

and the opportunity arose to suppress local languages. He and his confreres considered dialects and non-French languages as counterrevolutionary. "Federalism and superstitions speak Breton; emigration and hatred of the Republic speak German; counter-revolution speaks Italian and fanaticism speaks Basque," reported a French revolutionary to the Committee of Public Safety. Bertrand Barère, a revolutionary ally of Abbé Grégoire and author of this report, denounced "these instruments of injury and error": "The language of a free people must be one and the same for all." Barère called for linguistic legionnaires to be sent to each rural commune. "The instructors will be required to teach the French language and the Declaration of the Rights of Man on alternate days to all young citizens."[55]

Like a contemporary social scientist, Abbé Grégoire conducted a survey. To officialdom throughout France he sent out questions on the extent of local dialects or patois. "Is the usage of the French language universal in your region?" ran the first question. "Does one speak one or several patois?"[56] The implications of the questions were clear. Linguistic diversity sustained reactionary sentiments and terms. The survey served as the basis for Abbé Grégoire's report, the title of which speaks for itself: "Report on the Necessity and Means for Annihilating Patois and Universalizing the Usage of the French Language." For Abbé Grégoire, enlightenment, progress, and linguistic uniformity meant the same thing. To annihilate patois aids in the decline of prejudice, fosters virtues, and simplifies laws and government. "The unity of language is an integral part of the revolution."[57]

The cult of uniformity found determined critics, perhaps most notably the German philosopher Johann Gottfried

Herder—roughly coterminous with Kant; he stands as one of the most passionate champions of diversity. For this reason, he has appealed to modern-day pluralists such as Isaiah Berlin.[58] Herder upsets the usual categories. Is he part of the Enlightenment or the protest against it?[59] Even his contemporaries found him difficult to pin down. But his celebration of the particular and specific comes through loud and clear. In both the theoretical and material dimension, he upheld the unique against the systematizers of rationalized uniformity. He feared, according to one scholar, the "mechanization of life."[60] Berlin called him "one of the earliest opponents of uniformity."[61] A chapter in Herder's *Reflections on the Philosophy of the History of Mankind* (1780s) breathes of an exuberant celebration of diversity that we have seen in earlier thinkers. It opened this way, anticipating Hope Jahren's remarks: "No two leaves of any one tree in nature are to be found perfectly alike; and still less do two human faces, or human frames, resemble each other. Of what endless variety is our artful structure susceptible!"[62]

Like virtually all the figures of the Enlightenment, he returned often to the issue of language, its origins and diversity. In one of his earliest works, Herder defended the matchlessness of each language—including German; and this during the reign of Frederick the Great, who—as mentioned in Chapter One, above—preferred French to German. For Herder, every mother tongue should be prized. He judged the multiplicity of languages a "genuine good." Such diversity would persist so long as scholars are not ruled by "a monarch" who would "set one language upon the throne"; and "so long as the plans for a universal language belong among the empty projects and journeys to the moon."[63] So much for Esperanto—and the other efforts to establish a universal language.

Herder hammers away at the empty, universal, and abstract systems that constrict individual experience. A soft materialistic note pervades his writings. Social conditions, not just desiccated philosophies, constrain life. Unregulated experience grows rare and, along with it, original thinking. The sense of touch, he states in his early travel diaries, has become "dormant" and other senses cannot compensate. "There is no axiom more noteworthy," writes Herder, than that thought depends on our senses. "If the senses are crippled, the mind is crippled too." And this is occurring. He strikes the same notes as Humboldt. "Diverse, tangible and vivid sensations" that gave rise to original men with vigorous ideas dwindle. "These ages are past for us; we live in the century of ordinary experiences, of law and orderly government, of refinement and comfort, in which we must think like others because we learn to see what they see and as they see it."[64]

Herder's more systematic work—not very systematic—responded to the criticism that he romanticized past eras. We live in an age of progress and enlightenment, Herder declared with sarcasm in *Another Philosophy of History* (1774). Our age exports its "liquor and luxury to the world."[65] He mimics a contemporary cheerleader: "We have no highway robbers, no civil wars, no crimes anymore!" Herder rejoins, "Given how thoroughly our lands are regimented, plastered and violated with highways, and congested with garrisons; how wise the distribution of our fields; and how vigilant our wise justice is—where on earth could a poor scoundrel ply his rough trade . . . ?" For Herder, something has been lost; there is a "diminished strength and feeling of joy with which we are left as individuals." Uniformity increases, and originality and energy decline. "Where all the customs are the same, all equally level, right, and good, what need is there for any effort?"[66]

The protest against creeping uniformity surfaced among other thinkers, although the lines of influence often led back to Herder. This is true for one of the more compelling figures, Benjamin Constant, the Swiss-French liberal, who is linked to the larger-than-life figure of Madame de Staël. For decades Constant has been treated as a minor figure, but recently his star has begun to rise.[67] In his European peregrinations Constant almost met Herder; he arrived in Weimar as the German philosopher died there. At that moment Constant turned to study him.[68] Herder's condemnation of arid uniformity resonated with Constant. The lines of influence ran in several directions. The theologian Friedrich Schleiermacher, discussed above, took much from Herder and he, in turn, influenced Constant.[69]

Though Constant took inspiration from Schleiermacher and Herder, he went his own way.[70] He was also less a full-time philosopher than a full-time man of daily politics; he navigated the French Revolution and Napoleon's reign, and flourished in the Restoration, the era after Napoleon's final defeat, when he defended liberty against radicals of the Left and Right. Today Constant and Madame de Staël, whose lives were inextricably tangled, are credited as originators of French liberalism.[71] Again and again Constant affirmed his defense of individual liberty. In an 1815 preface to his writings, he proclaims that for twenty years he has professed the same ideas, "individual liberty, liberty of the press, absence of arbitrary arrest, respect for the rights of all." Fifteen years later, shortly before his death, he affirmed his credo: "For forty years I have defended the same principle, liberty in everything. . . . By liberty I mean the triumph of individuality, as much over . . . despotism as over the masses that claim the right to subject the minority to the majority."[72]

The allusion to the masses as a threat indicates the topic that would increasingly trouble liberal thinkers: not tyrants, but the masses and uniformity endangered the individual. Both Constant and Madame de Staël championed the individual against foibles of the age. While not the focus of her memoir *Ten Years of Exile*, Madame de Staël protests the "extraordinary mania" of French revolutionaries—and of Napoleon—for imposing the same structure everywhere. They love uniformity. Universal principles of freedom exist, she asserts, "but what matter whether the political organization is a limited monarchy like England, or a federal republic like the United States, or the thirteen Swiss cantons? It is surely not necessary to limit Europe to a single idea . . . !" She refers to Napoleon's despotism as "that great regulated system" that imposes the one edifice throughout his empire.[73]

Constant formulated the most forceful response to regimented uniformity in his broadside against Napoleonic rule, *The Spirit of Conquest and Usurpation and Their Relation to European Civilization*. The argument hinged on a distinction he employed in his most famous piece, "On the Liberty of the Ancients Compared with that of the Moderns." For Constant, the ancients conquered peoples but did not seek to dominate and regulate all activities. They were "satisfied with general obedience," and ignored the "charm" of everyday life—childhood, local customs, and gods. But the modern conquerors differ. They want to impose everywhere "the same code of law, the same measures, the same regulations, and if they could . . . the same language." They "wish their empire to present an appearance of uniformity, upon which the proud eye of power may travel without meeting any unevenness that could offend or limit its view." For Constant, the goal of "uniformity" drives the modern despot. For the contemporary tyrant, "it is a pity that one cannot destroy all towns to rebuild them according to the same plan, and level all mountains to make the ground even everywhere."

Constant's chapter "On Uniformity" in his *Spirit of Conquest* expanded on these points. He marvels at the paradox that the push toward uniformity found great favor with both French revolutionaries and their opponents such as Napoleon. The "two extremes" of revolutionaries and anti-revolutionaries "found themselves in agreement." Unlike the old tyrants, the new breed pursues people "into their most intimate aspects." The modern tyrant seeks to reduce the individual to "uniform proportions." In the past "conquerors expected the deputies of conquered nations to appear on their knees before them. Today it is man's morale that they wish to prostrate." For Constant, "this obsession with uniformity" undermines human vigor and spirit that are sustained by "diversities . . . demanded by nature and consecrated by experience." It throws men "like atoms onto a monotonous plain." In a ringing statement, Constant declaims, "Variety is life; uniformity, death."[74]

Constant harbored a special animus for Abbé de Mably, who is remembered today—if at all—as an associate of Rousseau. For Constant, Mably sought to subordinate all emotions, even love, to strict laws. "He detested individual liberty like a personal enemy." Under Mably's regime, "every relaxation, every need" was subject to legislation. "The monastic barracks appeared to him as the ideal of a free republic."[75] In life and letters Constant moved in the opposite direction. He and Madame de Staël worshipped a robust individuality and disdained lethargy. Early in his career Constant lamented that the individual had been squeezed between decades of royalty and anarchy. Liberty emerges in "a generation that is mutilated, fatigued, faded."[76] He wrote to a friend, "There are no more individuals, but only battalions wearing uniforms."[77]

In Constant's autobiographical novel, *Adolphe*, about a tragic love affair, the title character harbors "an insurmountable aversion from all hackneyed phrases and dogmatic formulae." He seeks a profound "emotional experience" and fears being overwhelmed by a "universal apathy." When he hears "people holding forth complacently about established and incontrovertible principles of morality, behavior, and religion," he feels "moved to contradict them." Adolphe mistrusts "general axioms uttered without any reservation, so innocent of any shade of distinction."[78] In an unpublished passage for the preface, Constant stated that he wanted to portray in *Adolphe* "one of the principal moral maladies of our century" that he identified as "this fatigue . . . this absence of force." Lassitude undermines not only love but also religion and liberty: "Fidelity in love is a force as in religion, as with liberty. But we no longer have any strength."[79]

Both Constant and de Staël praised individuality, which for them rested on an emotional foundation, a notion that showed up in Humboldt. The individual strove not simply for happiness, but for something more. De Staël celebrated an enthusiasm for life and openness. She contrasted it to fanaticism, which is exclusive and narrow. "To reach the heart of things, we need some impulse arousing us to get eagerly involved." She feared that young people seemed "disillusioned of enthusiasm" and were entering a premature senescence.[80] Constant uses a different vocabulary but makes a kindred point. The threat to ancient liberty came from tyrants, but "a different sort of danger" threatens modern liberty. Men sink into private happi-

folded but hardly considered their political consequences. is inaugural essay for the journal he launched, the *Journal of History of Ideas*, barely mentioned the world situation.[84]

Yet his *Great Chain of Being* dates from 1936. Lovejoy was riting amid the threat of fascism, to which his phrases about he cultivation" of national and racial peculiarities alluded. e continued in the text, "The belief in the sanctity of one's liosyncrasy . . . is rapidly converted into a belief in its superirity." Evidently referring to Germany, Lovejoy, who was born Berlin, wrote that "more than one great people . . . having rst made a god of its own peculiarities . . . presently began suspect there was no other god. A type of national culture alued at first because it was one's own . . . came in time to be onceived of as a thing which had a mission to impose upon thers."[85]

Five years later Lovejoy linked the rise of fascism to the otion that he dubbed "diversitarianism," which was a protest gainst the idea that "what is rational is uniform"—or what he called "uniformitarianism." For Lovejoy "the fateful political events of our time" are partly "animated by an intense and obsessing sense of the differentness" in which each people are separate and distinct. His piece closed by affirming a "specific historical connection" between the cult of diversity and "the tragic spectacle of Europe in 1940."[86]

Lovejoy put his finger on the dangerous side of "diversitarianism." In the name of differences, it renounces a commitment to universal rights. As Lovejoy indicated, this repudiation imbued Nazi ideology. For instance, the much-quoted line "When I hear the word culture, I reach for my gun" turned on a denunciation of universal ideas. "Culture" equaled liberal rights. The sentence derived from a Nazi play performed for Hitler's birthday in 1933,

ness and ignore the larger world and its possi
happiness alone our only aim? asks Constant.
witness to the better part of our nature, tha
which pursues and torments us, that desire
knowledge and develop our faculties. . . . It is
ment that our destiny calls to us."[81] But passiv
mity threaten the self.

Something must be said about the ambiguous pc
sity, which brings us back to Arthur Lovejoy. E
ebrated diversity, Lovejoy was aware of a prob
stated—as cited above—that, for better or wo
covery of the intrinsic worth of diversity" markec
in modern thought. In part it was for the wors
knew. He was a committed liberal. He believed ir
themselves founded not on principles of diversity, b
site, "universal formulas" that apply to all people. I
career Lovejoy resigned from Stanford Universit
the coerced resignation of a colleague. A Stanford
had earned the wrath of its matriarch, Mrs. Stanfo
of his political activities in general, and his attack
monopolies, the source of the Stanford wealth, in p
Later Lovejoy helped establish a professional assoc
defended academic freedom. A recent account of th
zation—the American Association of University Pr
calls him its "primary founder."[83] But does that con
to universal axioms conflict with diversity? With wha
terms "the cultivation of individual, national and rac
liarities?" Lovejoy was a man of ideas; he examined l

a few years before Lovejoy's *Great Chain of Being*. In the play, a veteran of World War I who had also witnessed the brief leftist German revolution of 1918 proclaims, "And the last thing I'll stand for is ideas to get the better of me! I know that rubbish from '18 . . . fraternity, equality . . . freedom . . . beauty and dignity. . . . No, let 'em keep their good distance with their whole ideological kettle of fish [*Weltanschauungssalat*]. . . . I shoot with live ammunition! When I hear the word culture . . . I release the safety on my Browning!"[87]

Nevertheless, despite its "ruinous uses," Lovejoy maintained that the discovery of the inherent value of diversity is "one of the great discoveries of the human mind."[88] And so it might be. Yet its dark underbelly keeps reappearing in history. At what point does the stress on diversity bury general notions of human solidarity? At what point does it turn into an ideology that exalts segregation and discrimination? After all, American slavery became known to its defenders as the "peculiar institution"—not universal, but peculiar because of its unique ties to the American South. An architect of South African apartheid appealed to diversity as its justification: "Our policy is a policy," he stated, "that accepts that there are differences between people and you have to recognize these differences. Differences should be celebrated."[89]

In the period of the 18th and early 19th centuries these ideas of diversity, particularism, and individualism composed what has been called the counter-Enlightenment—a rejection of universalism and reason. For some scholars, these ideas amounted to less an opposition to the Enlightenment than a modification of it.[90] For others, the counter-Enlightenment presaged right-wing 19th-century movements. For still others, such as the Israeli scholar Zeev Sternhell, the counter-Enlightenment, a term that may have originated with Nietzsche, contained the seeds of fascism. Herder shows up often in Sternhell's account of the baleful effects of the counter-Enlightenment. He notes, for instance, that Hans-Georg Gadamer, a student of Heidegger, a philosopher who initially embraced the Nazis, lectured on Herder in Paris at the Nazi German Institute in 1941. Sternhell claims that, at the moment of Nazi victory, Gadamer wanted to lord over the defeated French and show the superiority of German values. In Sternhell's view, Herder served him well. "Gadamer had totally assimilated Herder's critique of the French Enlightenment, rationalism, and the rights of man."[91]

There is something to this. But how much? Herder was very much a student of the Enlightenment even as he offered a sharp criticism of its (French) excesses. The same might be said of others who are corralled into the counter-Enlightenment, such as Edmund Burke. The Irishman is famous for his denunciation of the French Revolution, but less famous for his defense of the American Revolution and his condemnation of English misdeeds in India. Moreover, writers such as Constant and Madame de Staël boasted solid liberal credentials and, at the same time, offered criticism of "uniformitarianism."

Yet a defense of diversity and denunciation of uniformity inform conservative thought more than liberal. Why? A short answer might be that liberals, even Marxists, see themselves as improving modern society, while (some) conservatives see themselves as resisting it. Inasmuch as this conservativism is out of step with progress, it might be more alert to its costs; and the costs encompass many features of a modern commercial society, such as uniform standards. At the same time, this conservatism easily tilts into foggy notions of past differences between peoples and nations, which Sternhell foregrounds.

In a classic work, Karl Mannheim, the German sociologist who was himself a refugee, concluded that conservative thought arose "as a political argument against the revolutionary breach with the past" and everywhere upheld tradition, nobility, and even feudalism. Mannheim spotlighted the German 18th-century conservative, Justus Möser, who today garners little attention apart from specialists.[92] In his discussion Mannheim did not accent diversity, but as a theme it jumps out of Möser's writings. Möser was a reactionary who adored his corner of Germany—its rules, traditions, customs—and railed against an impending uniformity. He is sometimes dubbed a "German Burke," but his impact hardly compares to that of the Irishman. Mannheim signaled as archetypical Möser's essay "The Modern Taste for General Laws and Decrees is a Danger to Our Common Liberty" (1772). In it Möser champions diversity and variety against bureaucratic simplifications. He cites Montesquieu's comments on the topic to support his own argument that uniformity begets despotism.[93]

For Möser, government bureaucrats reduce everything to identical regulations and thereby subvert variety. He ridicules Voltaire, who himself ridicules the fact that someone can lose a court case in one village that he would win in a neighboring village with different rules. For Voltaire, this situation cries out for uniformity of legal codes, but for Möser the diversity is a blessing, not a curse. Voltaire can "find the same differences within two families" of one village. Uniform regulations injure the variety of nature and society. "In fact, we distance ourselves from the true plan of nature, which shows its wealth in diversity ["*Mannigfaltigkeit*"], and we move toward despotism, which subordinates everything to a few regulations, and in so doing lose the wealth of diversity."[94] To Möser, the links between diversity and conservatism stand out in sharp relief—in the same way, as in Abbé Grégoire, the links between uniformity and radicalism leap out.

Like many Germans, Möser was a bit of an Anglophile, and prefers, for instance, English gardens over French ones. The French garden, however tasteful with straight allées and trimmed hedges, can be sketched out in a few lines. But the English garden is Shakespearean in its thickets, ruins, and caves—in its "unending diversity."[95] As in gardens, so in art: general rules do not apply. Möser connects the aesthetic and the political. "It is a commonplace how general rules confine men of literary genius . . . [to] mediocrity unless they break through the tyranny of rules." In the same way, the state must not be constructed in the French mode in which "one should be able to describe its essential features upon a single sheet of paper."[96] Here as elsewhere, Möser prized variety in politics. As the distinguished Renaissance historian Hans Baron put it, for Möser the word "diversity" ["*Mannigfaltigkeit*"] served as "a battle cry against the hated uniformity of the age."[97]

Before dismissing the attack on uniformity as inevitably conservative, it must be appreciated that Constant made the same point—often with similar phrases. He also attacked Voltaire and kindred writers for "their love of symmetry." "'What,' they cry out, 'two portions of the same empire are subjected to different laws because they are separated by a hill or a stream of water! Is justice not the same on the two sides of a hill, or on the two banks of a stream of water?'" For Constant, however, two communities, although geographically close, may have "enjoyed a separate existence" and preserved "different forms," and perhaps cannot be judged by one standard. "The freest country in our old world, Great Britain, is governed by very diversified laws."[98] Elsewhere, he writes, it is "strange" that friends of liberty have "always heatedly worked" to impose a single abstract law, stripping people of memory and imagination. It is not so strange, Constant reflects, after the realization that "local memories contain a principle of resistance that the authorities only regret and hurriedly seek to uproot."[99]

The difference between Constant and counter-Enlighteners may be in the vector of their approach. Möser's does look backward, as Mannheim indicated, to a feudal past; he feared the rise of commerce.[100] But Constant looks forward to an industrial future.[101] Early and late in his career Constant planned to write about the idea of human progress, which he embraced.[102] If Möser and his intellectual kin are the conservatives, and Constant and his the liberals, they converged in privileging diversity and protesting uniformity. On these issues, at first glance they appear almost indistinguishable. However, they diverged in identifying the source of the ill. For the conservatives the danger emanated largely from the French Enlightenment, with its commitment to precision and homogeneity. But for the liberals the danger derived from the dynamics of a new commercial society-in-the-making.[103]

Constant's lecture on the liberty of the ancients and moderns pivots on this issue. He argued that liberty differed in the classical and modern world due to distinct economic systems. The ancients depended on a slave society that gave them the leisure to participate in public life. "Without the slave population of Athens, 20,000 Athenians could never have spent every day at the public square in discussions." Modern commerce and the abolition of slavery bring about a society in which the individual relies on his own self and activity. "Our freedom must consist of peaceful enjoyment and private independence."

For Constant this signaled many advances. "The progress of civilization" and the "commercial tendency of the age" have "infinitely multiplied and varied the means of personal happiness." There is no going back. To draw lessons from how the Greeks—or the Persians or the Egyptians—lived misses the point. "We are modern men, who wish each to enjoy our own rights, each to develop our own faculties as we like best." For this we need political liberty, which allows us to seek happiness and self-development. Political liberty, which encompasses "all the citizens, without exception . . . enlarges their spirits, ennobles their thoughts, and establishes among them a kind of intellectual equality which forms the glory and power of a people."[104] Yet moderns face a new problem as they seek to enfold their talents—a crush of uniformity that threatens the individual.

CHAPTER FIVE

Diversity and its Vicissitudes

The Modern Period

Misgivings about a uniformity that jeopardized the individual did not end with Constant. Unease beset other 19th-century thinkers, notably Alexis de Tocqueville and John Stuart Mill. Both loom large in the pantheon of liberal thinkers. But if they represent high points of liberalism, they also benchmark a low point in that they feared its dissolution. Both Tocqueville and Mill questioned the ability of the individual to stand up against society—against social homogenization and conformity. These were not just passing observations but structured their entire analyses. With the dwindling of diversity, the fate of the individual became uncertain.

As we approach the 20th century, shadows gather around liberalism. Questions about the vitality of the individual mount. Perhaps the individual lacks the backbone to maintain independence. Perhaps the forces of uniformity—newspapers, public opinion, social codes—overwhelm the individual. Perhaps the motor of history is less the individual than the crowd or the masses. Inasmuch as diversity rests on the well-being of the individual, what is the future of democracy? What prevents democracy from sliding into a popular dictatorship?

Historians have long complained about viewing the past

through the lens of the present; this entails distorting the past to fit contemporary imperatives. Such an approach implies that history is a one-way street to the present, as if there were no turns along the way. While this charge is well-taken, an approach of this kind proves almost impossible to avoid. We read and reread the past from the perspective of the present. Yesterday that might be the role of black people in history; today it might be the role of women. Since we live in the here and now, we cannot evade this; nor should we. For instance, many of those who fled Nazism became preoccupied with the demise of democracy. They witnessed and wanted to grasp democracy's collapse. Diversity or its absence entered the explanation by a side door. To some refugees, the fall of democracy coincided with the rise of the mass man, the antithesis of the individual. Uniformity in life spelled the end of democracy. Twentieth-century scholars turned to 19th-century liberals to figure out what happened to the individual.

Case in point: as mentioned in Chapter One, above, Jacob-Peter Mayer came to England as a German-Jewish refugee from Nazism. On the eve of World War II, he published the first biography of Tocqueville in English with the subtitle "Prophet of a Mass Age." He wanted to give an honest portrayal of Tocqueville, but also to inquire if the Frenchman anticipated something that upended Mayer's own life—namely, the breakdown of democracy and the onset of Nazi dictatorship. The man in the street probably views the victory of Nazism as a series of violent acts, symbolized by the conflagration of the Reichstag, the German parliament. This is not accurate. The belief that Hitler came to rule by a "seizure of power" belongs to the "mythology of the Third Reich," writes the historian Henry Ashby Turner Jr. Rather, the ordinary negotiations of a parliamentary democracy led to Hitler's appointment as chancellor, which opened the door to the Third Reich. "Hitler had not seized power; it had been handed to him."[1] Or, as Benjamin C. Hett puts it in his recent account, *The Death of Democracy: Hitler's Rise to Power and the Downfall of the Weimar Republic*, Hitler "had come to office in a constitutionally legitimate, even democratic way."[2]

The electoral strength of his party, the National Socialist German Workers' Party, or Nazis, formed the basis of the negotiations that led to his appointment as chancellor in 1933. The Nazis moved from a fringe outfit with 2 percent of the vote in the mid-1920s to the leading party in the 1930s. In the German elections of 1932, the Nazis had become by far the largest party in the Reichstag. They obtained 230 representatives and 14 million votes, almost twice that of the next most popular party, the social democrats. As an historian of Germany declares, the Nazis attracted "more votes than any party had done before."[3] A University of Chicago political scientist who visited Germany in 1932 noted that, in the weeks prior to the election, "Nazi meetings were unsurpassed in numbers and enthusiasm." He added that "an observer might have concluded that the Nazis controlled well over fifty per cent of the voters."[4] While the Nazi electoral draw may have peaked in 1932, their stunning electoral victories made Hitler's appointment as chancellor possible.[5]

For J.P. Mayer, these were obvious facts. "It was universal suffrage that led National Socialism to victory," he declared in his Tocqueville book.[6] He noted that "whole libraries" exist on Aristotle and Machiavelli, but Tocqueville had been little studied. The rise of fascism made an examination of Tocqueville "doubly urgent." To Mayer, Tocqueville understood something about "the rising of the masses" and the ease by which a democracy turns into a dictatorship. He understood the forces eroding the individual. Tocqueville put his finger on the weakening of diversity and its implications.

But it was not only Tocqueville who could aid in fathoming the decline of democracy and the emergence of the mass individual. A 19th-century political event could also: the mid-century rise of a French emperor. Louis Napoleon was the nephew of the much more famous Napoleon Bonaparte, who dazzled the world in the final stage of the French Revolution. The nephew, a much smaller figure than the uncle—Victor Hugo dubbed him "Napoleon the Little"—came to rule in the aftermath of the revolution of 1848, some fifty years after his uncle. What troubled Mayer—and he was not alone in his concern—was the speed with which a new French republic of 1848 passed into a popular dictatorship by 1851. The bedrock of democracy remained the individual. But what if the individual could be misled? What if individuals formed an unthinking mass? The demise of diversity correlates with the rise of the masses. The success of Louis Napoleon confirmed these suspicions.

The new French republic, which followed the overthrow of the monarchy in 1848, created a government with a presidency elected by universal male suffrage. To general amazement, in the very first presidential election Louis Napoleon, a peripheral figure who had never held a political office, had a somewhat disreputable past, and made vague promises to everyone, overwhelmingly defeated the other candidates. His popularity upset the National Assembly, which passed a law that restricted through residency requirements universal male suffrage. By excluding millions of voters, the assembly hoped to checkmate Louis Napoleon's future moves.

To no avail. Louis Napoleon possessed an undeniable populist touch that proved decisive. As he toured France he declared, "My sincerest and most devoted friends are not to be found in palaces but in cottages, not in rooms with gilded ceilings but in the workshops and fields."[7] Within three years, Louis Napoleon ended the republic with a coup d'état in which he announced the restoration of universal suffrage that would legitimate his rule with a plebiscite, which it did.[8] Even if the plebiscite was manipulated, the coup was nevertheless by most accounts popular. As one historian put it, to the Catholics Louis Napoleon "seemed a champion of the Papacy," to the socialists "he appealed as a friend of the poor," to the capitalists "he appeared the bulwark against socialism," and to the republicans "he seemed the champion of popular sovereignty."[9] Louis Napoleon adroitly played cards that would be played by future dictators. He ruled for twenty years.

Virtually all political commentators of the day, including Karl Marx and Victor Hugo, weighed in on these events. For those who came later, such as J.P. Mayer, the popular coup foreshadowed a singular feature of fascism, its use of elections; it indicated that "the people" had become "the masses," which could be easily manipulated. Mayer asked in his Tocqueville book whether "an analogy" existed between the "plebiscitary dictatorship" of Louis Napoleon and the "modern dictatorships of Germany and Italy."[10] The inner relationship of diversity and democracy informs these topics. Democracy rests on the resilience and autonomy of the individual. If the individual loses individuality, democracy becomes imperiled.

Before he fled Germany, Mayer edited two contemporary books on the topic of Louis Napoleon's coming-to-power; one by Karl Marx (*The Eighteenth Brumaire of Louis Napo-*

leon), the other by the little-known Constantin Frantz (*The Mass or the People: Louis Napoleon*). The socialist Mayer found that the socialist Marx missed the point. Too much a man of the Enlightenment, Marx did not grasp the historical regression that marked the "democratic basis" of Louis Napoleon. Frantz, on the other hand, apprehended the atomization that led to Louis Napoleon's democratic dictatorship. For Frantz, "the people" had become "the mass."[11] Mayer returned to these events after he became a refugee. "Louis Napoleon came to power by virtue of the universal suffrage" that European democrats had once considered their own best tool, he declared in 1943. "Quantity—the new democratic mass—had turned into a new quality: the modern dictator."[12]

Apprehension that the democratic individual would prove frail colored the thought of an increasing number of liberals in the 19th century, especially Mill and Tocqueville. Benjamin Constant had led the way, and Tocqueville and Mill pursued kindred ideas. The relationship or lack of relationship between the two Frenchmen, Constant and Tocqueville, has long puzzled scholars. Inasmuch as his ideas seem close to Constant's, how is it that Tocqueville hardly paid heed to his compatriot?[13] After all, Constant was not unknown. By the time of his death in 1830, he was widely celebrated. Crowds followed his casket to the Père-Lachaise cemetery. In 1830 Tocqueville was a 25-year-old lawyer, but apparently Constant did not draw his attention.[14]

The real issue, however, is not how little Constant influenced Tocqueville or, jumping ahead, how much Tocqueville influenced Mill, but rather how a coterie of 19th-century thinkers who were neither conservatives nor socialists moved in the same direction.[15] The weakening of diversity and individuality struck them. They registered the impact of a commercial society—call it industrialization or capitalism—on the individual. Unlike Möser and related conservatives, Tocqueville and Mill accepted progress, but worried that modern society undermined individual diversity. This is the key. And unlike contemporary diversity adherents bedazzled by superficial variety, these observers, who are sometimes dubbed aristocratic liberals or neo-republicans, perceived the threat that society posed to the values they cherished.[16] Social uniformity endangered robust individuals.

Since Mayer, scholarship on Tocqueville amounts to a small library. But even though diversity imbues his work, its place in Tocqueville's writings draws little attention.[17] One thing, however, is clear: Tocqueville's *Democracy in America* dealt with much more than democracy in America. Contemporary reviewers saw this. "I have one criticism to make," stated a reviewer in 1840. "The title of the book is misleading. It isn't really about democracy in America, but about the future of democracy in the world."[18] For Tocqueville, democracy faced perils such as the tyranny of the majority. But undergirding that tyranny was something more troubling: the accelerating uniformity of society that depleted the individual. Tocqueville voiced these concerns in his first impressions of the United States.

In "Two Weeks in the Wilderness," an essay that he wrote soon after his arrival (and which he did not publish during his lifetime), Tocqueville remarked on the diminished variety in the New World. With chagrin, he admitted he arrived with preconceptions. "I had imagined something quite different." In Europe sharp contrasts characterized adjacent areas: "I had noticed that in Europe, the more or less remote situation of any provincial region or town, its wealth or poverty, its size, big or small, would exercise great influence upon its inhabitants and would often establish the variations of several centuries between the different parts of the same area." Here Tocqueville ratified an observation made by Rousseau and others: adjoining domains in Europe often diverged. Tocqueville expected to find this spectrum of regions and customs "all the more so in the New World." He anticipated finding dramatic differences between bordering regions. But "nothing of that picture has any truth," he continued. "Of all the countries of the world, America is the least suited to provide the sight which I had come to seek." He found not differences, but similitude.[19]

Everywhere he came across the same people, customs, and stores. "The shopkeepers of Buffalo and Detroit are as well stocked as those in New York." Everywhere he discovered the same network. "In America, much more than in Europe, only one society exists." The same society extends throughout. "It may be rich or poor, modest or brilliant, engaged in commerce or farming, nevertheless, it consists everywhere of the same elements." Identical people seem to surface everywhere. "You will come across the man you left on the streets of New York in the middle of almost impenetrable solitudes—same clothes, same spirit, same language, same habits, same pleasures." The variations found in Europe disappear. As Tocqueville put it, "The plane of a uniform civilization has passed over."[20]

His traveling companion, Gustave de Beaumont, a lawyer and prison reformer, came to the same conclusion. He also imagined profound differences between regions and peoples in the United States and also did not find them. "Everywhere the same men, the same passions, the same mores; everywhere the same enlightenment and the same obscurities." Beaumont noted the paradox of Americanization, a term not yet in use.

"How strange! The American nation recruits from all the peoples of the earth, and none of those display such uniformity of traits and characteristics."[21]

These ideas flit throughout *Democracy in America*, especially the more reflective Volume Two, published five years after the first. Tocqueville observed a new commercial society in the making that rounded off individual edges and idiosyncrasies. He did not label it capitalism or even industrialization, which hardly interested him.[22] In the aftermath of Volume One, Tocqueville did visit factories in Manchester and Birmingham, England; and his observations about industrial pollution and degradation compare to those set down by Engels some ten years later in *The Condition of the Working Class in England* (1845).[23] Tocqueville noticed the dirt, noise, and darkness. The soil has been scratched away; stagnant water collects; fog envelops everything. "Heaps of dung, rubble from buildings, putrid, stagnant pools are found here and there among the houses." But look up and "you will see huge palaces of industry. . . . These vast structures keep air and light out of the human habitations. . . . From this filthy sewer pure gold flows. . . . Here civilization works its miracles, and civilized man is turned back almost into a savage."[24]

By Volume Two, Tocqueville seemed convinced, perhaps reinforced by his visit to industrial England, that as commercial society gained strength the individual lost vitality.[25] This impression informs much of Tocqueville's work: the rise of commercial society based on money and equality undermines the individual.[26] Tocqueville saw the advance of democracy and equality as irreversible, but worried about its consequences—uniformity, greyness, and even a new despotism. "Everything was different in earlier societies," he declared. "Unity and uniformity were nowhere to be found." Diversity was now ebbing. "Everything is threatening to become so much alike that the peculiar features of each individual will soon be altogether lost in the common physiognomy."[27]

Such points lead Tocqueville to some of his most counter-intuitive arguments—and the points most neglected by commentators.[28] Tocqueville believed that modern democratic societies are static and conservative, not revolutionary and dynamic. Commercial society promotes endless activity, but within narrow channels. Individuals are free and energetic, but similar and weak. His chapter titled "How Society in The United States Seems Both Agitated and Monotonous" captures the contradictory elements; things always move but always in the same way. Tocqueville foregrounds the dwindling of diversity, although "diversity" is not the term he employs. Rather, he notes that uniformity escalates and individuality retreats. "The appearance of American society is agitated, because men and things are constantly changing; and it is monotonous, because all changes are the same."[29]

Tocqueville emphasized that this phenomenon was not confined to the United States. "What I say about America applies, moreover, to nearly all men of the present day. Variety is vanishing from the human species. In all corners of the world we find the same ways of acting, thinking, and feeling." This is not because "all peoples have more to do with one another and copy each other more faithfully than in the past." Rather, the dwindling force of "caste, occupation, or family" and the strengthening of industry have led to similarities among people. Without imitating each other, men "are becoming more alike."[30]

A later work, *The Ancien Régime and the Revolution*, confirms that Tocqueville saw the tide of uniformity as more than

American. "How France was the Country Where Men Had Come to Resemble Each Other the Most," runs the title of one of its chapters. He noted that obvious markers once separated the nobility from the middle class. But now by merely scratching the surface, little separated them. "Deep down" they were increasingly alike. Aristocrat and commoner hardly differed. "They had the same ideas, the same habits, they pursued the same tasks, indulged in the same pleasures, read the same books and spoke the same language." Tocqueville found similitude across France. "Not only did the provinces increasingly resemble each other," he noted, but also "men of different social class . . . became ever more alike despite the individual differences of rank."[31]

It would be anachronistic to dub these remarks as addressing globalization. Yet it would be obtuse not to admit that Tocqueville is characterizing the homogenizing force of capitalism. In the 1840s and '50s, a good French liberal with aristocratic leanings and democratic commitments expressed fears of reduced diversity in the world. He did not attack diversity, which he prized, but he indicated the degree to which reality contravened it.

Tocqueville grasped the counterintuitive nature of his argument, as notes to himself show. "I must be careful to avoid the improbable and paradoxical." The twin movements of individual emancipation and individual conformity seemed as contradictory in the 19th century as they do today in the 21st. As "social equality" makes people independent, freeing them from past obligations and traditions, it should give rise to robust individuals, intellectual anarchy, and revolutions. Tocqueville puzzled over this and concluded that the opposite happens. "After examining things more closely," Tocqueville finds that "the human mind" becomes "too immobile" and "too stable."

In the commercial society, torpor and routine set in. "This idea is so extraordinary and so novel to the reader that it can only be limned in the background, presented as a kind of hypothesis."[32]

But Tocqueville hammers away at the "extraordinary" idea in his text. Despite equality and relentless activity, the denizens of democracy become more alike and more conservative. Tocqueville indicates that this conclusion contradicts the impression of "intellectual anarchy," which might seem endemic in an egalitarian society: every person is for himself or herself. However, Tocqueville is convinced that this anarchy at best evidences an "era of transition." The long-range trends suggest stability, not anarchy. I dread, declared Tocqueville, that "man will exhaust his energies in petty, solitary, and sterile changes, and that humanity, though constantly on the move, will cease to advance."[33]

The phenomenon seemed so important that Tocqueville devoted another chapter to trying to describe it, "What Kind of Despotism Democratic Nations Have to Fear." The Frenchman admitted he could not find an adequate name for it. "The old words 'despotism' and 'tyranny' will not do." Here Tocqueville begins to sound very much like Constant. A new species of despotism, both milder and more extensive than in the past, had appeared. It rests on uniformity—across peoples and government. The democratic sovereign enacts "a fine mesh of uniform, minute and complex rules. . . . He does not break men's wills but softens, bends, and guides them."

Past rulers abused their power but did not mold daily lives. "When the power of the Caesars was at its height, the various peoples that inhabited the Roman world preserved their diverse customs and mores." The new sovereigns accelerated the decline of that diversity. The uniformity was both horizontal—between peoples—and vertical—between the state and its peoples. "Little by little," the democratic state "robs each citizen of the use of his own faculties." The new Caesar does not tyrannize, but rather "inhibits, represses, saps, stifles, and stultifies, and in the end he reduces each nation to nothing but a flock of timid and industrious animals." Tocqueville pondered how men who had surrendered their independence could choose judicious leaders: "It is impossible to believe that a liberal, energetic, and wise government can ever emerge from the ballots of a nation of servants."[34] Tocqueville concluded his two volumes on a dark note. He wondered whether equality of conditions will bring about "servitude or liberty, enlightenment or barbarism."[35]

"Can you tell me anything of Tocqueville?" asked, in 1835, an appreciative English reader of a French acquaintance.[36] This was John Stuart Mill, the great 19th-century English liberal. He had just read the first volume of *Democracy in America*. He was much taken with the book. His own *On Liberty*, with its epigraph from Humboldt on individual diversity, lay decades in the future.

Mill and Tocqueville soon met, corresponded, and heaped praise on each other. "There is no living man in Europe whom I esteem more highly or of whose friendship I should be more proud than I am of yours," declared Mill.[37] Mill wrote glowing reviews of *Democracy in America*. His review of the second volume clocked in at more than eighty pages. The review thrilled Tocqueville. "Of all the articles written on my book, yours is *the only one* in which the author mastered my thought perfectly and was able to display it to others." Tocqueville announced he was having the review bound with a copy of his book.[38]

Scholars argue whether Tocqueville influenced Mill or whether their ideas ran along parallel lines. It seems clear that

Tocqueville redoubled Mill's doubts of democracy. In the aftermath of reading Tocqueville, he focused less on the state as a threat and more on the masses—and the weakening of the individual. In one of his first essays which cites Tocqueville, Mill presented the disjuncture between material and cultural progress as critical. While society advances in wealth, transport, and communication, the individual regresses in force or intensity. "Can it be said that there has been any corresponding quantity of intellectual power or moral energy unfolded among those individuals or classes who have enjoyed superior advantages?" Mill cannot confirm it. In fact, he registers "a very marked decrease of vigor and energy."

The individual seems to be retreating. "Power passes more and more from individuals . . . to masses." This means "the weight and importance of an individual, as compared with the mass, sink into greater and greater insignificance." It also signifies that, for the individual tradesman as well as the individual author, success depends on "puffery," not substance. In the crowded cities, individual quality makes little impression. Honesty, faithfulness, and prudence will not bring in customers. The tradesman is "driven to cry out on the housetops that his wares are the best of wares, past, present, and to come." This draws the crowd. For Mill, in a commercial society "any voice, not pitched in an exaggerated key, is lost in the hubbub." For the author as well, the "arts of attracting public attention" override any other skill.[39]

In his reviews of *Democracy in America* Mill picked out themes in Tocqueville's book that resonated with him. With a somewhat different accent than Tocqueville, Mill stressed the loss of diversity and the decline of the individual. For Mill, Westerners were relinquishing a robust individuality. Uniformity had become the watchword of the age. "When all are in nearly the same pecuniary circumstances," observed Mill in his 1835 review, "all educated nearly alike, and all employed nearly alike, it is no wonder if all think nearly alike."[40] In his lengthy 1840 review Mill cited verbatim long stretches of *Democracy in America*. As Mill read Tocqueville, the Frenchman accentuated the shift from an aristocratic to a democratic society that undermines differences.

Diversity devolved into homogeneity. For Mill, this phenomenon was visible in England, where newspapers and railroads flattened out distinctions, "rapidly effacing those local distinctions which rendered one part of our population strangers to another" and turning them into a "homogeneous people."[41] Tocqueville grasped this new reality. "The general character of old society was diversity: unity and uniformity were nowhere to be met with," stated Mill's Tocqueville. "In modern society, all things threaten to become so much alike, that the peculiar characteristics of each individual will be entirely lost in the uniformity of the general aspect."[42] After fifty pages Mill cites this passage from Tocqueville and declares it would be a good place to "close this article."

Yet Mill ventures "one criticism" without which Tocqueville's ideas sometimes have "an air of over-subtlety and false refinement." Mill's criticism proves damaging. He suggests the Frenchman has confused politics and economics; he has "confounded the effects of Democracy with the effects of Civilization." Mill explains that Tocqueville "has bound up in one abstract idea the whole of the tendencies of modern commercial society, and given them one name—Democracy." He has attributed to democracy the ills of capitalism.

For Mill, "modern commercial society" spells the reign of the middle class. "That class is now the power in society." Its imperatives inform all of society. "Accordingly, all the intellectual effects which M. de Tocqueville ascribes to Democracy are taking place under the Democracy of the middle class." This does not suggest that the rich and poor, the peers and proletarians, disappear. England is proof of that. It does indicate that a commercial society reigns supreme and brings in its wake what is essential for Mill, "the growing insignificance of individuals."[43]

This topic became Mill's signature issue, the fate of the individual. Mill returned to it twenty years later in *On Liberty* (1859). This book is so well-known, cited, and analyzed that it resists fresh interpretation. And that will not be attempted here. Yet nearly all the current appraisals, usually by philosophers and political scientists, focus on its theoretical principles or their consistency.[44] How does Mill's utilitarian ethic or harm principle stand up? How does his argument in *On Liberty* mesh with that of his *System of Logic* or *Utilitarianism*?

Academic thought proceeds by replacing half-truths with half-truths. Philosophers, who miss the point, correct previous philosophers, who missed the point. The commentary on Mill is not wrong, but rarely addresses central issues. Campus theorists stick to their bread and butter—logic, coherence, and evidence—but avoid the heart of the matter, what motivated Mill. "The case I have been trying to make out," writes a typical philosopher in his book about *On Liberty*, "is that Mill's principle of self-protection rests on a division of conduct into actions which either do or do not affect the interests of other persons rather than on what has generally been supposed to have been the division, namely, into conduct having or not having effects on others."[45] The political theorist Alan Ryan in his book on Mill tells us that "the discussion of the famous essay has been confused by a misunderstanding of its purpose." Ryan clears some brush, then announces, "I can now state what I believe to be the essence of Mill's argument in *Liberty*. People have failed to distinguish between acts which really are wrong and those which are foolish and unaesthetic."[46]

In this philosophical bluster, little attention—except by biographers, who often have a better sense—is given to what might be called the driving force of *On Liberty*, its Humboldtian ethos. A recent collection of scholarly work on Mill barely mentions Humboldt.[47] But Mill used Humboldt for the epigraph to *On Liberty* and returns to him in the text. For Mill, the development of the individual was key, as was the danger of the onset of uniformity. Variety in conditions nourished and partly defined the individual; the loss of variety undermined the individual. Many pages in *On Liberty* pursue this theme. They are hard to avoid, except by contemporary philosophers and political theorists. Indeed, the reviewers of Mill's own day understood the animus driving *On Liberty* much better than today's scholars. After noting that *On Liberty* is a "melancholy" book, a 19th-century reviewer stated in his second sentence that it "is written in the sincere foreboding that the strong individualities of the old types of English character are in imminent danger of being swallowed up."[48]

In his autobiography Mill does not mince words. He offers that *On Liberty* is "likely to survive longer than anything else that I have written." This is because the book became a "textbook of single truth" that is increasingly pertinent: "the importance, to man and society, of a large variety in types of character," and the importance of "giving full freedom to human nature to expand itself in innumerable and conflicting directions."[49] This does not seem obscure. Mill yells out his argument: this is my single truth. "Variety" is essential for individual development. Most philosophers miss it.

In Chapter 3 ("On Individuality, as One of the Elements of Well-Being") of *On Liberty* Mill elaborates on the importance of variety and the dangers to it. He swivels from the previous chapter that discusses what might be called top-down threats to liberty—censorship by state authorities—to bottom-up threats—censorship by social constrictions. The reason for the shift is simple. The argument for freedom of the press against despotic governments has been made often and well. Moreover, at least in England, although the law curtailing press freedom still existed, Mill believed there was "little danger of its being actually put in force." To that confident declaration Mill added a footnote with a quick qualification. The English government had just brought charges against a publisher, who had put out a pamphlet—*Tyrannicide: Is It Justifiable?*—that defended an assassination attempt on the French leader, Louis Napoleon. However, Mill notes that the prosecution was dropped, and Mill sees no reason to revise his text.

The chapter on individuality takes up not freedom of dissent, but freedom of life, or what might nowadays be called "lifestyle." The issue is not divergent opinions, but divergent modes of living. This meshes with Mill's endeavors over the decades. An image of Mill as a fuddy-duddy Victorian liberal misleads. Scholars argue as to whether, as a young fellow, Mill distributed illegal literature on contraception. Yet no doubt exists that everyday politics increasingly informed Mill's career. At the end of his life, as a member of Parliament, he punched away at numerous unpopular causes. One example: Mill led a campaign against government efforts to ban demonstrations in public parks, including Hyde Park, "a corner of which remains a symbol of free speech to this day," notes his biographer.[50] As a recent appraisal of Mill's activities puts it, "questions of suffrage, sexual equality, Ireland, Empire, secularism, and land reform" consumed Mill at the end of his life. He did not age quietly. Mill was "more hated at the moment of his death than at any other point in his career."[51]

For Mill, then, liberty was more than freedom of dissent and press. That is to say, if it is "useful" to have "different opinions," it is also useful to have "different experiments" in living. "Free scope should be given to varieties of character." In short, "individuality should assert itself." It is here where Mill turns to Humboldt, the "eminent" *savant* and politician. The true "end of man" consists of the "highest and most harmonious development of his power." Following Humboldt, this requires "'freedom, and variety of situations'"; and these combine to give rise to "'individual vigor and manifold diversity,' which combine themselves in 'originality.'"[52]

All this might seem obvious, but for Mill the obstacles to variety and individuality have gathered momentum. "There has been a time when the element of spontaneity and individuality was in excess," but that era is long past. "Society has now fairly got the better of individuality," and the danger is not excess, but deficiency. The pressure to conform, what Mill called a "wearing down into uniformity," has redoubled. Mill registered a standardization in opinion and life. People are more alike.

Using an old trope, Mill juxtaposed a European diversity and a Chinese homogeneity; the former led to progress, the latter to stagnation.[53] Mill clarified that Europeans are not superior to the Chinese as a people, but that Europeans do have a "remarkable diversity of character and culture." Our "individuals, classes, nations, have been extremely unlike one another:

they have struck out a great variety of paths." In my judgment, declares Mill, Europe is "wholly indebted to this plurality of paths for its progressive and many-sided development."

Unlike today's diversity boosters, Mill saw diversity not simply as choices or inherited characteristics, but as something deeper, modes of living. It is here that Mill returns to Tocqueville and Humboldt. He refers to Tocqueville's observation about "how much more the Frenchmen of the present day resemble one another than did those even of the last generation." Mill notes that "the same remark might be made of Englishmen in a far greater degree." He goes back to Humboldt, who posits that human development, which is another term for rendering "people unlike one another," requires two conditions: freedom and "variety of situations." It is the latter which worries Mill: "The second of these two conditions is in this country every day diminishing."

This reality distressed Mill. "The circumstances" that inform different classes and individuals are converging. "Formerly, different ranks, different neighborhoods, different trades and professions lived in what might be called different worlds." No longer. Now they live in the same world. "Comparatively speaking, they now read the same things, listen to the same things, see the same things, go to the same places, have their hopes and fears directed to the same objects, have the same rights and liberties, and the same means of asserting them."

All the great transformations of the age—commerce, manufacturing, communications—conspire to bring about "a general similarity among mankind." Mill gloomily raises an alarm. "It is not so easy to see" how individuality "can stand its ground." But, if it is possible, "the time is now," before complete assimilation has taken place. "If resistance waits till life is reduced *nearly* to one uniform type," it will be too late. Mankind will be "unable to conceive diversity, when they have been for some time unaccustomed to see it." Mill calls for non-conformity, a refusal "to bend the knee to custom." Indeed, he calls for people to be original, even eccentric. "Eccentricity has always abounded when and where strength of character has abounded"; today few "dare" to be eccentric.[54]

The clarion calls for diversity can be found elsewhere in Mill, but they barely elicit a nod from current academics who write on him. They have other fish to fry. But Mill's contemporaries addressed the issues, which is not to say they agreed with him. Several of his 19th-century critics challenged his belief in the decline of individuality. "Do ordinary Englishmen resemble each other every day more and more closely?" asked a reviewer. "Surely, if any one will run over in his mind the names of ten or twelve of his more immediate friends, he will arrive at the conclusion that they differ from each other as radically as the ash, the oak, the birch, and the elm."[55] The historian Lord Macaulay also thought that Mill missed his target. Macaulay believed boldness and inventiveness defined the times—to a fault. "Every writer seems to aim at doing something odd—at defying all rules and canons of criticism." To recommend eccentricity was exactly wrong. Mill, he declared, is "really crying 'Fire!' in Noah's flood."[56]

An anonymous critic in the *British Quarterly Review* agreed. He thought it "droll" to argue that the present epoch was witnessing a suppression of individuality. "As *we* read the present day," he claimed, eccentricities proliferate. "We can hardly see the 'green ground' in Truth's meadow for the dandelions, thistles, and poppies that have sprung up." For present-day England, individualism "inflicts far more on society than society inflicts on it."[57] Mill's *On Liberty* spurred a full-scale response by James Fitzjames Stephen, jurist and journalist, who pursued these themes. In *Liberty, Equality, Fraternity* he took exception to Mill's devotion to variety; nor did he appreciate Mill's ode to individual originality and eccentricity.

Stephen did not think that eccentricity should be promoted; nor that it should be defined as simply nonconformity. The eccentricity that Mill promotes "is far more often a mark of weakness than a mark of strength." To be original is not necessarily to be different. "Originality consists in thinking for yourself, not in thinking differently from other people." Moreover, Stephen protests what he called "the odd manner in which Mr. Mill worships mere variety." Mill confounds "the proposition that variety is good with the proposition that goodness is various." He throws up his hands. "The difference between Mr. Mill's views and mine is that he instinctively assumes that whatever is is wrong. I say, try each case on its own merits."[58]

James Stephen came from an illustrious family, and his brother Leslie—writer and father of Virginia Woolf and Vanessa Bell—joined in with an essay aptly title "Social Macadamisation," a reference to the level and graveled roads pioneered by the Scottish engineer, John McAdam. Mill feared "the macadamisation of society" or the "grinding down of the individual," declared Leslie Stephen. All variety and individuality would be lost. Like his brother, he would have none of it. He also did not like the harping on variety.

Mill supposes, according to this Stephen, that "variety of character" is an absolute good. For Stephen, it is "pretty plain" that this is not tenable. Diversity in itself is not desirable. "A nation in which everybody was sober would be a happier, better, and more progressive, though a less diversified nation, than one of which half the members were sober and the other half habitual drunkards." If this is diversity, England does not need it. A diversity of opinions might be acceptable, but only as a stage, not as an end. "The doctrine which says that variety of opinions is *per se* and in the ultimate resort a desirable state of things, is precisely analogous to the doctrine which made every man his own pope." For Stephen, "within certain limits" a variety of opinions and of character is desirable. But it is not the goal, which is concord. "We require, therefore, so much diversity as is compatible with, and indeed necessary to, harmony, but no more."[59]

Mill died in 1873, just as these criticisms by the Stephens appeared. Yet his *Autobiography* almost responds—or at least responds to earlier criticism he had seen. The autobiography, written and revised over many years, appeared in the year of his death. Mill is unbowed. To his critics he makes a telling point. He distinguishes between long-term and short-term trends. Mill explains that he is characterizing underlying social realities, but realizes they contradict everyday appearances.

It is in his *Autobiography* that Mill states that *On Liberty* might be considered a textbook expounding on a "single truth . . . the importance, to man and society, of a large variety in types of character." He admits that, "to superficial observation," the present times do not "stand much in need of such a lesson" and do not suffer from "an oppressive yoke of uniformity in opinion and practice." Mill alludes to the statement made by his critics then and today, that variegated individuals and larger-than-life characters proliferated in 19th-century England.[60] If this were true, he writes, then the fears that "we"—his late wife Harriet Taylor and himself—expressed about the eclipse of diversity and individuality would seem "chimerical."

Yet the critics are looking at "facts" and not "tendencies." We are living in an unsettled period in which opinions and variety multiply, argues Mill. Old convictions are challenged, but this flux marks an era of transition. It will not last. Appearances blind his critics. In the long run, the deeper forces of a noxious uniformity "stunting and dwarfing human nature" may win out. "It is then that the teachings of the *Liberty* will have their greatest value."[61] In other words, says Mill, history is on my side. My critics confuse a transient efflorescence of diversity with long-term decline. He might be right.

··●··

Mill's essay "should not be called *On Liberty*, but rather *On Diversity*." He correctly supposes that "the *peculiarity* and *diversity* of human nature" sustain humanity. But he proposes an "impossible antidote—he wants individual peculiarity and diversity in European thought without individual peculiarity and diversity in European life." So commented the 19th-century Russian critic Constantine Leontyev in "The Average European as an Ideal and Instrument of Universal Destruction."[62] Leontyev (1831–1891), who is not well-known, resists classification. He was an aesthete, mystic, and hedonist all rolled into one. One of his current editors calls him a minor philosopher, but a major critic with "an almost demonic clarity."[63] The philosopher Nicolas Berdyaev dubbed him a Renaissance type, "and for that reason he tended to be a reactionary in our own time."[64] Leontyev hated the uniformity of bourgeois life: that comes across loud and clear in his writings. "It is not vice that is to be feared nowadays; it is banality and facelessness that are frightening."[65] Like other conservatives such as Möser, he turns to nature as a counterpoint. "Organic nature thrives on diversity, on antagonisms and struggles" and "not in flat unison." Nature "loves the exuberance of form and it loves diversity. Our life must be patterned after it."[66]

Leontyev was on to something. Perhaps *On Liberty* should indeed be titled *On Diversity*. But Leontyev's comments suggest something else. By mid-century the denunciation of encroaching uniformity passed to outliers—reactionaries, philosophical malcontents, and Russian nationalists, who distrusted Western society. A case in point would be another Russian, coming from the Left, not the Right.

Like everyone else, it seems, Alexander Herzen, the Russian writer, was in Paris during the revolution of 1848; and like many others, he was shaken to the core by the events. Even before the election of Louis Napoleon and his coup, the ineptitude of the Left, as well as the savagery of the Right, disabused him of hopes for change. "It is the peculiar destiny of the Russians," he wrote in his brilliant reflections on the revolution of 1848 and its aftermath, *From the Other Shore*, "to see further than their neighbors, to see in darker colors and to express their opinions boldly."[67] And what did he see?

He saw that the liberators were weak, and "the masses" conformist and obedient. The masses are not only "indifferent to individual freedom, to freedom of speech," they "love authority" and "the arrogant glitter of power." Herzen admitted that, along with other socialists and liberals, he had been wrong about "the people." Liberals live "in large towns and small circles" among "books, journals, clubs." Liberals "did not know the people at all; they studied it with immense profundity from historical sources, antiquities, not in the villages and the market place."

The reality evaded liberals. "It was easier for liberalism to invent the people than to study it." If liberals had known the "inner life of France," they would not have been surprised that the people voted for Louis Napoleon. They would have realized that "the French people have not the faintest notion of freedom, of the Republic, but they have bottomless national pride."[68] To be sure, Herzen did not damn "the people." They were not ready to govern, and the state, he wrote elsewhere, did not give the people what it needed, education, but what it did not need, universal suffrage.[69]

Like many other refugees of the 1848 revolution—such as Marx—Herzen ended up in England. He lived in London for twelve years, but never warmed to the English. "Life here," he wrote to a Russian acquaintance, "is about as boring as that of worms in a cheese. There is not a spark of anything healthy, vigorous or hopeful."[70] He had arrived in England a defeated man; his hopes for a European revolution had been dashed. Moreover, he suffered a series of personal blows of the first magnitude. His mother and one of his sons had drowned in a boating accident. His wife had died in the aftermath of his devastating discovery of her passionate affair with his best friend.[71]

It would be difficult to imagine two figures more different than John Stuart Mill and Alexander Herzen—at least at first glance: the careful English state employee and the hot-blooded Russian aristocrat. Mill was the son of a state official and former clergyman; Herzen the illegitimate son of a wealthy landowner and his German common-law wife. The father bestowed on him the surname Herzen (German *Herz* = heart) as a token of his affection.[72] Herzen impressed virtually everyone by his energy and fire. Jane Carlyle, the wife of Thomas Carlyle, invited him for tea along with other political refugees. There were five us, she reported, speaking four languages, sometimes at the same time. "It was a madhouse!" She judged Herzen brave and fervent—too much so. "His tawny eyes have a hungry animal look that makes me feel as if he might easily spring at me and eat me."[73]

Herzen made a few friends during his years in London but seems never to have met Mill. He did encounter Mill's *On Liberty*, and it bespeaks something of the Zeitgeist that these two individuals whose intellectual and personal trajectories were so different—just for starters, a sober utilitarianism branded Mill's thought; and a Romantic Hegelianism, Herzen's—came to agree. Herzen himself was amazed. He identified Mill as a member of the establishment—"recently a member of the India Board"; and the beneficiary of a position offered by Lord Stanley. This is a man "accustomed to regard the world calmly, like an Englishman." He is no "angry socialist exile." Yet he had written a book that "goes far beyond anything I have said."

Mill came out swinging in defense of "liberty of thought, speech and the person." Herzen found this "strange," since Milton had already defended freedom of speech two centuries ago. But the times had changed. Milton defended freedom of speech against the government. "Mill's enemy is quite different." Mill was standing up for "liberty not against an educated government but against *society*, against custom, against the deadening force of indifference, against petty intolerance, against 'mediocrity.'" Mill was "horrified by the constant deterioration of personalities." What Tocqueville observed in France, Mill observed in England: the omnipresence of "standard, indistinguishable types." Individualities get "effaced" and "disappear among the masses." In Herzen's paraphrase, "Everything is moving towards *mediocrity*. . . . Faces are being lost in the crowd." This mediocrity "hates everything that is sharply defined, original, outstanding." A "viscous bog" spreads over society that "forestalls the disorderliness of eccentric individuals." Change takes place, but like fashion, it is monotonous or "senseless."[74] To cite Mill, "We have discarded the fixed costumes of our forefathers . . . for change's sake, not from any idea of beauty or convenience."[75]

Herzen agreed. Mill "was not exaggerating in the least when he talked of the narrowing of men's minds and energies, of the obliteration of individuality."[76] But he offered a criticism: Mill had no solution. How are we to wake the sleeping individual? asked Herzen. "In the name of what shall the flabby personality, magnetized by trifles, be inspired, be made discontented with its present life of railways, telegraphs, newspapers, and cheap goods?" Herzen banked on new political upheaval but lacked optimism in its prospects. The English workingman has numbers but not will. "Numbers prove nothing. Two or three Cossacks of the line with two or three garrison soldiers each of them take five hundred convicts from Moscow to Siberia." But if no upheaval takes place, Mill is on target, concludes Herzen. Rights will exist, but "the ability to make use of these rights and this freedom" will dwindle.[77]

Many of these 19th-century observers tapped a stereotype of a foreign land to highlight where uniformity dominated and individuality vanished. For Mill, China represented a stagnant society without individuals. For Herzen, it was Holland: "Where are her great statesmen, her great artists, her subtle theologians, her bold mariners?" Instead, she gives the world "drained marshes . . . laundered towns . . . ironed gardens." The Dutchman works and prospers but "has not the time to look round him, to enjoy some leisure, before he is carried off to 'God's acre' in an elegant, lacquered coffin, while his son is already harnessed to the trade-wheel."[78] For Constantine Leontyev, Switzerland incarnated a dull conformity. He railed against "the lot of industrialized societies" with "pitifully small variations" in which "the characters of individuals would become similar." Leontyev asked, in 1864, "what is better": the "spiritually seething period of the Renaissance" or the "meek, prosperous and sedate Switzerland?"[79]

Was he alluding to the Swiss historian Jacob Burckhardt and his *Civilization of the Renaissance in Italy*, published a few years earlier? He might have been, since Burckhardt was thinking along similar lines. For a literate public, Burckhardt remains the author of just that one book, which has gone through many editions and translations, and is deemed "an historical classic read in all western countries."[80] As one critic recently declared, "The study of the Renaissance can no more forget Burckhardt than biology can leave Darwin behind."[81]

But Burckhardt remains a bit of a cipher. His life had none of the "Sturm und Drang" of Herzen—or of Burckhardt's colleague, Nietzsche. He moved from religion and journalism to art history. He wrote a guide to Italian art, but he published little and kept a low profile, teaching at Basel, Switzerland for nearly fifty years. He even refused offers of more prestigious positions that came his way. Yet his professional and political asceticism can be seen as a protest against a world that had gone amuck, a stance that comes through in his unpublished writing and peeks through his Renaissance book. For this reason, he appealed to refugee scholars, both because he kept his integrity and because he alluded to future political disasters.

J.P. Mayer, who resurrected Tocqueville, also turned to Burckhardt during World War II; to Mayer, both anticipated the rise of popular authoritarian regimes. He classified Burckhardt and Tocqueville as "new liberals." That is, they were not conventional liberals who believed in automatic progress; nor were they socialists "chasing after a Utopian idea; nor reactionary conservatives trying to put the clock back." They accepted progress and remained committed to liberty and freedom but feared the onset of uniformity and popular dictatorships. Mayer called the Swiss professor a "lonely prophet" with contemporary relevance, noting the defeat of France by the Nazis that had just occurred. "The French collapse in June 1940," wrote Mayer in 1941, "is a terrible confirmation of the fears of the Basel prophet."[82] A year earlier another refugee scholar, Albert Salomon, also turned to Burckhardt and found insights into the current disaster. Almost a century ago, announced Salomon in 1940, a scholar "visualized the forthcoming debacle of European civilization . . . This man was Jacob Burckhardt."[83]

Although Burckhardt kept his loyalties veiled, they can be glimpsed in the manner he celebrated robust individuality in *The Civilization of the Renaissance in Italy*. In the section titled "The Development of the Individual," Burckhardt stated that the Italians of the 14th century "knew little of false modesty or of hypocrisy in any shape; not one of them was afraid of singularity, of being and seeming unlike his neighbors." Even those outside political power found ways to express their Renaissance individualism. Their "political impotence" did not "hinder the different tendencies and manifestations of private life from thriving in the fullest vigor and variety."[84] As the scholar Lionel Gossman wrote in his *Basel in the Age of Burckhardt*, the Renaissance book draws a comparison between an exuberant past individualism and the grey uniformity of contemporary Switzerland. Gossman believes that Burckhardt's "entire historical enterprise was an act of resistance to that modern way of life" he detested. He saw contemporary society as marked by "absolute uniformity" and empty novelty.[85]

Like Tocqueville and Mill, Burckhardt feared the onset of conformist masses and hollow diversity. He judged that people surrendered individuality for technological accoutrements. Mankind today, Burckhardt wrote to a friend, would willingly "give up their particular literature and culture for express overnight trains." People "really hate every kind of diversity."[86] Both Mayer and Salomon cite a passage in which Burckhardt declared that "the term liberty sounds beautiful and perfect," but "I know too much history." The masses could bring an end to liberty. "There is a popular mass, wherein slumber the seeds of a vast number of splendid characters, but which could be utilized as a mass in the hands of any rogue and would then behave like a wild beast."[87]

Burckhardt distrusted elections because, "if they want to be re-elected, the leaders of the people must win over the loudest-mouthed sections of the popular masses." The rise of Louis Napoleon in France and Bismarck in Germany worried him. Burckhardt's vision got darker and darker. "I feel it in my bones that something will erupt in the West." He anticipated stages of "confusion and disorder," until "by an act of pure violence, a new power emerges which will make damned short shrift of voting rights, popular sovereignty, material welfare, industry, etc."[88] Burckhardt wrote to a friend, "All power now lies with the forces of dissolution and uniformity."[89]

In his lectures on history Burckhardt sounded very much like Benjamin Constant. He criticized the short-lived Helvetic Republic that was established when Napoleon invaded Switzerland to set up a centralized government. For Burckhardt, this spelled the end of diversity that characterized Swiss localism. The new Republican leaders aimed to impose uniform regulations on the archaic practices of almost autonomous cantons. As an historian of Switzerland put it, for the Helvetic Republic "diversity embodied the corporatist society of the *ancien régime*, while uniformity in cultural and political matters was a sign of a truly modern and progressive (i.e. republican) state."[90] Burckhardt would have concurred. He saw Napoleon's principal representatives as misguided Enlighteners, who aimed to efface the diversity of Swiss society. "From the spirit of the century they had worked up a veritable indignation at everything varied and different."[91]

These comments come from Burckhardt's lectures, which he delivered in the 1860s, '70s, and '80s, a period that witnessed accelerating industrialization and empire-building. By the last quarter of the century, laments of encroaching uniformity had become common not only among maverick scholars like Burckhardt but also in the new field of sociology. Many of the discipline's founding texts, such as Ferdinand Tönnies's *Community and Society* (1887), Gabriel Tarde's *Laws of Imitation* (1890), and Émile Durkheim's *The Division of Labor in Society* (1893), rested on the observation that differences were contracting in modern society.

All these authors were murky—they were, after all, sociologists. Tönnies's basic concepts of "community" (*Gemeinschaft*) and "society" (*Gesellschaft*) puzzled readers and translators.[92] Nevertheless, the rough argument, which reflected Tönnies's own alienation from contemporary German society, comes through. Indeed, in his letters he often sounded like Burckhardt, unhappy with all political options. "It seems to me," he wrote in 1879, "as though the clouds draw closer and closer over our national life. Will the Lord soon take a look and exterminate the scoundrels?" Like Burckhardt, he felt estranged from the university.[93] A friend recalled that "uncompromising" and "altogether negative attitude toward the world we live in"; he saw about him "nothing but dissolution and ruin." He rejected the university and wanted to establish a "free academy" where learning could proceed unhampered by status and restriction.[94, *]

For Tönnies, the commercial transactions of an industrial society supplant the natural and organic relations of an agrarian community. A romantic note infuses his work. Industrial homogeneity succeeds rural diversity. "Every man . . . becomes in some measure a merchant," states Tönnies, quoting Adam Smith.[95] The merchant is "isolated from all necessary relationships, duties, and prejudices. . . . He is free from the ties of the life of the *Gemeinschaft*; the freer he is from them, the better for him." The categories of profit and trade remake the world. The denizen of *Gemeinschaft* looked inward, but the new trading class looks outward. "It is concerned only with the roads which connect towns and with the means of transit. . . . The whole country is nothing but a market in which to purchase and sell."[96]

The other sociological classic, Tarde's *Laws of Imitation*, accented quickening uniformity, which Tarde understood through a complex analogy to nature that oscillated between difference and regularity. In nature and history "difference is the cause and the goal, and harmony the means and the effect."[97] The Frenchman Tarde noted that uniformity marks our present

---

* If these sentiments evoke the Basel scholar, Tönnies was in fact only one degree separated from him. At age 27, Tönnies spent time in the Swiss Alps courting a 21-year-old with whom he had fallen in love and who was half in love with Burckhardt's colleague Nietzsche. Everyone from Nietzsche to Freud seems to have been enchanted by the Russian Lou-Andreas Salomé. So was Tönnies. "She is a phenomenon that must be seen from close up to be believed. . . . She is a genius," Tönnies reported to a friend.[98]

society, which is reflected in the military. In the 17th century, the king marveled at the diversity of costumes in his army, but by the following century "a uniform became general," which persists to the present. "Imagine the effect produced by a return in our day . . . to such an antique medley of military garments! Such diversity of costume would not be tolerated." As in the military so in life. Tarde concurred with Mill that without diversity "the world would be as monotonous as it is vast." He noted "the picturesque side of the 'rich diversity'" of the medieval period, while in the modern era uniformity dominates. He asked, "Is not our present civilization . . . cast in a single, unique mold? Nowadays, have we not to seek the depth of some African desert or Chinese village to avoid seeing the same hats and dresses, the same cigars, the same newspapers?"

Tarde ended his 1890 study of "imitation" on a bleak note, asking whether homogeneity will triumph or dissolve and give rise to a new individuality. "We may wonder," he declares in his final paragraph, "whether universal similarity under all its present or future forms, in regard to dress, to the alphabet, perhaps to language, to sciences, to law, etc., we may wonder whether it is the consummate fruit of civilization." Or, he continues, it is possible that civilization may "pause" and give rise to "distinctive traits of our individuality"—an "aesthetic life"—that will be more radical than anything witnessed before. If this is the case, then our present stage is just a "long, obscure, and tortuous transition" from an old to a new diversity.[99]

The final sociological classic belongs to Durkheim, whose reputation far eclipses that of Tarde and Tönnies. He also mulled on the forces of uniformity but offered a twist that would be rephrased by champions of globalization today. His *Division of Labor in Society* takes up the implications of increasing specialization. Even the scholar must specialize. "The time has passed" when one could study everything, he declares. Such a broad project appears as dilettantism, something "loose and flabby." We prefer the man "who has a restricted task, and devotes himself to it." Specialization in life and work typifies modern society.

Durkheim introduces two categories, mechanical and organic solidarity, to apprehend the core of past and present society. The terms are somewhat confusing—and virtually reverse Tönnies's vocabulary—but do capture a central element of an industrial world. "Organic" solidarity distinguishes advanced societies. In a pre-industrial society the individual acquired food and shelter on his own, and with that autonomy the relationship to others became external or mechanical. In industrial societies we do not bake our own bread or sew our own clothes. We specialize—and increasingly rely on others. With specialization our relationship to others is indispensable. For Durkheim, "organic" alludes to the fact that our specialized organs—the eye or ear—cannot function in isolation. As we become more and more specialized, the links to society become more and more biological or "organic."[100]

What does this mean for diversity or the development of the individual? On one hand, the reality of homogeneity cannot be denied. Echoing Tarde—and Rousseau and Tocqueville—Durkheim asked, "Are not the differences which separate a Frenchman from an Englishman or a German less today than heretofore?" The French sociologist declares that "in almost all European societies, law, morality, customs, even fundamental political institutions are nearly identical." This can be observed not only across countries but also within countries. Differences between provinces and regions decline. "We no longer find today the same contrasts that we used to find." Social life "no longer varies so much from one province to another." In France "it is nearly the same in all regions."[101]

Yet Durkheim flips the switch here. Homogenization increases, but so does individuality, which might be treated as a form of specialization. As differences between countries and regions decline, individuality increases. The relationship is inverse. The particularities of the region, group, or tribe retreat as individuality advances. "There is now less distance than heretofore between the Frenchman and the Englishman, generally speaking, but that does not stop the contemporary Frenchmen from differing among themselves more than the Frenchmen of yesteryear." The same configuration exists within the country. Distinctions between regions of France diminish, but individuality grows. "There are no longer as many differences as there are great regions, but there are almost as many as there are individuals." The modern division of labor fuels this diversity, believes Durkheim. Though jobs look more and more alike, their specialization engenders differences. Homogeneity coexists with cultivated diversity.[102]

This is almost the argument today of those like economist Tyler Cowen who celebrate the global market. Global homogenization is set against the opposite, global heterogeneity. They are "two sides of the same coin," as Cowen writes in *Creative Destruction*. Critics have failed to distinguish two types of diversity that move in opposite directions. Globalization "tends to favor diversity within society, but to disfavor diversity across societies." This means that "different regions may look more similar than in times past," but individuals in those regions "have a more diverse menu of choice for their cultural consumption." Mass marketing and niche marketing complement each other. "In some ways the world was very diverse in 1450, but not in a way that most individuals could benefit from." Today it is the opposite. "Only in a world of globalized culture can I collect nineteenth-century Japanese prints, listen to the music of Pygmy tribes, read the Trinidadian author V.S. Naipaul, and enjoy the humor of Canadian Jim Carrey, while my neighbors pursue different paths of their own choosing."[103]

There is undoubtedly a truth to this, but a question leaps out for both Durkheim and others who present these arguments: does specialization and increased "menu of choice" constitute enhanced individuality? It is at least as convincing to suggest the opposite; they connote an attenuated individual. Already Adam Smith expressed fear that specialization would maim, not enhance, the individual. He worried that "the progress of the division of labor" led most people to do only a few tasks each, and that "dexterity" in one specialized trade over a lifetime "corrupts" the mind, leading to a "drowsy stupidity."[104] (Note to followers of Ayn Rand: for this reason Smith supported state education.) Undoubtedly the menu of choices has increased, which Cowen celebrates: "We can go anywhere and see Javanese puppet theater, look at French Impressionist pictures, eat sushi, and hear Afro-Cuban music." As positive as this scenario may be, its vision of the individual does not extend beyond that as a consumer. Humboldt would be aghast. As the individual dwindles, purchasing options widen.

The consumption angle does not appear in Durkheim, but he did wrestle with the antinomies of individualism; and, as with many fin-de-siècle social thinkers, a certain darkness imbues his work. On one hand, the division of labor gives rise to the modern individual—on the other, it leads to breakdown. Besides *The Division of Labor in Society*, Durkheim's most famous work is *Suicide*, where he employed the term "anomie," which refers to the dissolution of norms.[105] *Suicide* can be clumped with a number of somber works that appeared towards the end of the century, such as Henry Morselli's *Suicide: An Essay on Comparative Moral Statistics* (1879) and Thomas G. Masaryk's *Suicide and the Meaning of Civilization* (1881).[106] These books established a relationship between industrial civilization and suicide.[107]

Durkheim recognized that the division of labor engendered social disorganization—and suicide.[108] But something else reared up at the end of the century that illuminated dwindling diversity and its dangers: the emergence of the mass man in the guise of popular anti-Semitism. The new anti-Semitism upset many, including Durkheim. The Dreyfus Affair, in which a Jewish French army captain was framed in 1894 for treason, ripped France apart for a decade. Rabbi Moses Durkheim's son became a famous sociologist; but the son dropped his first name, David, for his middle name, Émile, and preferred that his last get pronounced in a French manner with a short 'e'—Durkhem—rather than the more German and Jewish "Durkhime."[109] Professor Durkhem kept a very low, perhaps nonexistent, Jewish profile. But the Dreyfus Affair ensnared him and caused a small blip in his worldview. In the few writings that he devoted to the Affair, he struggled to fathom what he called the "state of social malaise," this "public madness." When Dreyfus was found guilty by a military court, Durkheim noted, "There was a fervent joy in the streets. People celebrated. . . . People finally knew whom to blame for the economic troubles and the moral distress through which they lived. Evil came from the Jews."[110]

With limited success Durkheim struggled to reconcile the

antipodes of his own theories. On one hand, the advanced division of labor led to a "diversity of situations and constantly changing circumstances" that allowed a new kind of individual to flourish. On the other, these same conditions destabilized society. "There remains nothing that men may love and honor in common." He noted that the Jewish faith in France was no "less ardent" 20 or 30 years ago, while anti-Semitism had increased, which reflects "the serious moral disturbance from which we suffer."[111] Yet Durkheim did not offer much insight into why these disturbances gathered strength.

The ineptness of the opposition to anti-Semitism troubled Durkheim. He wrote to a friend in 1898 that he just "spent the saddest winter; all these deplorable events, the impression they give of our moral isolation, the disgusting spectacle of so much cowardice." This got the "better of my courage."[112] However, he rallied and called for intellectuals, who in their commitment to justice and rights must resist the "enthusiasms of the crowd" which celebrates the condemnation of Dreyfus. "May the common danger we confront at least help us by shaking us out of our torpor and giving us again the taste for action!"[113] He wanted to keep his intellectual protesters together beyond the Dreyfus Affair. We must not "disband," he wrote to a friend, "but must draw the consequences of the crisis and do whatever possible to prevent its return. Otherwise, it will reproduce itself in another form." After some renewed personal attacks by anti-Semites, he wrote to an acquaintance that he was "becoming discouraged," but "at bottom I am an optimist."[114]

Perhaps too much so. The crisis did return—in other decades and forms, as Burckhardt and others anticipated. The years that Durkheim cemented his reputation as a rationalist sociologist who banked on progress saw a new kind of sociological literature appear that foregrounded the opposite, regression—or the underside of industrialization and democracy. Amid the Dreyfus Affair, Gustav Le Bon published *Psychology of Crowds*, which has been called "the first best-seller of social science since Thomas Paine's *Rights of Man*."[115] In overheated rhetoric, he announced the "advent to power of the masses." The old ideas are "tottering and disappearing"; the old pillars of society are "giving way one by one," but one thing is gaining power: the masses. Scarcely a century ago, the opinion of the masses "did not count at all." Today it is the opposite: "The destinies of nations are elaborated in the heart of the masses, and no longer in the council of princes."[116]

Psychology of Crowds belonged to a series of works from the end of the century that underscored the emergence of the crowd, the mob, or the masses. Tarde also wrote a book on crowds. But most of the authors owed nothing to Mill or Tocqueville. They were not liberals, but illiberals and reactionaries. They regretted democratic society. Le Bon was an anti-Dreyfusard—and a colonialist, racist, and misogynist. Mussolini thought highly of him.[117] Nevertheless, the new illiberal literature on the crowd suggested that the fears of Tocqueville and Mill were not misplaced.

This is what J.P. Mayer understood when, in the wake of Nazism, he returned to Tocqueville as a prophet of the masses. He was not alone. Virtually at the same time, another left-leaning German-Jewish refugee visited the issue. At one time the star of Emil Lederer shined brightly. But "he has more or less been forgotten," an Israeli sociologist recently commented, adding that "the time for a renewal of interest in this great social scientist" has come.[118] Lederer found refuge in the United States, co-founded the "University in Exile" at the New School, and became the first dean of its graduate faculty. One year after his death in 1939, his final work, *The State of the Masses*, was published. As a student of his wrote in a foreword, the manuscript was "written after Czechoslovakia had been wiped off the map of Europe but before the German army and secret police invaded Poland."[119] In other words, at the same moment that Mayer reexamined the place of the masses, so did Lederer.

Lederer noted that socialists had long been wrong about the masses in two regards. Because of Le Bon and his ilk, socialists believed that the "masses (as we now know them) are only an invention of reactionary thinkers." In addition, the socialists imagined that the masses would "follow their own interests" toward a rational and egalitarian society. In both respects socialists were wrong. The masses do exist, and they do not necessarily follow their own interests, Lederer declared. Because socialists never understood these phenomena, the "fascist reality was the great surprise." In the same way, liberals do not understand fascism. They stress "the terror, the suppression of free press and speech," and ask, "How this can be possible?" Yet Lederer, like J.P. Mayer, notes that "the suppression of free speech and thinking" is only "the last step." The people have already been atomized, ground down, and turned into a mass.[120]

Lederer had identified this process decades earlier in an analysis of World War I, written during the war's first months. He glimpsed in the conflict an intensification of "depersonalization and mechanization" that had been unfolding for decades. These realities affected all sides—Germans, Russians, French, English. "National differences of social and economic structure have become irrelevant." What is happening is an "historical mass homogenization of people," he declared in 1915.[121] In other words, the eclipse of real diversity opened the way for a dangerous mass politics. Welcome to the future.

••●••

An American also glimpsed something of the same sort during World War I. This was a young writer, Randolph Bourne, who was visiting Germany the day the war broke out. As German reservists paraded down Berlin's Unter den Linden, Bourne feared the worst for Europe. "This civilization that I have been admiring so much seems so palpably about to be torn to shreds," he lamented.[122] Bourne "rued how rapidly the fever for war had eroded civility and cultural tolerance," summarizes an historian.[123] He hurried back to the States, where he wrote a series of essays that damned the warmongers and championed American diversity.

The American contribution to diversity overlapped with the European but addressed a reality unique to the United States, namely the millions of immigrants that poured into North America. These circumstances defined American diversity. Between 1901 and 1910 almost one million immigrants entered each year. For politicians and citizens, the issue was how or even why to transform this varied population into one nation. The prevailing goal often appealed to the metaphor of the melting pot, popularized by Israel Zangwill's play, *The Melting Pot.* This theatrical celebration of melding all peoples into similar Americans opened in 1908 with President Theodor Roosevelt, who apparently loved it, in attendance.[124] For Bourne, however, the war demonstrated "the failure of the 'melting pot.'" The time had come, he declared, "to assert a higher ideal than the 'melting pot'" of narrow Americanization. He rejected the idea of a homogeneous America for a "cosmopolitan federation" where "heterogeneous peoples" live harmoniously together.[125]

Bourne was not alone in the early decades of the 20th century in defending diversity against a repressive American homogeneity; other critics such as Horace Kallen and Alain Locke joined him. Not only did their lives intersect, these three writers could serve as an advertisement for the diversity they celebrated. Bourne came from an old American Puritan family; at birth, forceps mangled him, and a spinal disease struck him as an infant. These misfortunes left him disfigured. He bore "a crooked back and an unsightly face," he wrote in the essay "The Handicapped"; "no one but the deformed man can realize just what the mere fact of sitting a foot lower than the normal means."[126]

Kallen came from Silesia, Austria—now Poland—to the United States; his father was an Orthodox rabbi, but Kallen rebelled and frequently fled his home. He described his father as "among the last of the old school of Jews who would make absolutely no concession to their environment."[127] Locke was a gay African American from a Philadelphia family of educators. His parents called him "Allan," but he changed it to "Alain," which he thought more stylish.[128]

Both Kallen and Locke studied at Harvard during philosopher William James's tenure; Bourne became entranced with James as a student of John Dewey at Columbia. Herein lies part of the American diversity story: American pragmatism and pluralism laid a foundation for challenging total philosophies that were pitched in one register. James defended what might be called the anarchism of pluralism against the law-and-order of monism. "An antiauthoritarian principle" marked James's pluralism, Locke observed.[129] Its "radical protest" attracted him.[130] "The world is a pluralism," James wrote in the preface to *The Will to Believe*. It consists of "real possibilities, real indeterminations, real beginnings, real ends, real evil, real crises, catastrophes," all of which escape philosophical monism.[131]

One of James's essays, "On a Certain Blindness in Human Beings," collected quotations of poets, dreamers, and loafers who reveled in a natural world to which absolutist philosophers and "highly educated classes (so called)" seem immune. "We are stuffed with abstract conceptions, and glib with verbalities and verbosities." What is the point of this collection of quotations? asks James in conclusion. "It absolutely forbids us" to damn lives other than our own. "It commands us to tolerate, respect, and indulge those whom we see harmlessly interested and happy in their own ways." More generally, awareness of the world of these dreamers means, "Hands off: neither the whole of truth nor the whole of good is revealed to any single observer." He adds, "Even prisons and sick-rooms have their special revelations."[132]

This indelible pluralism pervades James's writings. Indeed, the title of his most famous work is *Varieties of Religious Experience*.[133] Elsewhere, in a review of a book by Benjamin Paul Blood, an obscure New York State philosopher, he seconds the author: "Variety, not uniformity, is more likely the key to progress."[134] The political and cultural conclusions, if they are not front and center, peek out. Even in this review James endorses what he calls a "a sort of 'left-wing' voice of defiance . . . what to my ear has a radically pluralistic sound."[135] Kallen, in a collection of James's writings that he edited, cites a letter in which the philosopher declares that he is always for the "underdogs." James stated, "I am against bigness and greatness in all their forms, and with the invisible molecular moral forces that work from individual to individual. . . . The bigger the unit you deal with, the hollower, the more brutal, the more mendacious is the life displayed."[136] In *A Pluralistic Universe* James explains that part of the world always eludes the rational monist. "Things are 'with' one another in many ways, but nothing includes everything, or dominates over everything. The word 'and' trails along after every sentence. Something always escapes. . . . The pluralistic world is thus more like a federal republic than an empire or a kingdom."[137]

Inspired by William James, Bourne, Kallen, and Locke proposed "cultural pluralism" as the response to American immigrant diversity—and to some extent racial diversity.[138] Bourne's idea of a "cosmopolitan federation" of nationalities seems directly borrowed from James.[139] Kallen claimed the phrase "cultural pluralism" emerged out of conversations with Locke when they both studied philosophy at Harvard.[140] In a 1915 essay, "Democracy versus the Melting-Pot," Kallen lambasted those who wanted to turn everyone into identical Americans. "What troubles them is *difference*." The point, for Kallen, is to build on difference. Each nationality would retain "its own peculiar dialect or speech, its own individual and inevitable esthetic and intellectual forms." In this essay Kallen declares, "Men can change their clothes, their politics, their wives, their religions, their philosophies, to a greater or lesser extent; they cannot change their grandfathers."[141] In the book that included this essay, Kallen announced his "standpoint . . . as Cultural Pluralism." For Kallen, democracy involves "not the elimination of differences, but the perfection and conservation of differences. It aims . . . not at uniformity, but at variety."[142]

"Culture and the Ku Klux Klan" runs the title of the volume's preface. For Kallen, the Ku Klux Klan incarnated the opposition to American pluralism, which is founded upon "variation of racial groups and individual character; upon spontaneous differences of social heritage, institutional habit, mental attitude and emotional tone." The strength of the United States lies in its "manyness, variety, differentiation." Kallen closed his preface with a call to arms. "The alternative before Americans is Kultur Klux Klan or Cultural Pluralism."[143]

Both Kallen and Locke had long careers ahead of them. Kallen taught at the New School for decades and identified as a liberal Zionist. Locke taught for almost as long at Howard University and wrote often about race. Henry Louis Gates Jr. has called him "the veritable 'dean' of the fabled Harlem Renaissance."[144] In his thirties Locke joined the Bahá'í faith. Though he died in 1954, his ashes were not buried until 2014, beneath a tombstone that included two phrases, "Herald of the Harlem Renaissance" and "Exponent of Cultural Pluralism," alongside symbols suggesting his sexual and religious identities.[145]

The influenza epidemic at the end of World War I cut down the ailing Bourne; he died at age 32. His brief life has led to debates about what his future contributions might have been. In his final writings he wrestled with new issues and formulations. Not simply the war, but popular support for it disillusioned Bourne. "The mass of the people" succumb to the "irresistible forces for uniformity." Bourne bemoaned the emergence of a "herd-feeling" he saw all around him. Even the beliefs of the socialists, "millions strong, did not insulate them against that electric thrill of panic and patriotism."[146] For some critics, Bourne glimpsed the future, the emergence of "the technocratic state and a mass man."[147]

At one point Kallen's cry—Kultur Klux Klan or Cultural Pluralism—seemed dated.[148] John Higham's comprehensive history of Americanization, *Strangers in the Land: Patterns of American Nativism, 1860–1925*, which was published first in 1955, cautiously concluded that the days of illiberal populism and the Ku Klux Klan were over—over, but perhaps not out.

The new prosperity, with its promise of two chickens in every pot and two cars in every garage, sapped the animus of the American homogenizers.[149] Even into the 1990s a scholar opined that the era of Americanization had ended. "The historian can only express astonishment at the alteration of national ethos," declared Brandeis University professor Stephen J. Whitfield in 1996. "Diversity has ceased to be something to be feared and has become something to be celebrated. The ideal of heterogeneity has displaced homogeneity." He observed that "almost no monoculturalists remain standing."[150] But times change—and regress. The monoculturalists are back. They are more than standing; they are commanding. The backlash against immigrant diversity runs deep and wide—in the United States and elsewhere.

Yet the salience of cultural pluralism à la Kallen should not obscure its limits. It mainly addresses group diversity and assumes individual diversity. Men cannot change their grandfathers, declared Kallen, who continued, "Jews or Poles or Anglo-Saxons, in order to cease being Jews or Poles or Anglo-Saxons, would have to cease to be. . . . The selfhood which is inalienable in them . . . is ancestrally determined."[151] Or as he wrote elsewhere, "An Irishman is always an Irishman, a Jew always a Jew. . . . Irishman and Jew are facts in nature."[152] But this biological notion of group identity has proved both dangerous and misleading. Kallen himself departed from the Jewish orthodoxy of his father; and his children and grandchildren did even more so.[153] The issue in these pages, however, is less group diversity than individual diversity. Can the former wax and the latter wane? Can we have more groups and fewer individuals? More "diversity" and at the same time more homogeneity? To these questions the American pluralists had little to offer.

Epilogue

"Variety is life, uniformity, death." So said Benjamin Constant in 1814. Perhaps few would challenge the sentiment. But the point is to move beyond sentiment. When does the ideology of variety blind us to the reality of uniformity? How does the individual flourish in an age of Americanization? Constant worried about the health of the individual. He asked when individuals "cast like atoms upon an immense flat plain," stripped and isolated, formed "people *en masse*."[1] He was not alone in his disquiet. The great liberal thinkers of the 19th century shared his unease. They honored individual diversity and dreaded its eclipse.

The evidence for the weakening of diversity is everywhere. Today's celebrants do not notice or want to notice. They serve English-spoken-only diversity as they wear Nike garb, check their Facebook pages, and text their friends. Dwindling biodiversity makes no impression. Global homogenization passes them by. A Mexican journalist recently complained of the impact of the United States: "It's made us one of the most obese people on earth, because we are now mass consumers of American junk food."[2] The diversity celebrants can't be bothered. They love diversity, but rarely ask what it means or what its reality is in an age of massification.

Groups and diversity get conflated everywhere. If you have the first, you have the second. A university sets out prerequisites for a course to be eligible to meet new campus "diversity requirements." In the inimitable language of academics, the first reads: "The course must substantially address conditions, experiences, perspectives, and/or representations of at least two groups using different frames that include but are not limited to race, ethnicity, gender, socioeconomic status, sexual orientation, religion, disability, age, language, nationality, citizenship status and/or place of origin."[3] Do these courses teach diversity—or how to enter data on spreadsheets? Once you tabulate the group and the frame, you know everything worth knowing. Today, diversity spells taxonomy.

The conservative criticism, at least of the campuses, cannot be brushed aside. Conservatives charge that group heterogeneity does not mean intellectual heterogeneity. What is group diversity, these critics ask, with intellectual homogeneity? It's a good question. Unfortunately, the conservatives rarely use the same optic on other parts of society. They might find a more troubling homogeneity. It's not language or clothes that is distressing, but the pith of society, including the pastimes of children. Infant strollers with iPad holders do not bode well for individual diversity. Nor does a population that gets its information from tweets and video snippets. This should be more alarming to conservatives than Oppression Studies 101 taught by a tenured radical. Leftists populate some humanities departments, but all these outfits combined hardly compare to the heft of ExxonMobil, Walmart, or Apple. Moreover, unlike these corporations, the humanities suffer serious decline. Each year support and enrollment fall. Construction cranes dot science, medical, and business schools as humanities departments contract and shed faculty. This too should bother conservatives.

Once upon a time, conservatives—or at least one strain of conservatives—offered sharp criticisms of unbridled capitalism. Consider the blast delivered by Thomas Carlyle in his 1829 "Sign of the Times" that denounced "the Age of Machinery." "Men are grown mechanical in head and in heart, as well as in hand." He feared the loss of individual diversity. We "stand lashed together, uniform in dress and movement." Our "civil Liberty" is secured, but "our moral Liberty is all but lost."[4] That conservatism has faded. Today conservatives think the market is dandy for everything from cancer to poverty and first grade. They write books with titles like *Two Cheers for Capitalism*.[5]

Diversity has become the ambient noise of our era. We are all diverse all the time: this is the message we hear incessantly. "Diversity at Johnson & Johnson is about your unique perspective. It's about you." The advice from high and low, corporate advertisers and private therapists, is "Be Yourself." Alluring adverts tell us to reach for the sky. Counselors suggest we listen to our inner selves. *Must You Conform?* asked the title of a classic book of the 1950s by the psychologist Robert Lindner, who also authored *Rebel Without a Cause*.[6] His answer, of course, was "No," and history has followed him. Today everyone is a rebel and nonconformist—or so we believe. In the age of Americanization we are all different.

To challenge the ideology of diversity smacks of elitism. The critic of society—to follow T.W. Adorno—evokes a "flagrant contradiction." The critic is not happy with civilization to which "alone he owes his discontent." He speaks as if he represents something higher. "Yet he is necessarily of the same essence as that to which he fancies himself superior."[7] This problem—to put it less philosophically—dogs the critic of diversity. He or she is the individual that others are not, but at the same time shares the general fate. The great Viennese critic Karl Kraus once declared that, "according to a census, Vienna has 2,030,834 inhabitants—that is, 2,030,833 souls and me." He stood apart. How else could he denounce a society in which "everyone has individuality, and everyone [is] the same"?[8]

The "flagrant contradiction" cannot be wished away; at best, it can be recognized and regretted, but not denied. An elite that cocoons in toney neighborhoods often succumbs to self-satisfaction, if not self-delusion. It risks attributing to the common folk the ills that are common to all folk. Talk of the "masses" can easily mislead, as if the masses exist apart from the society that makes us all. The difference between a Porsche SUV and a Ford Fiesta is money, not substance.

We live in an age of populism, however, where elites fall under suspicion. Populism assumes various forms. In the dominant version, liberals, journalists, big city denizens, professors, and government employees constitute an insular class unfamiliar with 'real' people. That the attacks on an elite are orchestrated by an elite does not alter the phenomenon. "Political mass meeting: the stadium filled to the last seat, a veritable carpet of people and faces in the ascending tiers; the orator going full steam. He says, 'The mass culture is to blame for everything.' Tumultuous applause."[9] This is a fictional event from the 1950s, but captures a truth alive and well today, the riven mentality of a phony populism. Elites attack elites in the name of the masses that partake of resentment toward a society that has turned them into masses.

The minor form of populism flourishes among the liberals and professors themselves; they too believe in the people or least a subsection of it. To any criticism of any advocacy group they respond with celerity and anger. The critic has impugned the integrity and righteousness of those criticized. He or she is an elitist. This pose has long marked leftist scholars of mass culture; they protest any criticism of popular culture as a slur on the people. They find individuality and rebellion everywhere. "Lee Cooper is made to be different so that you can wear your clothing and footwear with a gritty individual look," runs an advert for jeans and shoes. The critical scholar tags closely behind. It is an illusion, writes a French sociologist, to see "mass standardization" or "the negation of individualism" in blue jeans and current fashions. "Jeans, like any other fashion, are selected, not imposed. . . . Private individuals are always free to accept or reject the latest fad." Jeans are "the expression of individuality."[10] This stance marks the liberal version of populism; the people are always right.

Some truths are worth repeating. The people are not always right. Nor are their representatives. Nor are the liberals and leftists who defend unreservedly any marginal grouping. Nor are conservatives who govern in the name of the people, however deluded. Worse than elitism is pandering, which is the ill of contemporary populism in its liberal and illiberal forms.

The 19th-century critics of diversity knew something about populism, although the term did not exist. They recognized that the forces of uniformity threatened the individual and democracy. J.P. Mayer was not the only refugee who returned to these 19th-century figures to help understand what had gone amuck in the 20th-century democracies. These scholars grasped that it was not an assault from without, but corrosion from within that ended democracy. We might follow their lead in assessing 21st-century democracies.

Mill and Tocqueville identified trends, not passing events. Neither were optimists. Yet it should not be ignored that they both participated in everyday politics.[11] Pessimism does not preclude action; neither does it mystify action, an old disorder. The motto derived from the French humanist Romain Rolland, "pessimism of the intellect, optimism of the will," may be too simple, but retains its truth. Towards the end of his long life, during the occupation of France by the Nazis, Rolland encouraged a young partisan, Elie Walach, to retain confidence in the future. "I don't have to burst my lungs shouting: Mankind marches like a snail (it's already something if it isn't like a crab)." Rolland added what Galileo supposedly uttered when forced to recant his assertion that the Earth circled the sun: "*E pur si muove!* (But still it moves!)."[12]

And still it does. But today we lack a platform to apprehend the motion and find a way out. The path forward is not clear. Every solution is the wrong one. Nevertheless, it is better to see the situation for what it is than to pretend it is something else. The insistence that all criticism should conclude with ten bullet points of recommendations is part of the problem. "It is what it is" has become a popular phrase to address almost anything; it suggests an angry helplessness or acceptance for things large and small. "It is what it isn't" might be offered as a counterpoint. Things are not always as they appear. That is the hope.

Notes

CHAPTER ONE—THE MYTH OF DIVERSITY

1 The University of Michigan staffs diversity offices with nearly one hundred employees. Apparently, this is typical. The University of Texas at Austin and the University of California, Berkeley report similar numbers. What do all these diversity officials do? A trade organization, the National Association of Diversity Officers in Higher Education (NADOHE), came into being a dozen years ago to figure this out or, in its words, "to guide the nascent diversity profession." ["History," National Association of Diversity Officers in Higher Education, undated, https://www.nadohe.org/history] The organization now prospers with dues, annual conferences, and a journal. I'm taking the figures of the size of the diversity offices from Mark Pulliam, "The Campus Diversity Swarm," *City Journal*, October 10, 2018. One prestigious liberal arts college, Amherst College, boasts a staff of twenty in its Office of Diversity & Inclusion—this in a school of 1800 students. All those listed do not work full-time in the office, but at Amherst we know how some officials passed their time. This office published a 36-page glossary, *Common Language Guide*, which it modestly described as "a list of carefully researched and thoughtfully discussed definitions for key diversity and inclusion terms." [Resource Center Team, *Common Language Guide* (Amherst, MA: Amherst College, Office of Diversity & Inclusion, March 2019)]. The guide thoughtfully included such key terms as "cisheteronormativity" and "homonationalism." The publication caused a stir when it found its way online and elicited a retraction from Amherst's president. See Rand Richards Cooper, "Is This 'Common' Language? A College's Misguided Guide," *Commonweal*, April 22, 2019, https://www.commonwealmagazine.org/common-language. Probably in response to unwanted criticism about the size or activities of its diversity enterprise, Amherst, as of September 2019, lists only seven employees in its Office of Diversity & Inclusion. This appears to be a bureaucratic masquerade inasmuch as the larger staff of diversity officers still exist but have been simply been removed from the page. A visit to the Internet Archive WayBack Machine confirms that twenty were listed as late as June 5, 2019. By

July 14, 2019 the extra thirteen names had been removed. ["Meet us," (Amherst, MA: Amherst College, Office of Diversity & Inclusion, June 5, 2019. September 11, 2019.) Internet Archive. https://web.archive.org/web/20190201061633/https://www.amherst.edu/amherst-story/diversity/office-of-diversity-inclusion/meet-us].

2 Some of these paragraphs are drawn from my article "The Cult of Diversity," *Chronicle of Higher Education*, Vol. 62 No. 30 (April 8, 2016), B7–9.

3 *Encyclopaedia of the Social Sciences*, eds. Edwin R.A. Seligman and Alvin Johnson, 15 vols. (New York: Macmillan Company, 1930–1935).

4 *Dictionary of the History of Ideas: Studies of Selected Pivotal Ideas*, ed. Philip P. Wiener (New York: Scribner, 1973–74).

5 *Routledge International Handbook of Diversity Studies*, ed. Steven Vertovec (London: Routledge, 2015).

6 *Encyclopedia of Diversity in Education*, ed. James A. Banks (Thousand Oaks, CA: SAGE Publications, 2012).

7 The University of California, Los Angeles library catalog kicks out 877 books in a keyword search of "diversity" for books published in 2018. This means that diversity shows up in the book's title or subtitle—or sometimes in a chapter title, subheading, or the book's description.

8 Peter Wood, *Diversity: The Invention of a Concept* (San Francisco: Encounter Books, 2003), 112.

9 "Appendix to Opinion of Powell, J.: Harvard College Admissions Program," *University of California Regents v. Bakke (1978)*, No. 76811, United States Supreme Court. Argued: October 12, 1977; Decided: June 28, 1978.

10 See Jon A. Shields and Joshua M. Dunn Sr., *Passing on the Right: Conservative Professors in the Progressive University* (New York: Oxford University Press, 2016).

11 Marcus Lee Hansen, cited in my book *Dogmatic Wisdom: How the Culture Wars Divert Education and Distract America* (New York: Doubleday, 1994), 155–56.

12 Robert D. Putnam, "*E Pluribus Unum*: Diversity and Community in the Twenty-First Century," *Scandinavian Political Studies*, Vol. 30 No. 2 (June 2007), 137.

13 Amanda Hess, "Asian-American Actors are Fighting for Visibility. They Will Not be Ignored," *New York Times*, May 25, 2016,.

14 Ira Wagler, *Growing Up Amish* (Carol Stream, IL: Tyndale House Publishers, 2011), 7–9.

15 Deborah Feldman, *Unorthodox: The Scandalous Rejection of My Hasidic Roots* (New York: Simon & Schuster, 2012), 89, 35.

16 Quotes from Annie Lowrey, "After Charlottesville, Business Leaders are Dumping the Trump Administration," *The Atlantic*, August 15, 2017 For some other references of corporate support for diversity, see Peter Baehr and Daniel Gordon, "Paradoxes of Diversity," in *The SAGE Handbook of Political Sociology*, eds. William Outhwaite and Stephen P. Turner (London: SAGE Publications, 2018), 977–78. The authors also note what they call "a 'conundrum,' how difficult it is to talk about diversity without praising it." (p. 991).

17 The "No Enemy on the Left" slogan marked a popular frontism that goes back to the Russian Revolution of 1905. See Donald W. Treadgold, *Lenin and His Rivals:*

The Struggle for Russia's Future, 1898–1906 (New York: Frederick A. Praeger, 1955), 130–33 and 255–72

18 "The Family of Man" exhibition and book have been a favorite whipping target for leftist critics, subject to what one scholar has called "several decades of critical disdain." [Fred Turner, *The Democratic Surround: Multimedia and American Liberalism from World War II to the Psychedelic Sixties* (Chicago: University of Chicago Press, 2013), 197]. You know the riff. The exhibit represents American triumphalism and imperialism. It "elides" colonialism, genocide, poverty. All this can be found in a recent collection, *The Family of Man 1955–2001: Humanismus und Postmoderne: eine Revision von Edward Steichens Fotoausstellung = Humanism and Postmodernism: A Reappraisal of the Photo Exhibition by Edward Steichen*, eds. Jean Back and Viktoria Schmidt-Linsenhoff (Marburg, Germany: Jonas Verlag, 2004). For a more measured discussion, see Janine Marchessault, *Ecstatic Worlds: Media, Utopias, Ecologies* (Cambridge, MA: MIT Press, 2017); and Turner's *The Democratic Surround*. Indeed, Turner argues that the "Family of Man" project was less American propaganda than a "promotion of diversity as the basis of national unity." (p. 201).

19 Edward O. Wilson, *The Diversity of Life* (Cambridge, MA: Harvard University Press, 1992/2010), 254.

20 Johan Rockström et al., "A Safe Operating Space for Humanity," *Nature*, Vol. 461, Issue 7263 (September 24, 2009), 472–75.

21 Pim Martens and Carijn Beumer, "Biodiversity Keeps People Healthy," in *Health of People, Places and Planet*, eds. Colin D. Butler, Jane Dixon, and Anthony G. Capon (Canberra, Australia: ANU Press, 2015), 480, http://www.jstor.org/stable/j.ctt1729vxt.46.

22 Daisy Chung and Michael Greshko, "Silent Spring on the Farm," *National Geographic* (September 2018), 17.

23 "Self-Reliance," in *The Works of Ralph Waldo Emerson*, Four Volumes in One (New York: Tudor Publishing, n.d. [1930]), 54–55.

24 Walter Benjamin, "The Storyteller," *Illuminations*, ed. Hannah Arendt, tr. Harry Zohn (New York: Harcourt, Brace & World, 1968), 84.

25 Joe L. Frost, *A History of Children's Play and Play Environments* (New York: Routledge, 2010), 261.

26 Robert Paul Smith, *Where Did You Go? Out. What Did You Do? Nothing* (New York: Norton, 1957/2010), 105.

27 It is not only the decline of play that troubles Horwitz but also the popular opinion that ratifies it. Although most Americans probably grew up playing in the outdoors without adults, these same citizens now opine that such activity is too dangerous for children—and even should be outlawed. "Almost half of Americans would like to criminalize all pre-teenagers playing outside on their own." Steven Horwitz, "Cooperation over Coercion: The Importance of Unsupervised Childhood Play for Democracy and Liberalism," *Cosmos + Taxis*, Vol. 3 No. 1 (2015): 4, 8; and Steven Horwitz, *Hayek's Modern Family: Classical Liberalism and the Evolution of Social Institutions* (New York: Palgrave Macmillan, 2015), 200–205.

Of course, the topic of how to educate for democracy is hardly new; it has marked progressive education for more than a century. "For the creation of a democratic society we need an educational system," declared John Dewey, where moral-intellectual development is "a cooperative transaction of inquiry engaged in by free, independent human beings." John Dewey, Introduction to Elsie Ripley Clapp's *The Use of Resources in Education* (New York: Harper & Brothers Publishers, 1952), reprinted in *Dewey on Education: Selections*, ed. Martin S. Dworkin (New York: Teachers College Press, 1959), 133–34. Typically this tradition of progressive education paid little attention to the value of play itself.

28 John Stuart Mill, *On Liberty*, ed. Gertrude Himmelfarb (Middlesex: Penguin Books, 1985), 125–27.

29 Alexis de Tocqueville, *Democracy in America*, tr. Arthur Goldhammer (New York: Library of America, 2004), 829.

30 Joseph Brodsky, *Less than One: Selected Essays* (New York: Farrar, Straus and Giroux, 1986), 385.

31 For a careful examination, see Koenraad W. Swart, "'Individualism' in the Mid-Nineteenth Century (1826–1860)," *Journal of the History of Ideas*, Vol. 23 No. 1 (January–March 1962): 77–90.

32 See Jerrold Seigel, *The Idea of the Self: Thought and Experience in Western Europe since the Seventeenth Century* (Cambridge: Cambridge University Press, 2005), 469–71.

33 Viktor Orbán, "Prime Minister Viktor Orbán's Speech at the Hungarian Chamber of Commerce and Industry's Ceremony to Mark the Start of the 2017 Business Year," tr. uncredited, Miniszterelnok.hu, February 28, 2017, http://www.miniszterelnok.hu/prime-minister-viktor-orbans-speech-at-the-hungarian-chamber-of-commerce-and-industrys-ceremony-to-mark-the-start-of-the-2017-business-year/.

34 J.P. Mayer, *Prophet of the Mass Age: A Study of Alexis de Tocqueville*, trs. M.M. Bozman and C. Hahn (London: J.M. Dent and Sons, 1939). Matthew Mancini, in his *Alexis de Tocqueville and American Intellectuals* (Lanham, MD: Rowman & Littlefield Publishers, 2006), expends much effort in refuting what he sees as the "myth" that Tocqueville was ignored until after World War II. Nevertheless, Mayer's point still stands, even for the United States. No book-length biographies appeared. The partial exception, George Wilson Pierson's *Tocqueville and Beaumont in America*, was published in 1938 and, as Mayer notes, looks at the Frenchman "without the intention of interpreting his political ideas as a whole." (Mayer, *Prophet of the Mass Age*, trs. M.M. Bozman and C. Hahn, 215).

35 J.P. Mayer, *Alexis de Tocqueville: A Biographical Essay in Political Science*, trs. M.M. Bozman and C. Hahn (New York: Viking Press, 1940), 186, 203. This is the retitled American edition of *Prophet of the Mass Age*.

36 Nancy Scheper-Hughes, as quoted in Thomas Fuller, "Let Right-Wing Speakers Come to Berkeley? Faculty is Divided," *New York Times*, September 22, 2017.

37 One of the signers of this protest was Judith Butler, a chaired professor at the University of California, Berkeley. "The idiocy of American left academia can easily be explained through an example of Judith Butler, because she at the same

time considers an academic essay as . . . violence and Hamas and Hezbollah as part of the broad left." Unattributed, cited in Juraj Katalenac, "'American Thought': From Theoretical Barbarism to Intellectual Decadence," *Adidas Marxism* blog, August 25, 2017, https://adidasmarxism.wordpress.com/2017/08/25/american-thought-from-theoretical-barbarism-to-intellectual-decadence/#_ftnref5. Butler was also one of the academic luminaries who wanted a feminist philosophy journal to retract an article because of the "harm" it caused. This letter, signed by hundreds of professors, offers an incomparable example of academic thuggery and political correctness. The complainants charge, among other things, that an article on "transracialism" "fails to seek out and sufficiently engage with scholarly work by those who are most vulnerable to the intersection of racial and gender oppression (women of color)." "Open Letter to Hypatia," Google Docs, initiated April 29, 2017, https://docs.google.com/forms/d/1efp9CoMHch_6KfgtlmoPZ76nir-WtcEsqWHcvgidl2mU/. In 2012 the city of Frankfurt awarded Butler its Adorno Prize. A real shanda.

38 Nancy Scheper-Hughes as quoted in Fuller, "Let Right-Wing Speakers Come to Berkeley?"; and Nancy Scheper-Hughes, "The Great Wall of UC Berkeley vs. Baby Face Shapiro," *CounterPunch*, September 13, 2017, https://www.counterpunch.org/2017/09/13/the-great-wall-of-uc-berkeley-vs-baby-face-shapiro/.

39 In a democratic age, the commissars of censorship are the professors themselves, who feel "harmed" or "damaged" by various writings and demand censorship and retraction. The incidents pile up. In addition to those mentioned in previous endnotes, one petition signed by more than fifteen thousand insisted on having an academic journal, *Third World Quarterly*, retract an article. See Colleen Flaherty, "Is Retraction the New Rebuttal?" Inside Higher Ed, September 19, 2017, https://www.insidehighered.com/news/2017/09/19/controversy-over-paper-favor-colonialism-sparks-calls-retraction; and Peter Wood, "The Article That Made 16,000 Ideologues Go Wild," Minding the Campus, October 4, 2017, https://www.mindingthecampus.org/2017/10/04/the-article-that-made-16000-profs-go-wild/.

40 Daniel Bell, *The End of Ideology* (New York: Free Press, 1960/1962), 404–405.

41 Francis Fukuyama, "The End of History?" *National Interest*, 16 (Summer 1989), 3–18. Note that I'm referencing the essay, rather than the book published a few years later, *The End of History and the Last Man* (New York: Free Press, 1992).

42 The exchange took place first in the writers' fictions, and then spilled over into nonfictional life.

43 Thomas Piketty, *Capital in the Twenty-First Century*, tr. Arthur Goldhammer (Cambridge, MA: Harvard University Press, 2014).

44 I'm borrowing a few sentences from my piece "Piketty v. Marx," *New Republic*, June 7, 2014.

45 Harry G. Frankfurt, in his *On Inequality* (Princeton, NJ: Princeton University Press, 2015), tries to stand outside the pack, but barely does. He argues that equality is not an intrinsic value, though he approves its pursuit. That does not take us very far. He does make a good case that economic equality can become a fetish. He could be reminded that Marx said it better (although Marx himself

borrowed the formulation): "From each according to his ability, to each according to his needs!" Karl Marx, "Critique of the Gotha Program," in *Selected Writings*, tr. uncredited, ed. Lawrence H. Simon (Indianapolis, IN: Hackett Publishing, 1994), 321.

46 Kenichi Ohmae, *The End of the Nation State: The Rise of Regional Economies* (New York: Free Press, 1995), 1.

47 I'm combining two translations: G.W.F. Hegel, *The Philosophy of History*, tr. J. Sibree (New York: Dover, 1956), 20–21; and G.W.F. Hegel, *Reason in History*, tr. Robert S. Hartman (Indianapolis, IN: Bobbs-Merrill Company, 1953), 26–27. For the original, see G.W.F. Hegel, *Vorlesungen über die Philosophie der Weltgeschichte: Die Vernunft in der Geschichte*, ed. J. Hoffmeister (Berlin: Akademie Verlag, 1970), 79–80.

48 Marx's term "radical chains" is from his Introduction to "A Contribution to the Critique of Hegel's Philosophy of Right," first published in two parts in the journal *Deutsch-Französische Jahrbücher* (February 7 and 10, 1844); the translation, by Gregor Benton, is from Karl Marx's *Early Writings* (London: Pelican Books, 1975).

49 Malcolm Bull, "Vectors of the Biopolitical," *New Left Review*, 45 (May/June 2007), 7. Bull edited the special edition of *New Left Review* in which this is the lead article.

50 Perry Anderson, *The H-Word: The Peripeteia of Hegemony* (London: Verso, 2017). "In considering the fortunes of the concept [hegemony], the approach adopted here will in the first instance be an exercise in comparative historical philology." (pp. vii–viii).

51 Herbert Marcuse cited these words of Beckett in his dark conclusion to *One-Dimensional Man* (Boston: Beacon Press, 1964), 243. I follow his lead.

CHAPTER TWO—"A DIVERSITY CRISIS!": SNEAKERS, SPECIES, AND SPEECH

1 Niall Ferguson, *Civilization: The West and the Rest* (New York: Penguin Press, 2011), 197, 240–43.

2 For instance, Michael Zakim underlines the relationship of ready-made clothes and capitalism but confines himself to the United States. See his *Ready-Made Democracy: A History of Men's Dress in the American Republic, 1760–1860* (Chicago: University of Chicago Press, 2003).

3 "Cloth and clothmaking are often seen as rather frivolous." Kassia St. Clair, "Embarrassment of Obscurities: Women, Weaving and History," *Times Literary Supplement*, October 26, 2018, 25.St. Clair explains that the study of textiles has been neglected in part because it was the work of women.

4 Thomas Carlyle, *Sartor Resartus*, eds. Kerry McSweeney and Peter Sabor (New York: Oxford University Press, 1987/1999), 12, 41.

5 Sven Beckert, *Empire of Cotton: A Global History* (New York: Penguin Random House, 2014/2015), xii, 81.

6 Beverly Lemire, *Fashion's Favourite: The Cotton Trade and the Consumer in Britain, 1660–1800* (Oxford: Oxford University Press, 1991), 24–25.

7 Woodruff D. Smith, in *Consumption and the Making of Respectability, 1600–1800* (New York: Routledge, 2002), 136–38, discusses the new fashion of clean white cotton underwear.

8 Stephen Yafa, *Cotton: The Biography of a Revolutionary Fiber* (New York: Penguin Books, 2005), 59.

9 Eric Hobsbawm, *The Age of Capital: 1848–1875* (London: Weidenfeld & Nicolson, 1975). The Degas painting appears on the cover of the paperback edition published in London by Abacus in 1997.

10 Marilyn R. Brown, *Degas and the Business of Art: A Cotton Office in New Orleans* (University Park, PA: Pennsylvania State University Press, 1994), 16–18.

11 See Douglas A. Farnie, "The Role of Merchants as Prime Movers in the Expansion of the Cotton Industry, 1760–1990," in *The Fibre That Changed the World: The Cotton Industry in International Perspective, 1600–1990s*, eds. Douglas A. Farnie and David J. Jeremy (Oxford: Oxford University Press, 2004), 29–30.

12 Beckert, *Empire of Cotton*, xiv.

13 Quentin Bell, *On Human Finery*, 2nd ed. (New York: Schocken Books, 1976), 105..

14 Lee Simonson, "Fashion and Democracy," *Metropolitan Museum of Art Bulletin*, New Series, Vol. 3 No. 3 (November 1944), 65–72.

15 Friedrich Vischer, "Fashion and Cynicism," tr. Kelly Barry, in *The Rise of Fashion*, ed. Daniel Leonhard Purdy (Minneapolis, MN: University of Minnesota Press, 2004), 155–56.

16 Claudia B. Kidwell and Margaret C. Christman, *Suiting Everyone: The Democratization of Clothing in America* (Washington, DC: Smithsonian Institution Press, 1974), 115.

17 Simonson, "Fashion and Democracy," 72.

18 Johann Georg Korb, *Scenes from the Court of Peter the Great: Based on the Latin Diary of John G. Korb, a Secretary of the Austrian Legation at the Court of Peter the Great*, tr. Charles MacDonnell, ed. F.L. Glaser (New York: Nicholas L. Brown, 1921), 31–32. To call Peter's actions 18thth- century measures is a small stretch. Peter returned from Europe in 1698.

19 Peter's decree, cited in Christine Ruane, "Subjects into Citizens: The Politics of Clothing in Imperial Russia," in *Fashioning the Body Politic: Dress, Gender, Citizenship*, ed. Wendy Parkins (New York: Berg Publishers, 2002), 49–70. See also Robert K. Massie, *Peter the Great: His Life and World* (New York: Alfred A. Knopf, 1980), 234–39.

20 In another example, Alecu Russo, a 19th-century Moldavian Romanian writer, noted and partly regretted the introduction of Western clothes in his corner of the Ottoman Empire. He called the frock-coat and waistcoat "the clothes of equality." He stressed the link between Enlightenment and fashion: "[N]ew ideas took our country by storm at the same time as the trousers . . . The change in costume signalled the new spirit of awakening. The new ideas and progress emerged from the tails of the frock coat and the pocket of the waistcoat." Alecu Russo, cited and translated by Angela Jianu, "Women, Fashion, and Europeanization: The Roma-

nian Principalities, 1750–1830," in *Women in the Ottoman Balkans: Gender, Culture and History*, eds. Amila Buturović and İrvin Cemil Schick (London: I.B. Tauris, 2007), 214–15.

21 Liza Crihfield Dalby, *Kimono: Fashioning Culture* (New Haven, CT: Yale University Press, 1993), 76–77.

22 Selçuk Esenbel, "The Anguish of Civilized Behavior: The Use of Western Cultural Forms in the Everyday Lives of the Meiji Japanese and the Ottoman Turks during the Nineteenth Century," *Japan Review*, 5 (1994), 157.

23 Citations from Camilla T. Nereid, "Kemalism on the Catwalk: The Turkish Hat Law of 1925," *Journal of Social History*, Vol. 44 No. 3 (Spring 2011), 707–728; and Alev Çınar, "Subversion and Subjugation in the Public Sphere: Secularism and the Islamic Headscarf," *Signs*, Vol. 33 No. 4 (Summer 2008), 891–913.

24 All my information derives from Leander Schneider, "The Maasai's New Clothes: A Developmentalist Modernity and Its Exclusions," *Africa Today*, Vol. 53 No. 1 (Fall 2006), 101–131. A later campaign, Operation Vijana, sought to go in the opposite direction. See Andrew M. Ivaska, "'Anti-mini Militants Meet Modern Misses': Urban Style, Gender, and the Politics of 'National Culture" in 1960s Dar es Salaam, Tanzania," in *Fashioning Africa: Power and the Politics of Dress*, ed. Jean Allman (Bloomington, IN: Indiana University Press, 2004), 104–121. Other essays in this volume deal with the issues of Westernization, colonialism, and nationalism as they play out through clothing in Africa.

25 Zehra Ayman and Ellen Knickmeyer, "Ban on Head Scarves Voted Out in Turkey. Parliament Lifts 80-Year-Old Restriction on University Attire," *Washington Post*, February 10, 2008.

26 Lisa Trivedi, *Clothing Gandhi's Nation: Homespun and Modern India* (Bloomington, IN: Indiana University Press, 2007), 76–80, 124–25, 155.

27 Emma Tarlo, *Clothing Matters: Dress and Identity in India* (Chicago: University of Chicago Press, 1996), 324–28.

28 Eric Hobsbawm, *Interesting Times: A Twentieth-Century Life* (New York: Pantheon Books, 2002), 261.

29 Jonas Hanway, cited in Neil McKendrick, "Commercialization and the Economy," in *The Birth of a Consumer Society: The Commercialization of Eighteenth-Century England*, eds. Neil McKendrick, John Brewer, and J.H. Plumb (London: Europa Publications, 1982), 53.

30 Frank Trentmann, *Empire of Things: How We Became a World of Consumers, from the Fifteenth Century to the Twenty-First* (London: Allen Lane, 2016), 73–74.

31 Michael Harrington, *The Other America: Poverty in the United States* (Baltimore, MD: Penguin Books, 1964), 12–13.

32 Erving Goffman, *The Presentation of Self in Everyday Life* (New York: Anchor Books, 1959).

33 Wilhelm von Humboldt, *Linguistic Variability and Intellectual Development*, trs. George C. Buck and Frithjof A. Raven (Philadelphia, PA: University of Pennsylvania Press, 1972), 5.

34 Ibid., 141, 127–28.

35 Wilhelm von Humboldt to Karl Gustav Brinckmann, October 22, 1803, cited and translated by Paul R. Sweet, *Wilhelm von Humboldt: A Biography, Vol. 1: 1767–1808* (Columbus, OH: Ohio State University Press, 1978), 278.

36 James W. Underhill, *Humboldt, Worldview and Language* (Edinburgh: Edinburgh University Press, 2009), 3.

37 Michael C. Gavin et al., "Toward a Mechanistic Understanding of Linguistic Diversity," *BioScience*, Vol. 63 No. 7 (July 2013), 524.

38 Martin Luther, tr. George V. Schick, cited in Theodore Hiebert, "The Tower of Babel and the Origin of the World's Cultures," *Journal of Biblical Literature*, Vol. 126 No. 1 (Spring 2007), 48. I'm citing Luther against the grain of Hiebert, who argues that the conventional interpretation of the Tower of Babel is mistaken, and that the story bespeaks a positive idea of God diversifying mankind.

39 René Centassi and Henri Masson, cited and translated by Esther Schor, *Bridge of Words: Esperanto and the Dream of a Universal Language* (New York: Henry Holt and Company, 2016), 16.

40 Zamenhof, cited and translated by Schor, *Bridge of Words*, 16, 63.

41 Umberto Eco, *The Search for the Perfect Language (The Making of Europe)*, tr. James Fentress (Oxford: Blackwell Publishing, 1995), 19.

42 Joseph H. Greenberg, "The Measurement of Linguistic Diversity," *Language*, Vol. 32 No. 1 (January–March 1956), 109–111.

43 Michael Krauss, "The World's Languages in Crisis," *Language*, Vol. 68 No. 1 (March 1992), 10.

44 Paul Newman, "The Endangered Languages Issue as a Hopeless Cause," in *Language Death and Language Maintenance,* eds. Mark Janse and Sijmen Tol (Amsterdam: John Benjamins Publishing Company, 2003), 1.

45 "UNESCO Atlas of the World's Languages in Danger," UNESCO, 2010, updated July 5, 2017, http://www.unesco.org/new/en/culture/themes/endangered-languages/atlas-of-languages-in-danger/.

46 David Crystal, *Language Death* (Cambridge: Cambridge University Press, 2000), i.

47 Mark Janse, "Introduction: Language Death and Language Maintenance—Problems and Prospects," in *Language Death and Language Maintenance*, eds. Mark Janse and Sijmen Tol, ix.

48 Crystal, *Language Death*, 1.

49 Tove Skutnabb-Kangas, "The Stakes: Linguistic Diversity, Linguistic Human Rights and Mother-Tongue-Based Multilingual Education—or Linguistic Genocide, Crimes Against Humanity and an Even Faster Destruction of Biodiversity and Our Planet," keynote presentation at Bamako International Forum on Multilingualism, Bamako, Mali, January 19–21, 2009, http://www.tove-skutnabb-kangas.org/pdf/Tove_Skutnabb_Kangas_Keynote_presentation_at_Bamako_International_Forum_on_Multilingualism_Bamako_Mali_19_21_Jan_2009.pdf. See Tove Skutnabb-Kangas, *Linguistic Genocide in Education—or Worldwide Diversity and Human Rights?* (Mahwah, NJ: Lawrence Erlbaum Associates, 2000), esp. 291–378.

50 Krauss, "The World's Languages in Crisis," 7–8.

51 Luisa Maffi, "On the Interdependence of Biological and Cultural Diversity," in *On Biocultural Diversity: Linking Language, Knowledge, and the Environment*, ed. Luisa Maffi (Washington, DC: Smithsonian Institution Press, 2001), 8.

52 "The Loss of Diversity," Terralingua, undated, http://terralingua.org/biocultural-diversity/the-loss-of-diversity/.

53 David Harmon, "On the Meaning and Moral Imperative of Diversity," in *On Biocultural Diversity*, ed. Luisa Maffi, 61.

54 L.J. Gorenflo, Suzanne Romaine, Russell A. Mittermeier, and Kristen Walker-Painemilla, "Co-Occurrence of Linguistic and Biological Diversity in Biodiversity Hotspots and High Biodiversity Wilderness Areas," *PNAS* (*Proceedings of the National Academy of Sciences of the United States of America*), Vol. 109 No. 21 (May 22, 2012), 8037.

55 Wilson, *The Diversity of Life*, 301.

56 Julie Lockwood and Michael McKinney, "Preface," in *Biotic Homogenization*, eds. Julie L. Lockwood and Michael L. McKinney (New York: Kluwer Academic/Plenum Publishers, 2001), vii; John L. Gittleman, "Foreword," in *Biotic Homogenization*, eds. Julie L. Lockwood and Michael L. McKinney, v.

57 Julian D. Olden and N. LeRoy Poff, "Toward a Mechanistic Understanding and Prediction of Biotic Homogenization," *American Naturalist*, Vol. 162 No. 4 (October 2003), 457.

58 Christoph Bühler and Tobias Roth, "Spread of Common Species Results in Local-Scale Floristic Homogenization in Grassland of Switzerland," *Diversity and Distributions*, Vol. 17 No. 6 (November 2011), 1089–1098.

59 Jeffrey R. Duncan and Julie L. Lockwood, "Spatial Homogenization of the Aquatic Fauna of Tennessee," in *Biotic Homogenization*, eds. Julie L. Lockwood and Michael L. McKinney, 245–58.

60 Dian Spear and Steven L. Chown, "Taxonomic Homogenization in Ungulates: Patterns and Mechanisms at Local and Global Scales," *Journal of Biogeography*, Vol. 35 No. 11 (November 2008), 1963.

61 David M. Richardson, "Biodiversity versus Biomonotony," *Diversity and Distributions*, Vol. 8 No. 2 (March 2002),126.

62 Julian D. Olden, Michael E. Douglas, and Marlis R. Douglas, "The Human Dimensions of Biotic Homogenization," *Conservation Biology*, Vol. 19 No. 6 (December 2005), 2036–2038.

63 Eric A. Smith, "On the Coevolution of Cultural, Linguistic, and Biological Diversity," in *On Biocultural Diversity*, ed. Luisa Maffi, 99. For this argument, see also Gorenflo, Romaine, Mittermeier, and Walker-Painemilla, "Co-Occurrence of Linguistic and Biological Diversity in Biodiversity Hotspots and High Biodiversity Wilderness Areas."

64 John Edwards, *Language and Identity* (New York: Cambridge University Press, 2009), 232–33.

65 George Steiner, *After Babel: Aspects of Language and Translation* (New York: Oxford University Press, 1975), 122–23.

66 James W. Underhill, *Creating Worldviews: Metaphor, Ideology and Language* (Edinburgh: Edinburgh University Press, 2011), 226–27.

67 Joshua A. Fishman, cited by Jane H. Hill, "'Expert Rhetorics' in Advocacy for Endangered Languages: Who is Listening, and What Do They Hear?" *Journal of Linguistic Anthropology*, Vol. 12 No. 2 (December 2002), 129.

68 Underhill, *Creating Worldviews*, 228.

69 Skutnabb-Kangas, "The Stakes: Linguistic Diversity, Linguistic Human Rights and Mother-Tongue-Based Multilingual Education."

70 H.E. Baber, *The Multicultural Mystique: The Liberal Case against Diversity* (Amherst, NY: Prometheus Books, 2008), 32.

71 Max Horkheimer, "Vernunft und Selbsterhaltung," *Gesammelte Schriften*, Vol. 5: >Dialektik der Aufklärung< und Schriften 1940–1950, ed. Gunzelin Schmid Noerr (Frankfurt am Main: Fischer Verlag, 1987), 328..

72 Walter Benn Michaels, *The Trouble with Diversity: How We Learned to Love Identity and Ignore Inequality* (New York: Picador, 2016), 148–67.

73 Victor Ginsburgh and, Shlomo Weber, *How Many Languages Do We Need? The Economics of Linguistic Diversity* (Princeton, NJ: Princeton University Press, 2011), pp. 147,. 203. A Belgian economist of Russian-Jewish-Austrian origin, Ginsburgh was born in what is today Rwanda and identifies himself as a native Swahili speaker.

74 Christopher Clark, *Iron Kingdom: The Rise and Downfall of Prussia, 1600–1947* (Cambridge, MA: Harvard University Press, 2006), 184.

75 Edwin H. Zeydel, "The German Language in the Prussian Academy of Sciences," *PMLA*, Vol. 41 No. 1 (March 1926), 126–50.

76 See Harold Mah, "The Epistemology of the Sentence: Language, Civility, and Identity in France and Germany, Diderot to Nietzsche," *Representations*, 47 (Summer 1994), 64–84.

77 "Passport Conference: Resolution Adopted by the Conference on Passports, Custos [*sic*] Formalities and Through Tickets in Paris on October 21st, 1920," (League of Nations Advisory and Technical Committee for Communications and Transit: Geneva, November 1, 1925), 5. Martin Lloyd, in *The Passport: The History of Man's Most Travelled Document* (Stroud, Gloucestershire: Sutton Publishing, 2003), summarizes the response to the League of Nation passport requirements (pp. 121–30).

78 See Adrian Tahourdin, "Globish Lit.," *Times Literary Supplement*, February 15, 2019, 26, https://www.the-tls.co.uk/articles/public/globish-lit/; and Alison Flood, "'An Insult': French Writers Outraged by Festival's Use of 'Sub-English' Words," *The Guardian*, February 4, 2019, https://www.theguardian.com/books/2019/feb/04/an-insult-french-writers-outraged-by-festivals-use-of-sub-english-words.

79 Minae Mizumura, *The Fall of Language in the Age of English*, trs. Mari Yoshihara and Juliet Winters Carpenter (New York: Columbia University Press, 2015), 52.

80 Mizumura, *The Fall of Language in the Age of English*, 169, 66. For an outsider's—and more upbeat—view of the effect of English on Japanese, see Mark Abley, *The Prodigal Tongue: Dispatches from the Future of English* (London: Arrow Books, 2009), 101–121.

81 Peter Hessler, "Talk Like an Egyptian," *New Yorker*, April 17, 2017, 56.

82 Mizumura, *The Fall of Language in the Age of English,* 78–81.
83 Mizumura, *The Fall of Language in the Age of English*, 41, 202–203.
84 Karl Marx, "Preface to the First Edition," *Capital*, Vol. 1, tr. Ben Fowkes (London: Penguin Books, 1990), 90.
85 Kenneth Pomeranz, *The Great Divergence: China, Europe, and the Making of the Modern World Economy* (Princeton, NJ: Princeton University Press, 2000), 13. For a critique, see Robert Brenner and Christopher Isett, "England's Divergence from China's Yangzi Delta: Property Relations, Microeconomics, and Patterns of Development," *Journal of Asian Studies*, Vol. 61 No. 2 (May 2002), 609–662.
86 Deirdre Nansen McCloskey, *Bourgeois Equality: How Ideas, Not Capital or Institutions, Enriched the World* (Chicago: University of Chicago Press, 2016), 153.
87 See David Crystal, *English as a Global Language*, 2nd ed. (Cambridge: Cambridge University Press, 2003).
88 Mizumura, *The Fall of Language in the Age of English*, 202.
89 Colleen Flaherty, "Not a Small World After All," Inside Higher Ed, February 11, 2015, https://www.insidehighered.com/news/2015/02/11/mla-report-shows-declines-enrollment-most-foreign-languages.
90 Russell A. Berman, "The Real Language Crisis," *Academe*, Vol. 97 No. 5 (September–October 2011), https://www.aaup.org/article/real-language-crisis#.WWMWTITyuDI.
91 See Richard D. Brecht, "America's Languages: Challenges and Promise," American Councils for International Education, November 15, 2015, https://www.amacad.org/sites/default/files/academy/multimedia/pdfs/AmericasLanguagesChallengesandPromise.pdf.
92 See Saul Rosenzweig, *The Historic Expedition to America (1909): Freud, Jung and Hall the King-Maker*, 2nd ed. (St. Louis, MO: Rana House, 1994).
93 Jean-Nicolas Beisel and Simon Devin, "Biomonotony: Definition and Assessment for Macroinvertebrates in European Running Waters," in *Biological Invaders in Inland Waters: Profiles, Distribution and Threats*, ed. Francesca Gherardi (Dordrecht, Netherlands: Springer, 2007), 369.
94 Immanuel Kant, *Critique of Pure Reason*, tr. Norman Kemp Smith (London: Macmillan & Co,, 1963), 668.

CHAPTER THREE—PLAYING WITH DIVERSITY

1 Philippe Ariès, *Centuries of Childhood: A Social History of Family Life*, tr. Robert Baldick (New York: Vintage Books, 1962), 129.
2 Nicholas Orme, *Medieval Children* (New Haven, CT: Yale University Press, 2001), 5. Another historian notes that Ariès was "an amateur 'weekend historian.'" Colin Heywood, *A History of Childhood: Children and Childhood in the West from Medieval to Modern Times* (Cambridge, UK: Polity Press, 2001/2003), 12. Heywood in fact offers a judicious appraisal of Ariès. For a good and skeptical overview of the field, see Linda A. Pollock, *Forgotten Children: Parent–Child Relations from 1500 to 1900* (Cambridge: Cambridge University Press, 1983).

3 Even Bruegel's painting, as compelling as it is, raises more questions than it answers. As one recent study put it, "Bruegel's *Children's Games* has no precedent." It is "so unique . . . that there is no adequate explanation for the fundamental question it raises: in 1560 who would commission a painting with this unusual subject and why would they want it?" Margaret A. Sullivan, *Bruegel and the Creative Process, 1559–1563* (Farnham, Surrey: Ashgate Publishing, 2010), 75. For a thoughtful study, see Edward Snow, *Inside Bruegel: The Play of Images in Children's Games* (New York: Farrar, Straus and Giroux, 1997).

4 Plutarch, "A Consolation to His Wife," in *Selected Essays and Dialogues*, tr. Donald Russell (New York: Oxford University Press, 1993), 297–98.

5 Orme, *Medieval Children*, 86, 52.

6 Daniel Defoe, *The Complete English Tradesman*, in *The Complete Daniel Defoe Collection* (Amazon Digital Services LLC: Coyote Canyon Press, 2010).

7 Jean-Jacques Rousseau, *Emile; or, On Education*, tr. Allan Bloom (New York: Basic Books, 1979), 33–34.

8 Ellen Key, *The Century of the Child* (New York: G.P. Putnam's Sons, 1909), 45–46. The original Swedish version was first published in Stockholm by Albert Bonniers Förlag in 1900. See Torborg Lundell, "Ellen Key and Swedish Feminist Views on Motherhood," *Scandinavian Studies*, Vol. 56 No. 4 (Autumn 1984), 351–69. Key took the phrase from Swedish feminist Frida Stéenhoff's 1896 play *Lejonets unge*, published under the pseudonym Harold Gote. On Key and Stéenhoff, see *Is There a Nordic Feminism? Nordic Feminist Thought on Culture and Society*, eds. Drude von der Fehr, Anna G. Jónasdóttir, and Bente Rosenbeck (London: Routledge, 2003), 31–33.

9 Neil Postman, *The Disappearance of Childhood* (New York: Delacorte Press, 1982), 128.

10 Viviana A. Zelizer, *Pricing the Priceless Child: The Changing Social Value of Children* (Princeton, NJ: Princeton University Press, 1994), 5.

11 Walter Benjamin, *The Correspondence of Walter Benjamin, 1910–1940*, eds. Gershom Scholem and Theodor W. Adorno, trs. Manfred R. Jacobson and Evelyn M. Jacobson (Chicago: University of Chicago Press, 1994), 524. According to Scholem, Lieb "was the only person in the years of Benjamin's emigration whom Benjamin addressed with the familiar *du* after only a few encounters." Gershom Scholem, *Walter Benjamin: The Story of a Friendship*, tr. Harry Zohn (London: Faber & Faber, 1981/1982), 207. On Lieb and Benjamin, see Chryssoula Kambas, *Walter Benjamin im Exil: Zum Verhältnis von Literaturpolitik und Ästhetik* (Tübingen: Max Niemeyer Verlag, 1983), 203–215. See also her "Actualité politique: Le concept d'histoire chez Benjamin et l'échec du Front Populaire," in *Walter Benjamin et Paris: Colloque international 27–29 juin 1983*, ed. Heinz Wismann (Paris: Les Éditions du Cerf, 1986), 273–84.

12 Walter Benjamin, tr. Rodney Livingstone, "The Handkerchief," *Selected Writings, Volume 2: 1927–1934*, eds. Michael W. Jennings, Howard Eiland, and Gary Smith (Cambridge, MA: Harvard University Press, 1999), 658; and Benjamin, tr. Livingstone, "Experience and Poverty," *Selected Writings, Volume 2*, 731.

13 Benjamin, tr. Livingstone, "Experience and Poverty," *Selected Writings, Volume 2*, 731–32. See also Martin Jay, *Songs of Experience: Modern American and European Variations on a Universal Theme* (Berkeley, CA: University of California Press, 2005), 312–43.

14 Benjamin, tr. Livingstone, "The Handkerchief," *Selected Writings, Volume 2*, 658.

15 Walter Benjamin, tr. Edmund Jephcott, "The Storyteller," *Selected Writings, Volume 3*, eds. Howard Eiland and Michael W. Jennings (Cambridge, MA: Harvard University Press, 2002), 143–44.

16 "Everything that was to become important during the twentieth century—from quantum physics to women's emancipation, from abstract art to space travel, from communism and fascism to the consumer society, from industrialized slaughter to the power of the media—had already made deep impressions in the years before 1914." Philipp Blom, *The Vertigo Years: Europe, 1900–1914* (New York: Basic Books, 2008), 3.

17 Larry McMurtry, *Walter Benjamin at the Dairy Queen: Reflections at Sixty and Beyond* (New York: Simon & Schuster, 1999).

18 McMurtry, *Walter Benjamin at the Dairy Queen*, 16.

19 Ibid., 45, 25.

20 Ibid., 20–21.

21 Benjamin, tr. Livingstone, "The Handkerchief," *Selected Writings, Volume 2*, 658.

22 McMurtry, *Walter Benjamin at the Dairy Queen*, 81.

23 Stefan Zweig, *The World of Yesterday*, tr. Anthea Bell (Lincoln, NE: University of Nebraska Press, 2013), 46–47.

24 At least two essays deal with the "Walter Benjamin Industry": See Noah Isenberg, "The Work of Walter Benjamin in the Age of Information," *New German Critique*, 83 (Spring–Summer 2001), 119–50; and Udi E. Greenberg, "The Politics of the Walter Benjamin Industry," *Theory, Culture & Society*, Vol. 25 No. 3 (2008), 53–70. Both take up the popularity of Benjamin, although neither address the absence of a discussion of McMurtry. Isenberg, in fact, uses as an epigraph a quote from McMurtry but does not return to him in the text.

25 Walter Benjamin, tr. Howard Eiland, "Berlin Childhood around 1900," in Benjamin, *Selected Writings, Volume 3*, eds. Howard Eiland and Michael W. Jennings (Cambridge, MA: Harvard University Press, 2002). 350.

26 McMurtry, *Walter Benjamin at the Dairy Queen*, 105–106.

27 Walter Benjamin, *The Arcades Project*, trs. Howard Eiland and Kevin McLaughlin (Cambridge, MA: Harvard University Press, 1999), 105. See Carlo Salzani for a comprehensive discussion of Benjamin and boredom: "The Atrophy of Experience: Walter Benjamin and Boredom," in *Essays on Boredom and Modernity*, eds. Barbara Dalle Pezze and Carlo Salzani (Amsterdam: Rodopi, 2009), 127–54.

28 Jude Stewart, "Making Time for Boredom," *Atlantic* (June 2017), 23

29 "Programme," International Interdisciplinary Boredom Conference, June 16–17, 2017, http://boredomconference.com/?page_id=760.

30 Lars Svendsen, *A Philosophy of Boredom*, tr. John Irons (London: Reaktion Books, 2005) and Peter Toohey, *Boredom: A Lively History* (New Haven, CT: Yale University Press, 2011).

31 Benjamin, *The Arcades Project*, trs. Howard Eiland and Kevin McLaughlin, 108. For a good overview of the boredom literature, see the introduction, "The Delicate Monster: Modernity and Boredom," to *Essays on Boredom and Modernity*, 5–34.

32 Svendsen, *A Philosophy of Boredom*, tr. John Irons, 21.

33 Søren Kierkegaard, *Either/Or: A Fragment of Life*, tr. Alastair Hannay, ed. Victor Eremita [a pseudonym for Kierkegaard] (London: Penguin Books, 1992), 227–28.

34 Anton Chekhov, *The Plays of Anton Chekhov*, tr. Paul Schmidt (New York: HarperCollins Publishers, 1997), 209.

35 For a (jargon-clotted) discussion of subjectivization of boredom, see Elizabeth S. Goodstein, *Experience Without Qualities: Boredom and Modernity* (Stanford, CA: Stanford University Press, 2005), esp. 101–246.

36 See Patricia Meyer Spacks, *Boredom: The Literary History of a State of Mind* (Chicago: University of Chicago Press, 1995), 7–8.

37 Robert Paul Smith, *Where Did You Go? Out. What Did You Do? Nothing* (New York: Norton, 1957/2010), 106–107.

38 Johan Huizinga, *America: A Dutch Historian's Vision, from Afar and Near*, transl. Herbert H. Rowen (New York: Harper & Row, 1972), pp. 237, 115-–116. This book is in fact composed of two separate pieces by Huizinga "Man and Masses in America," from 1918, before he visited the States;, and "Life and Thought in America," from 1926, after his visit.

39 Johan Huizinga, *Homo Ludens: A Study of the Play-Element in Culture*, tr. Johan Huizinga (Boston: Beacon Press, 1955), 8–9.

40 J. Huizinga, *In the Shadow of Tomorrow*, tr. J.H. Huizinga (New York: Norton & Co., 1936), 15.

41 Huizinga, *Homo Ludens*, tr. Johan Huizinga, 205–206. Two good—not new, but insightful—overviews of Huizinga are Robert Anchor, "History and Play: Johan Huizinga and His Critics," *History and Theory*, Vol. 17 No. 1 (February 1978), 63–93; and Henry M. Pachter, "Masters of Cultural History III: Johan Huizinga—The Historian as Magister Ludi," *Salmagundi*, 46 (Fall 1979), 103–119.

42 For a recent assessment of its impact, see Lisa Jardine, "The Afterlife of Homo Ludens: From Johan Huizinga to Natalie Zemon Davis and Beyond," *Temptation in the Archives: Essays in Golden Age Dutch Culture* (London: University College London Press, 2015), 84–101

43 For a survey of the scholarly debate, see Thomas Henricks, "The Nature of Play: An Overview," *American Journal of Play*, Vol. 1 No. 2 (Fall 2008), 157–80,.

44 William Wells Newell, *Games and Songs of American Children* (New York: Harper & Brothers, 1883), 11–12. On Newell, see Alexander F. Chamberlain, "William Wells Newell—1839–1907," *American Anthropologist*, New Series, Vol. 9 No. 2 (April–June 1907), 366–76.

45 Howard P. Chudacoff, *Children at Play: An American History* (New York: New York University Press, 2007), 126–53.

46 Bruce Watson, *The Man Who Changed How Boys and Toys Were Made: The Life and Times of A.C. Gilbert, the Man Who Saved Christmas* (New York: Viking, 2002), 6.

47 Henry Petroski, "Engineering: Work and Play," *American Scientist*, Vol. 87 No. 3 (May–June 1999), 208.

48 Harold Kroto, "Biographical" and "Addendum, July 2012," NobelPrize.org, 1996/2012, https://www.nobelprize.org/nobel_prizes/chemistry/laureates/1996/kroto-bio.html.

49 All information and quotes from Maaike Lauwaert, "Playing Outside the Box—On LEGO Toys and the Changing World of Construction Play," *History and Technology*, Vol. 24 No. 3 (2008), 221–37. Lauwaert argues that Lego has backed away from some of the extreme theme-centered sets.

50 Tim Walsh, *Timeless Toys: Classic Toys and the Playmakers Who Created Them* (Kansas City, MO: Andrews McMeel Publishing, 2004), 26.

51 Amanda Dargan and Steven Zeitlin, *City Play* (New Brunswick, NJ: Rutgers University Press, 1990), 166.

52 Stuart Brown, with Christopher Vaughan, *Play: How It Shapes the Brain, Opens the Imagination, and Invigorates the Soul* (New York: Avery (Penguin Books), 2009), 107.

53 Ginger Adams Otis, "What Happened to New York's Storied Street Games?" *New York Post*, May 9, 2010, https://nypost.com/2010/05/09/what-happened-to-new-yorks-storied-street-games/.

54 Brian Sutton-Smith, *A History of Children's Play: The New Zealand Playground, 1840–1950* (Philadelphia, PA: University of Pennsylvania Press, 1981), 249–53, 288–89.

55 Richard F. Ward, *A Lifetime's Non-Ordinary Events: A Modified Autobiography* (Victoria, BC: Trafford, 2010), 3.

56 See, for instance, Jane Martinson, "Apple's In-App Game Charges: How My Kids Ran Up Huge Bills," *Guardian*, March 26, 2013.

57 Aldous Huxley, *Brave New World* and *Brave New World Revisited* (New York: Harper Perennial, 2004), 37–38.

58 *New York Street Games* DVD, PBS Distribution, directed by Matthew Levy, produced by Craig Lifschutz and Matthew Levy, 2009/2011.

59 Senator Robert Hendrickson, cited in James Gilbert, *A Cycle of Outrage: America's Reaction to the Juvenile Delinquent in the 1950s* (New York: Oxford University Press, 1986), 75. For a more recent overview, see Jason Barnosky, "The Violent Years: Responses to Juvenile Crime in the 1950s," *Polity*, Vol. 38 No. 3 (July 2006), 314–44.

60 See, for instance, Stephanie Pappas, "As Schools Cut Recess, Kids' Learning Will Suffer, Experts Say," Live Science, August 14, 2011, https://www.livescience.com/15555-schools-cut-recess-learning-suffers.html.

61 Hara Estroff Marano, *A Nation of Wimps: The High Cost of Invasive Parenting* (New York: Broadway Books, 2008), 88.

62 Cited in Malcolm Harris, *Kids These Days: Human Capital and the Making of Millennials* (New York: Little, Brown and Company, 2017); excerpted as "The Working Classroom" in *Harper's* (November 2017), 11

63 Henry S. Curtis, "Public Provision and Responsibility for Playgrounds," *Annals of the American Academy of Political and Social Science*, Vol. 35 No. 2 (March 1910), 121.

64 The advertisement is reproduced in Brenda Biondo, *Once Upon a Playground: A Celebration of Classic American Playgrounds, 1920–1975* (Lebanon, NH: University Press of New England, 2014), xviii.

65 See the website of the National Program for Playground Safety (NPPS) at the University of Northern Iowa: http://www.playgroundsafety.org/ [accessed August 22, 2019].

66 See Deborah K. Tinsworth and Joyce E. McDonald, *Special Study: Injuries and Deaths Associated with Children's Playground Equipment*, U.S. Consumer Product Safety Commission, Washington, DC, April 2001, https://www.cpsc.gov/s3fs-public/playgrnd_0.pdf. Most of the injuries are falls and fractures.

67 Vivian Wang, "After Recall, Devoted Playground Crowd Asks: Where Did the Slides Go?" *New York Times*, June 10, 2017.

68 For a good survey that highlights counter-trends, see Carroll Pursell, *From Playgrounds to PlayStation: The Interaction of Technology and Play* (Baltimore, MD: Johns Hopkins University Press, 2015), 30–51.

69 John Tierney, "Can a Playground be Too Safe?" *New York Times*, July 18, 2011.

70 Susan G. Solomon, *American Playgrounds: Revitalizing Community Space* (Lebanon, NH: University Press of New England, 2005), 79–85.

71 Michael Gotkin, cited in Pursell, *From Playgrounds to PlayStation*, 49. Another landscape designer concurs about the American playground: "It's a rubber floor, a little structure surrounded by a fence, it's like a play jail," declares Meghan Talarowski, cited in Ellen Barry, "In Britain's Playgrounds, 'Bringing in Risk' to Build Resilience," *New York Times*, March 10, 2018. See the study Talarowski authored, *London Study of Playgrounds: The Influence of Design on Play Behavior in London vs New York, San Francisco, and Los Angeles* (Philadelphia, PA: Studio Ludo, 2017).

72 Darell Hammond, *Kaboom! How One Man Built a Movement to Save Play* (New York: Rodale, 2011), 224–26.

73 Hanna Rosin, "The Overprotected Kid," *The Atlantic* (April 2014)

74 Ibid.

75 "U.S. Travel Data Show Decline in Walking and Bicycling to School Has Stabilized," Safe Routes Partnership, April 8, 2010.

76 Mayer Hillman, John Adams, and John Whitelegg, *One False Move . . . A Study of Children's Independent Mobility* (London: Policy Studies Institute, 1990), 45. I'm averaging the numbers for both eight- and nine-year-olds.

77 Sandra Hofferth, David A. Kinney, Janet S. Dunn, "The 'Hurried' Child: Myth vs. Reality," Maryland Population Research Center, February 29, 2008.

78 Donald F. Roberts and Ulla G. Foehr, "Trends in Media Use," *The Future of Children*, Vol. 18 No. 1 (Spring 2008), 11–37.

79 Rhonda Clements, "An Investigation of the Status of Outdoor Play," *Contemporary Issues in Early Childhood*, Vol. 5 No. 1 (March 2004), 72.

80 Some dips in obesity rates have recently been recorded: "Early childhood obesity rates have begun to level off and even decline." [Laura M. Segal, Jack Rayburn, and Stacy E. Beck, "The State of Obesity: Better Policies for a Healthier America," Trust for America's Health/Robert Wood Johnson Foundation, 2017, 31, https://media.stateofobesity.org/wp-content/uploads/2019/02/19162039/stateofobesity2017.pdf] Three points about these numbers: 1) As this report notes, "Despite these positive trends, childhood obesity remains an American epidemic." [p. 27] 2) The trend for adolescents continues to increase. [See Cheryl D. Fryar, Margaret D. Carroll, and Cynthia L. Ogden, "Prevalence of Overweight and Obesity Among Children and Adolescents Aged 2–19 Years: United States, 1963–1965 through 2013–2014," National Center for Health Statistics, https://www.cdc.gov/nchs/data/hestat/obesity_child_13_14/obesity_child_13_14.pdf] 3) These findings about the recent decline have been challenged. A new study concludes, "Despite previous reports that obesity in children and adolescents has remained stable or decreased in recent years, we found no evidence of a decline in obesity prevalence at any age. In contrast, we report a significant increase in severe obesity among children aged 2 to 5 years since the 2013–2014 cycle, a trend that continued upward for many subgroups." [Asheley Cockrell Skinner et al., "Prevalence of Obesity and Severe Obesity in US Children, 1999–2016," *Pediatrics*, Vol. 141 No. 3 (March 2018)].

81 Jaak Panksepp, "Attention Deficit Hyperactivity Disorders, Psychostimulants, and Intolerance of Childhood Playfulness: A Tragedy in the Making?" *Current Directions in Psychological Science*, Vol. 7 No. 3 (June 1998), 91.

82 Peter Gray, "The Decline of Play and the Rise of Psychopathology in Children and Adolescents," *American Journal of Play*, Vol. 3, No. 4 (2011), 443–63.

83 See Peter Gray, *Free to Learn: Why Unleashing the Instinct to Play Will Make Our Children Happier, More Self-Reliant, and Better Students for Life* (New York: Basic Books, 2013).

84 Sherry Turkle, *Reclaiming Conversation: The Power of Talk in a Digital Age* (New York: Penguin Press, 2015), 108–109.

85 All quotes in this paragraph and following from Stefan Zweig, tr. Don Reneau, "The Monotonization of the World," in *Weimar Republic Sourcebook*, eds. Anton Kaes, Martin Jay, and Edward Dimendberg (Berkeley, CA: University of California Press, 1994), 397–400.

86 W.T. Stead, *The Americanization of the World* (New York: Horace Markley, 1901), 1–2.

87 Georges Duhamel, *America the Menace: Scenes from the Life of the Future*, tr. Charles Miner Thompson (Boston: Houghton Mifflin, 1931), 201, 194, 71. On Duhamel and other interpretations of the United States by French intellectuals, see Jean-Philippe Mathy, *Extrême Occident: French Intellectuals and America* (Chicago: University of Chicago Press, 1993), esp. 52–103.

88 Oliver Matuschek, *Three Lives: A Biography of Stefan Zweig*, tr. Allan Blunden (London: Pushkin Press, 2011), 92.

89 Georg Simmel, tr. Edward Shils, "The Metropolis and Mental Life," in *The Blackwell City Reader*, eds. Gary Bridge and Sophie Watson (Malden, MA: Blackwell Publishers, 2002), 11–19.

90 George Miller Beard, *American Nervousness, Its Causes and Consequences* (New York: G.P. Putnam's Sons, 1881), 13–14.

91 Sigmund Freud, "'Civilized' Sexual Morality and Modern Nervousness," in his *Collected Papers*, Vol. II, tr. Joan Riviere, ed. Ernest Jones (London: Hogarth Press/Institute of Psycho-Analysis, 1949), 79–80. See Philip P. Wiener, "G.M. Beard and Freud on 'American Nervousness,'" *Journal of the History of Ideas*, Vol. 17 No. 2 (April 1956), 269–74.

92 Beard, *American Nervousness*, 52, 193–291.

93 Ibid., 125, 138.

94 Ibid., 135–36.

95 McMurtry, *Walter Benjamin at the Dairy Queen*, 105.

96 Tim Wu, *The Attention Merchants: The Epic Scramble to Get Inside Our Heads* (New York: Knopf, 2016), 350.

97 Dr. Seuss, *And to Think That I Saw It on Mulberry Street* (New York: Vanguard Press, 1937).

CHAPTER FOUR—DIVERSITY AND ITS VICISSITUDES: ACROSS THE CENTURIES

1 Charles Darwin, cited in Jonathan Weiner, *The Beak of the Finch: A Story of Evolution in Our Time* (New York: Vintage Books, 1995), 157.

2 Charles Darwin, *The Origin of Species* (New York: Bantam Classics, 1999), 8–38.

3 Hope Jahren, *Lab Girl* (New York: Vintage Books, 2017), 63.

4 William Fitzgerald, *Variety: The Life of a Roman Concept* (Chicago: University of Chicago Press, 2016), 4–5.

5 Chrysippus, "Beauty of Living Things," in Władysław Tatarkiewicz, *History of Aesthetics*, Volume 1: *Ancient Aesthetics*, tr. uncredited, ed. J. Harrell et al. (The Hague: De Gruyter Mouton, 1970), 195; and Plutarch, tr. uncredited, "The Contradictions of the Stoics," *Complete Works of Plutarch* (Hastings, East Sussex/Amazon Digital Services LLC: Delphi Classics, 2013), section 21. I'm combining the two translations.

6 Epicurus, tr. Cyril Bailey, "Letter to Herodotus," NewEpicurean.com, http://newepicurean.com/epicurus/letter-to-herodotus-elemental-edition/.

7 Lucretius, cited in Steven J. Dick, *Plurality of Worlds: The Origins of the Extraterrestrial Life Debate from Democritus to Kant* (Cambridge: Cambridge University Press, 1982), 10–11. The English translation, as *On the Nature of Things*, is by W.H.D. Rouse (London: Loeb Classical Library (William Heinemann), 1924).

8 See David Cressy, "Early Modern Space Travel and the English Man in the Moon," *American Historical Review*, Vol. 111 No. 4 (October 2006), 961–82.

9 Bernard Le Bovier de Fontenelle, *Conversations on the Plurality of Worlds*, tr. H.A. Hargreaves (Berkeley, CA: University of California Press, 1990), 16, 45–46. If

a French philosopher of the Enlightenment gave us an elegant presentation of the plurality of worlds, it is not surprising that an American philosopher of the campus gave us an inane version. To follow an (unsympathetic) review of *On the Plurality of Worlds* by David Lewis, whom the *Stanford Encyclopedia of Philosophy* calls "one of the most important philosophers of the 20th century," the Princeton professor posited the existence of "fabulous alternative universes that are never empirically detected by us." Fontenelle's diverse faces are left far behind. In Lewis's alternative world anything and everything proliferates, including "tiny purple anthropologists who study human culture unobserved," "colossal human-eating monsters 50 feet in height" and, best of all, "professional philosophers earning salaries in excess of 37 million dollars." This is diversity à la American philosophy. See Nathan Salmon, Review of Lewis, *On the Plurality of Worlds* (Oxford: Blackwell, 1986) in *Philosophical Review*, Vol. 97 No. 2 (April 1988), 237.

10 Desiderius Erasmus, *On Copia of Words and Ideas*, trs. Donald B. King and H. David Rix (Milwaukee, WI: Marquette University Press, 1963), 16–17, 38–42.

11 G.W. Leibniz, *Theodicy*, tr. E.M. Huggard, ed. Austin Farrer (Chicago: Open Court, 1985), 198, sec. 124.

12 See the collection *The Language of Nature: Reassessing the Mathematization of Natural Philosophy in the Seventeenth Century*, eds. Geoffrey Gorham et al. (Minneapolis, MN: University of Minnesota Press, 2016).

13 Galileo, "The Assayer," *Discoveries and Opinions of Galileo*, tr. Stillman Drake (Garden City, NY: Doubleday & Company, 1957), 238.

14 Darwin, *The Origin of Species*, 399–400.

15 Francis Darwin, cited in Mea Allan, *Darwin and His Flowers: The Key to Natural Selection* (London: Faber and Faber, 1977), 18; and Tim Wing Yam, Joseph Arditti, and Kenneth M. Cameron, "'The Orchids have been a Splendid Sport'—An Alternative Look at Charles Darwin's Contribution to Orchid Biology," *American Journal of Botany*, Vol. 96 No. 12 (December 2009), 2128–54. For a lovely appreciation of Darwin's devotion to flowers, see Oliver Sacks, "Darwin and the Meaning of Flowers," *New York Review of Books* (November 20, 2008).

16 Galileo, tr. Stillman Drake, "The Assayer," 238.

17 Mary J. Henninger-Voss, "How the 'New Science' of Cannons Shook Up the Aristotelian Cosmos," *Journal of the History of Ideas,* Vol. 63 No. 3 (July 2002), 375.

18 Arthur O. Lovejoy, *The Great Chain of Being* (New York: Harper & Brothers, 1960), 293–94.

19 Friedrich Schleiermacher, *On Religion: Speeches to Its Cultured Despisers*, tr. John Oman (New York: Harper & Row, 1958), 55, 110, 281.

20 See Paul R. Sweet, *Wilhelm von Humboldt: A Biography*, Volume 1: 1767–1808 (Columbus, OH: Ohio State University Press, 1978), 60–62.

21 On Humboldt and the French Revolution, see Frederick C. Beiser, *Enlightenment, Revolution, and Romanticism: The Genesis of Modern German Political Thought, 1790–1800* (Cambridge, MA: Harvard University Press, 1992), 111–37.

22 Wilhelm von Humboldt, *The Limits of State Action*, tr. and ed. J.W. Burrow (Indianapolis, IN: Liberty Fund, 1993), 10.

23 Ibid. For the original German version, see Wilhelm von Humboldt, *Über die Grenzen der Wirksamkeit des Staates*, ed. Rudolf Pannwitz (Nürnberg: Verlag Hans Carl, 1946), 27.

24 For this, see Ulrich Muhlack, *Das zeitgenössische Frankreich in der Politik Humboldts* (*Historische Studien*, Vol. 400) (Hamburg: Matthiesen Verlag, 1967), 14; and Gerald N. Izenberg, *Impossible Individuality: Romanticism, Revolution, and the Origins of Modern Selfhood, 1787–1802* (Princeton, NJ: Princeton University Press, 1992), 48.

25 See Paul R. Sweet, "Young Wilhelm Von Humboldt's Writings (1789–93) Reconsidered," *Journal of the History of Ideas*, Vol. 34 No. 3 (July–September 1973), 477–78. Sweet argues that this dimension of Humboldt has been neglected by commentators.

26 Humboldt, *The Limits of State Action*, tr. J.W. Burrow, 14.

27 Newton and others reached for the metaphor of the pygmy sitting on the shoulders of giants to explain why the moderns achieved more. See Robert K. Merton's wonderful *On the Shoulders of Giants: A Shandean Postscript* (Chicago: University of Chicago Press, 1993). See, in general, Joseph M. Levine, *The Battle of the Books: History and Literature in the Augustan Age* (Ithaca, NY: Cornell University Press, 1991).

28 Quoted in Hans Baron, "The *Querelle* of the Ancients and the Moderns as a Problem for Renaissance Scholarship," *Journal of the History of Ideas*, Vol. 20 No. 1 (January 1959), 19.

29 Fontenelle, "Discourse Concerning the Ancients and Moderns," in *The Achievement of Bernard le Bovier de Fontenelle*, ed. and tr. Leonard M. Marsak (New York: Johnson Reprint, 1970), 1–8.

30 See, in general, Robert Leroux, *Guillaume de Humboldt: La formation de sa pensée jusqu'en 1794* (Paris: Société d'edition: Les Belles lettres, 1932), 264–78; and Siegfried Battisti, *Wilhelm von Humboldts 'Ideen zu einem Versuch, die Grenzen der Wirksamkeit des Staats zu bestimmen' und das Subsidiaritätsprinzip* (Berlin: Duncker & Humblot, 1987), 78–80.

31 Humboldt, *The Limits of State Action*, tr. J.W. Burrow, 18. Of course, as all commentators and biographers indicate, Humboldt's own life contradicts the main message of *The Limits* inasmuch as he becomes a state employee and educational reformer.

32 Jean-Jacques Rousseau, *Emile; or, On Education*, tr. Allan Bloom (New York: Basic Books, 1979), 452–53.

33 Jean-Jacques Rousseau, *The Government of Poland*, tr. Willmoore Kendall (Indianapolis, IN: Hackett Publishing Company, 1985), 11.

34 Lovejoy, *The Great Chain of Being*, 298.

35 See Melvin Richter, "'That Vast Tribe of Ideas': Competing Concepts and Practices of Comparison in the Political and Social Thought of Eighteenth-Century Europe," *Archiv für Begriffsgeschichte*, Vol. 44 (2002), 199–219.

36 For a recent restatement of this issue, see Keegan Callanan, "Liberal Constitutionalism and Political Particularism in Montesquieu's *The Spirit of the Laws*," *Political Research Quarterly*, Vol. 67 No. 3 (September 2014), 589–602.

37 Montesquieu, *The Spirit of the Laws*, tr. Thomas Nugent (New York: Hafner, 1949), Vol. I, 298–99.

38 Ibid., Vol. II, 170–71.

39 Pierre-Simon Laplace, cited in Charles W.J. Withers, *Zero Degrees: Geographies of the Prime Meridian* (Cambridge, MA: Harvard University Press, 2017), 107–108.

40 Arthur Young, *Travels during the Years 1787, 1788 and 1789 of the Kingdom of France* (Dublin: R. Cross et al., 1793), 43–44. Web.

41 See Ronald Edward Zupko, *Revolution in Measurement: Western European Weights and Measures since the Age of Science* (Philadelphia, PA: American Philosophical Society, 1990), 113–17.

42 C. Doris Hellman, "Jefferson's Efforts towards the Decimalization of United States Weights and Measures," *Isis*, Vol. 16 No. 2 (November 1931), 266–314; Marcello Maestro, "Going Metric: How It All Started," *Journal of the History of Ideas*, Vol. 41 No. 3 (July–September 1980), 479–86.

43 John Bemelmans Marciano, *Whatever Happened to the Metric System? How America Kept Its Feet* (New York: Bloomsbury, 2014), 6.

44 Romme, cited in Jacques Costagliola, *Romme. Le mulet d'Auvergne (1750–1795)* (Paris: Dualpha, 2008), 435–36.

45 See Eviatar Zerubavel, "The French Republican Calendar," *American Sociological Review*, Vol. 42 No. 6 (December 1977), 868–77.

46 Richard A. Carrigan Jr., "Decimal Time: Unlike the Metric System of Measurements, Decimal Time Did Not Survive the French Revolution. But is Dividing the Day by Tens a Possibility for the Future?" *American Scientist*, Vol. 66 No. 3 (May–June 1978), 305–313.

47 Romme, cited in Sanja Perovic, *The Calendar in Revolutionary France: Perceptions of Time in Literature, Culture, Politics* (New York: Cambridge University Press, 2012), 112.

48 Zupko, *Revolution in Measurement*, 149.

49 Matthew Shaw, *Time and the French Revolution: The Republican Calendar, 1789 – Year XIV* (Woodbridge, Suffolk: Royal Historical Society/Boydell Press, 2011), 122.

50 William Bright, "Notes: A Language is a Dialect with an Army and a Navy," *Language in Society*, Vol. 26 No. 3 (September 1997), 469.

51 See Alyssa Goldstein Sepinwall, *The Abbé Grégoire and the French Revolution: The Making of Modern Universalism* (Berkeley, CA: University of California Press, 2005).

52 Peter Galison, *Einstein's Clocks, Poincaré's Maps: Empires of Time* (New York: W.W. Norton & Company, 2003), 128–29.

53 Abbé Grégoire remained a symbol of French universalism and egalitarianism. In 1942 the Nazis "destroyed his statue during their occupation of Lunéville," which was close to his birthplace. Sepinwall, *The Abbé Grégoire and the French Revolution*, 233–34.

54 Abbé Grégoire, *An Essay on the Physical, Moral, and Political Reformation of the Jews*, tr. uncredited (London: C. Forster, 1791), 199–200. Translation slightly altered. See Abbé Grégoire, *Essai sur la régénération physique, morale et politique des Juifs* (Metz: Claude Lamort, 1789), 160–61. [Google Books]

55 "Le Rapport Barère," republished in Michel de Certeau, Dominique Julia, and Jacques Revel, *Une politique de la langue. La Révolution française et les patois* (Paris: Gallimard, 1975), 295. The quoted phrases are translated in Leo Gershoy, *Bertrand Barère: A Reluctant Terrorist* (Princeton, NJ: Princeton University Press, 1962), 230–31; and see, in general, David A. Bell, *The Cult of the Nation in France: Inventing Nationalism 1680–1800* (Cambridge, MA: Harvard University Press, 2001), 169–97.

56 The questions are in Certeau, Julia, and Revel, *Une politique de la langue*, 12–14.

57 "Le Rapport sur la nécessité et les moyens d'anéantir les patois et d'universaliser l'usage de la langue française," republished in Frank Paul Bowman, *L'Abbé Grégoire. Évêque des lumières* (Paris: Éditions France-Empire, 1988), 129–48. The quoted phrases are translated by the present author. The issue of overcoming local languages remained a contested issue in French well into the 19th century. For the later period, see Eugen Weber's classic *Peasants into Frenchmen: The Modernization of Rural France, 1870–1914* (Stanford, CA: Stanford University Press, 1976), esp. 310–18.

58 See his "Herder and the Enlightenment," in Berlin, *The Proper Study of Mankind: An Anthology of Essays*, eds. Henry Hardy and Roger Hausheer (New York: Farrar, Straus and Giroux, 1997), 359–435. A contemporary and voluminous debate, which often bounces off Berlin, centers on the ideas of pluralism. The task for these political theorists and philosophers is usually how to reconcile pluralism and liberalism. As a recent commentator put it, how "can we best make sense of Berlin's simultaneous advocacy of pluralism—the claim that there are multiple, incompatible 'ultimate ends' which cannot be reconciled or rank ordered—and his commitment to liberalism . . . ?" Ella Myers, "From Pluralism to Liberalism: Rereading Isaiah Berlin," *Review of Politics*, Vol. 72 No. 4 (Fall 2010), 605. For instance, one of the principals in this debate declares "there is indeed a link between value pluralism and political liberalism." William A. Galston, *Liberal Pluralism: The Implications of Value Pluralism for Political Theory and Practice* (Cambridge: Cambridge University Press, 2002), 57. But these arguments barely pursue the issues raised here. For the most part the participants seek to reconcile various theoretical "claims," often of a legal or policy nature. Moreover, the exchanges are often premised on the notion that society is increasingly diverse, and therefore the necessity to evaluate conflicting demands arises. "U.S. civil society is becoming increasingly diverse. . . . The application of general public principles to diverse associations . . . is perhaps more complex now than ever before." (Galston, *Liberal Pluralism*, 110). For outsiders these debates seem incestuous and anodyne: two dozen political theorists and philosophers reference each other's work ad nauseam. "In this chapter," writes Galston, "I continue to examine the major challenges to my account of liberal pluralism that have thus far emerged. These include, first,

that my conception. . . ." Galston, *The Practice of Liberal Pluralism* (Cambridge: Cambridge University Press, 2005), 187. Presumably another chapter will take up the "minor" challenges to his conception of liberal pluralism "that have thus far emerged." In addition to the debate on pluralism, a kindred one on historicism, which has a longer trajectory, has drawn in philosophers of history. Herder is often considered the originator of historicism, which prizes the particular in history, not the general. An ongoing issue, again, is to what degree this leads to relativism—or pluralism, and what the difference between them is. For an overview and recent airing of the topics, see Anne Löchte, *Johann Gottfried Herder: Kulturtheorie und Humanitätsidee der Ideen, Humanitätsbriefe und Adrastea* (Würzburg: Königshausen & Neumann, 2005), esp. 203–221.

59 The chapter dealing with this issue in the standard American biography of Herder is titled "Break with the Enlightenment." See Robert T. Clark Jr., *Herder: His Life and Thought* (Berkeley, CA: University of California Press, 1955), 179–213. For a discussion that places Herder in the tradition of critics of bourgeois society, see Andreas Herz, *Dunkler Spiegel—helles Dasein: Natur, Geschichte, Kunst im Werk Johann Gottfried Herders* (Heidelberg: Winter, 1996), 317–30.

60 See Siegfried Birkner, *Die Mechanisierung des Lebens im Werk Johann Gottfried Herders* (Frankfurt am Main: Johann Wolfgang Goethe-Universität, 1957).

61 Berlin, "Herder and the Enlightenment," 392. Berlin translates a passage from "Another Philosophy of History," in which Herder stated that the ferment of the Middle Ages at least kept at bay a despotism whose tendency is "to crush everything into a deadly uniformity." (p. 392) This seems a generous translation of Herder. The current translation by Evrigenis and Pellerin (see note 67, below) renders the passage as keeping at bay "death and uniform demolition." (p. 34) The original phrase is "in Tod und einförmige Zermalmung." Herder, *Sämmtliche Werke*, Vol. 5, ed. Bernhard Suphan (Berlin: Weidmannsche Buchhandlung, 1891), 516.

62 J.G. Herder, *Reflections on the Philosophy of the History of Mankind*, ed. Frank E. Manuel (Chicago: University of Chicago Press, 1968), 3.

63 Herder, "On Diligence in the Study of Several Learned Languages," *Selected Early Works, 1764–1767*, trs. Ernest A. Menze and Michael Palma, eds. Ernest A. Menze and Karl Menges (University Park, PA: Pennsylvania State University Press, 1992), 31.

64 "Journal of My Voyage in the Year 1769 (Travel Diary)," in *J.G. Herder on Social and Political Culture*, tr. and ed. by F.M. Barnard (Cambridge: Cambridge University Press, 1969), 83.

65 Wulf Koepke, *Johann Gottfried Herder* (Boston: Twayne, 1987), 32.

66 J.G. Herder, *Another Philosophy of History and Selected Political Writings*, eds. and trs. Ioannis D. Evrigenis and Daniel Pellerin (Indianapolis, IN: Hackett, 2004), 80, 69, 89, 84.

67 For a discussion of Constant's eclipse in the 19th century, see Helena Rosenblatt, *Liberal Values: Benjamin Constant and the Politics of Religion* (Cambridge: Cambridge University Press, 2008), 234–48.

68 See Kurt Kloocke, "Johann Gottfried Herder et Benjamin Constant," *Annales Benjamin Constant*, Vol. 29 (2005), 55–72. Kloocke is mainly interested in how the writings of Constant and Herder on religion converge. "In Weimar . . . Constant's major discovery was the work of Herder. . . . [Herder] was his daily reading matter in January and February of 1804, as he indicated in his diary." Etienne Hofmann, "The Theory of the Perfectibility of the Human Race," in *The Cambridge Companion to Constant*, ed. Helena Rosenblatt (New York: Cambridge University Press, 2009), 255.

69 "Schleiermacher . . . was above all following in the philosophical footsteps of one predecessor in particular: Herder." Michael Forster, "Friedrich Daniel Ernst Schleiermacher," *The Stanford Encyclopedia of Philosophy* (Summer 2015 Edition), ed. Edward N. Zalta, April 17, 2002, http://plato.stanford.edu/archives/sum2015/entries/schleiermacher/.

70 Klooke argues that Constant and Schleiermacher converge on basic issues. See his "Benjamin Constant et l'Allemagne. Individualité—Religion—Politique." *Annales Benjamin Constant*, Vol. 27 (2003), esp. 151–59.

71 The literature on Constant is growing exponentially. One of the best recent studies is K. Steven Vincent, *Benjamin Constant and the Birth of French Liberalism* (New York: Palgrave Macmillan, 2011).

72 Benjamin Constant, "Principes de politiques"; and "Mélanges de littérature et de politique," both in *Écrits politiques*, ed. Marcel Gauchet (Paris: Gallimard, 1997), 306–307, 623. In fact, Constant's consistency is much in question, especially in regard to his support for Napoleon's return to power—his 100 days.

73 Madame de Staël, *Ten Years of Exile*, tr. Doris Beik (New York: Saturday Review Press, 1972), 52–53, 169.

74 Constant, "The Spirit of Conquest and Usurpation and Their Relation to European Civilization," in his *Political Writings*, tr. and ed. Biancamaria Fontana (Cambridge: Cambridge University Presss, 1988), 71–78; and one phrase from "Des Idées D'Uniformité" in *Les 'Principes de politique' de Benjamin Constant*, Vol. 2, ed. Etienne Hofmann (Geneva: Librarie Droz, 1980), 385–89. In both these texts Constant cites Montesquieu's passage on uniformity.

75 Constant, "The Spirit of Conquest and Usurpation," in *Political Writings*, tr. and ed. Biancamaria Fontana, 106–109. Constant expands on his indictment of Mably in *Les 'Principes de politique' de Benjamin Constant*, Vol. 2, 438ff. For a recent reconsideration of Mably that partly takes up Constant's critique, see Johnson Kent Wright, *A Classical Republican in Eighteenth-Century France: The Political Thought of Mably* (Stanford, CA: Stanford University Press, 1997).

76 Constant, "Discours pour la plantation de l'arbre de la liberté," in *Oeuvres complètes*, Vol. 1, eds. Lucia Omacini and Jean-Daniel Candaux (Tübingen: Max Niemeyer Verlag, 1998), 553.

77 "Lettres de Benjamin Constant à Prosper de Barante," (February 25, 1808), ed. Baron de Barante, *Revue des deux mondes*, Vol. 34 (1906), 250. On Prosper de Barante, see Annelien de Dijn, *French Political Thought from Montesquieu to*

Tocqueville: Liberty in a Levelled Society? (Cambridge: Cambridge University Press, 2008), 101–110.

78 Benjamin Constant, *Adolphe*, tr. Leonard Tancock (London: Penguin Books, 1964), 41.

79 Cited in K. Steven Vincent, "Character, 'Sensibilité,' Sociability and Politics in Benjamin Constant's *Adolphe*," *Historical Reflections / Réflexions Historiques*, Vol. 28 No. 3 (Fall 2002), 366.

80 "On Germany," in *An Extraordinary Woman: Selected Writings of Germaine de Staël*, tr. Vivian Folkenflik (New York: Columbia University Press, 1987), 321–24. For a discussion of enthusiasm in de Staël (and its difference from fanaticism), see Lucien Jaume, *L'Individu effacé: ou le paradoxe du libéralisme français* (Paris: Éditions Fayard, 1997), 54–59.

81 "The Liberty of the Ancients Compared to That of the Moderns," in *Political Writings*, tr. and ed. Biancamaria Fontana, 326–27.

82 See James C. Mohr, "Academic Turmoil and Public Opinion: The Ross Case at Stanford," *Pacific Historical Review*, Vol. 39 No. 1 (February 1970), 39–61; and Warren J. Samuels, "The Firing of E.A. Ross from Stanford University: Injustice Compounded by Deception?" *Journal of Economic Education*, Vol. 22 No. 2 (Spring 1991), 183–90. The sociologist was E.A. Ross, but his case cannot be presented as a simple story of academic freedom and its violation. Ross was not only some sort of political activist and socialist, but also a racist and eugenicist who decried the immigration of Asian laborers. However, Stanford's vendetta against Ross began on economic grounds, as disdain for his vocal support of the Free Silver movement.

83 Hans-Joerg Tiede, *University Reform: The Founding of the American Association of University Professors* (Baltimore, MD: Johns Hopkins University Press, 2015), 29.

84 Arthur O. Lovejoy, "Reflections on the History of Ideas," *Journal of the History of Ideas*, Vol. 1 No. 1 (January 1940), 3–23.

85 Lovejoy, *The Great Chain of Being*, 312–13.

86 Arthur O. Lovejoy, "The Meaning of Romanticism for the Historian of Ideas," *Journal of the History of Ideas*, Vol. 2 No. 3 (June 1941), 257–78.

87 *Hanns Johst's Nazi Drama* Schlageter, tr. Ford B. Parkes-Perret (Stuttgart: Akademischer Verlag Hans-Dieter Heinz, 1984), 89. The Browning refers to the automatic pistol, widely adopted in Europe, that was designed by the American John Browning. Gavrilo Princip, who initiated World War I with the assassination of an archduke, used a Browning.

88 Lovejoy, *The Great Chain of Being*, 312–13.

89 Hendrik Verwoerd, cited in Sasha Polakow-Suransky, *Go Back to Where You Came From: The Backlash Against Immigration and the Fate of Western Democracy* (New York: Nation Books, 2017), 39–40.

90 See Darrin M. McMahon, *Enemies of the Enlightenment: The French Counter-Enlightenment and the Making of Modernity* (New York: Oxford University Press, 2001). For an older study, see Paul H. Beik, *The French Revolution Seen from the*

Right: Social Theories in Motion, 1789–1799 (Philadelphia, PA: American Philosophical Society, 1956).

91 Zeev Sternhell, *The Anti-Enlightenment Tradition*, tr. David Maisel (New Haven, CT: Yale University Press, 2010), 17–118.

92 Karl Mannheim, "Conservative Thought," in his *Essays on Sociology and Social Psychology*, trs. Karl Mannheim and Paul Kecskemeti, ed. Paul Kecskemeti (New York: Oxford University Press, 1953), 74–164. See, in general, Jonathan B. Knudsen, *Justus Möser and the German Enlightenment* (Cambridge: Cambridge University Press, 1986). Knudsen presents Möser as a moderate reformer with a "complicated, ambivalent attachment to the Enlightenment." (p. 149) In various writings Reiss presents him as a traditionalist. See Hans Reiss, "Justus Möser und Wilhelm von Humboldt: Konservative und liberale politische Ideen im Deutschland des 18. Jahrhunderts," *Politische Vierteljahresschrift*, Vol. 8 No. 1 (March 1967), 23–39.

93 He defends Montesquieu in this matter against one of his critics, Simon-Nicholas Henri Linguet, a French lawyer and journalist. The latter's *Théorie des loix civiles* (1767) attacks Montesquieu for equating simplification of laws and despotism. For a recent assessment of Linguet, see Amalia D. Kessler, "Searching for a 'New System' of Government: Linguet and the Rise of the Centralized, Administrative State," *Historical Reflections / Réflexions Historiques*, Vol. 28 No. 1 (Spring 2002), 93–117.

94 Justus Möser, *Patriotische Phantasien*, 2nd ed., Vol. II, ed. by I.W.J. von Voigts, Möser's daughter (Berlin: Verlag der Nicolaischen Buchhandlung, 1842), 21–24.

95 Möser, "Über die deutsche Sprache und Literatur. Schreiben an einen Freund," *Patriotische Phantasien—Ausgewählte Schriften aus den Patriotischen Phantasien* [http://gutenberg.spiegel.de/buch/patriotische-phantasien-4232/1].

96 Möser, cited in Klaus Epstein, *The Genesis of German Conservatism* (Princeton, NJ: Princeton University Press, 1966), 314.

97 Hans Baron, "Justus Mösers Individualitätsprinzip in seiner geistesgeschichtlichen Bedeutung," *Historische Zeitschrift*, Vol. 130 No. 1 (1924), 38.

98 Constant, "The Spirit of Conquest and Usurpation," *Political Writings*, tr. and ed. Biancamaria Fontana, 154–55. Constant carefully qualifies this argument. He does not want to justify injustices in the name of local mores.

99 Constant, *Les 'Principes de politique' de Benjamin Constant*, Vol. 2, 389.

100 See the chapter on Möser in Jerry Z. Muller, *The Mind and the Market: Capitalism in Modern European Thought* (New York: Anchor Books, 2003), 84–103.

101 See the discussion in Jaume, *L'individu effacé*, 86–91.

102 See Hofmann, "The Theory of the Perfectibility of the Human Race," 248–71.

103 See de Dijn, *French Political Thought from Montesquieu to Tocqueville*, 80–88.

104 Constant, "The Liberty of the Ancients Compared with That of the Moderns," *Political Writings*, tr. and ed. Biancamaria Fontana, 314–27.

CHAPTER FIVE—DIVERSITY AND ITS VICISSITUDES: THE MODERN PERIOD

1 Henry Ashby Turner Jr., *Hitler's Thirty Days to Power: January 1933* (New York: Basic Books, 1996), 161.

2 Benjamin Carter Hett, *The Death of Democracy: Hitler's Rise to Power and the Downfall of the Weimar Republic* (New York: Henry Holt, 2018), 3.

3 Richard Bessel, "The Formation and Dissolution of a German National Electorate: From Kaiserreich to Third Reich," in *Elections, Mass Politics, and Social Change in Modern Germany: New Perspectives*, eds. Larry Eugene Jones and James Retallack (Cambridge: Cambridge University Press, 1992), 403. See, in the same volume, Jürgen W. Falter, "The Social Bases of Political Cleavages in the Weimar Republic, 1919–1933), 371–97.

4 Jerome G. Kerwin, "The German Reichstag Elections of July 31, 1932," *American Political Science Review*, Vol. 26 No. 5 (October 1932), 922. The preceding issue of this journal noted that Kerwin was visiting Germany.

5 The Cambridge University historian Richard J. Evans argues against what he considers the new "conventional" view that Hitler came to power legally. For him, Hitler's rule begins with a "seizure of power." Yet he is not convincing. (See "Coercion and Consent" in Richard J. Evans, *The Third Reich in History and Memory* (New York: Oxford University Press, 2015), 87–117.)) Yes, after January 30, 1933, when Hitler was appointed chancellor, the Nazis used force to consolidate their rule, but what about before that date? To state, as Evans does, that a "power vacuum" existed in Germany; and that conservatives in the cabinet sought to "outmaneuver" Hitler when he became chancellor (which they failed to do) hardly suggests violence. The question is this: what allowed Hitler to demand, and get, the chancellorship in early 1933? Surely the answer points to Nazi popular support, even if it were ebbing.

6 J.P. Mayer, *Alexis de Tocqueville*(New York: Viking, 1940), 203.

7 Louis Napoleon, translated in Fenton Bresler, *Napoleon III: A Life* (London: HarperCollins, 1999), 229.

8 See Philippe Blachèr, "L'Étendue du suffrage universel: Sous la IIe République," *Revue Française d'Histoire des Idées Politiques*, No. 38 (2nd semester, 2013), 257–68.

9 Frederick B. Artz, "Bonapartism and Dictatorship," *South Atlantic Quarterly*, Vol. 39 No. 1 (January 1940), 40. Artz concludes by comparing Bonapartism and contemporary fascism.

10 Mayer, *Alexis de Tocqueville*, 201.

11 Constantin Frantz, in *The Impact of the 18th Brumaire*, tr. and ed. J.P. Mayer (New York: Arno Press, 1979), 5–6. This includes several texts, including those by Marx and Frantz. In 1932 and 1933 Mayer published separately Marx's book and Frantz's in editions I have not seen. But his remarks here on Marx and Frantz, sandwiched between their two texts, which are photo offsets of earlier editions, are dated 1933. The Frantz text in this Mayer 1979 collection is from a 1933 edition retitled as *Masse oder Volk: Louis Napoleon*, ed. Franz Kemper. J. Salwyn Schapiro, in *Liberalism and the Challenge of Fascism: Social Forces in England and France (1815–1870)*

(New York: Octagon Books, 1964; first edition, 1949) identifies Kemper as a Nazi. (p. 328) Iain McDaniel identifies Kemper as a pseudonym for Mayer. For this and an appraisal of Frantz, see Iain McDaniel, "Constantin Frantz and the Intellectual History of Bonapartism and Caesarism: A Reassessment," *Intellectual History Review*, Vol. 28 No. 2 (2018), 317–38 [http://dx.doi.org/10.1080/17496977.2017.1361218]. Marxists turned to Marx's *18th Brumaire* and the Louis Napoleon coup as prefiguring 20th-century fascism as early as 1922, with a contribution by the Austrian socialist Julius Braunthal, who analyzed Mussolini's 'March on Rome.' (Braunthal, "Der Putsch der Faschisten," *Der Kampf*, Vol. 15 (1922), 320–33). For a survey of these 20th-century Marxist discussions, see Wolfgang Wippermann, *Die Bonapartismustheorie von Marx und Engels* (Stuttgart: Klett-Cotta, 1983), 201–215. Schapiro, in his *Liberalism and the Challenge of Fascism: Social Forces in England and France*, compares Louis Napoleon and fascist leaders—and notes important differences. (pp. 308–331)

12 J.P. Mayer, *Political Thought in France from Sieyès to Sorel* (London: Faber and Faber, 1943), 60.

13 He did utilize Constant in his later work, *The Ancien Régime and the Revolution.* See Robert T. Gannett Jr., *Tocqueville Unveiled: The Historian and His Sources for* The Old Regime and the Revolution (Chicago: University of Chicago Press, 2003), 32–35.

14 George Armstrong Kelly, in *The Humane Comedy: Constant, Tocqueville, and French Liberalism* (Cambridge: Cambridge University Press, 1992), 3–6, carefully sifts through the evidence.

15 Constant was a sharp critic of the socialist St. Simonians—for reasons that could be anticipated: they were all about rules, regulations, and uniformity. He said the St. Simonians wanted to create an "industrial papacy." See "L'Industrie et la morale considérés dans leur rapport avec la liberté," in *Benjamin Constant, Publiciste, 1825–1830*, ed. Ephraïm Harpaz (Paris: Champion, 1987), 100–101.

16 See Alan S. Kahan, *Aristocratic Liberalism: The Social and Political Thought of Jacob Burckhardt, John Stuart Mill, and Alexis de Tocqueville* (New York: Oxford University Press, 1992); and Annelien de Dijn, *French Political Thought from Montesquieu to Tocqueville: Liberty in a Levelled Society?* (Cambridge: Cambridge University Press, 2008).

17 For instance, diversity does not figure at all in Lucien Jaume's *Tocqueville: The Aristocratic Sources of Liberty*, tr. Arthur Goldhammer (Princeton, NJ: Princeton University Press, 2013). Nor does it figure in *The Cambridge Companion to Tocqueville*, ed. Cheryl B. Welch (New York: Cambridge University Press, 2006). Arthur Kaledin mentions it several times in passing in his *Tocqueville and His America: A Darker Horizon* (New Haven, CT: Yale University Press, 2011).

18 Silvestre de Sacy, Review of *Democracy in America*, reprinted in Jaume's *Tocqueville*, tr. Arthur Goldhammer, 328.

19 Alexis de Toccqueville, "Two Weeks in the Wilderness," in *Democracy in America and Two Essays on America*, tr. Gerald E. Bevan, ed. Isaac Kramnick (London: Penguin Books, 2003), 879–80.

20 Here I'm using part of the translation of the text included in George Wilson Pierson, *Tocqueville and Beaumont in America* (New York: Oxford University Press, 1938), 236–37. The original reads, "Le niveau d'une civilisation égale a passé sur elle." Tocqueville, *Quinze jours au désert*, ed. Jean Edmond Mansion (Oxford: Clarendon Press, 1904), 7.

21 Beaumont, cited in Leo Damrosch, *Tocqueville's Discovery of America* (New York: Farrar, Straus and Giroux, 2010), 67.

22 Seymour Drescher, *Dilemmas of Democracy: Tocqueville and Modernization* (Pittsburgh, PA: University of Pittsburgh Press, 1968), 53.

23 Friedrich Engels, *The Condition of the Working Class in England*, tr. F. Kelley Wischnewetzky (New York: J.W. Lovell Co., 1887).

24 Alexis de Tocqueville, *Journeys to England and Ireland*, trs. George Lawrence and K.P. Mayer, ed. J.P. Mayer (London: Faber and Faber, 1958), 106–108. For a refreshing correction to the standard interpretation that Tocqueville ignored industrialization, see Benjamin Storey, "Tocqueville on Technology," *The New Atlantis*, No. 40 (Fall 2013), 48–71.

25 Seymour Drescher, in "Tocqueville's Two *Démocraties*," *Journal of the History of Ideas*, Vol. 25 No. 2 (April–June 1964), 201–216, argues that the two volumes fundamentally diverge in part because of the visit to England.

26 Tocqueville defended the individual but not individualism, which he saw as its antithesis. True individuality emerged in the informal networks of society, but individualism bespoke the mass democratic society characterized by isolation; here everyone pretends to be different, but everyone is the same. The historian Yehoshua Arieli noted the "paradox" that Tocqueville upheld the individual but not individualism. "Tocqueville distinguished between individuality and individualism." (Arieli, *Individualism and Nationalism in American Ideology* (Baltimore, MD: Penguin Books, 1966), 192) Tocqueville's *The Ancien Régime and the Revolution,* ed. and tr. Gerald Bevan (New York: Penguin Books, 2008) makes the case clearly. In the forward Tocqueville complains about "narrow individualism" in which shared interests and understanding recede before atomized citizens. (p. 13) Later in the book he comments that "our ancestors had no word for *individualism*, a word we have coined for our own use because, in their time, there was no individual who did not belong to a group or who could consider himself to be entirely alone." But today individualism suggests the end of the individual. "All these men standing apart from each other had become so alike one to another than you would not have seen any recognizable difference if you had made them change places." (p. 102) Tocqueville was hardly unique in drawing this distinction. "A variety of French thinkers" in the mid–19th century, writes Steven Lukes, "stressed the opposition between '*individualisme*,' implying anarchy and social atomization, and '*individualité*,' implying personal independence and self-realization." Lukes, "The Meaning of 'Individualism,'" *Journal of the History of Ideas*, Vol. 32 No. 1 (January–March 1971), 49. For a more recent discussion, see Dana Villa, "Hegel, Tocqueville, and 'Individualism,'" *Review of Politics*, Vol. 67 No. 4 (Autumn 2005), 659–86.

27 Tocqueville, *Democracy in America*, tr. Arthur Goldhammer (New York: Library of America, 2004), 829.

28 Here I'm following Seymour Drescher, "'Why Great Revolutions Will Become Rare': Tocqueville's Most Neglected Prognosis," *Journal of Modern History*, Vol. 64 No. 3 (September 1992), 429–54.

29 The chapter "Why Great Revolutions Will Become Rare" reprises these points. This chapter is also one that Tocqueville revised most thoroughly, and he contemplated various titles for it. One of these dropped titles virtually repeats an earlier one, "Why the Americans Seem So Agitated Yet are So Unchanging." Again see Drescher, "'Why Great Revolutions Will Become Rare': Tocqueville's Most Neglected Prognosis"; and the discussion in Jean-Claude Lamberti, *Tocqueville and the Two Democracies*, tr. Arthur Goldhammer (Cambridge, MA: Harvard University Press, 1989), 198–99. On this and many others matters—such as the relationship of Constant and Tocqueville—Lamberti is a thoughtful and careful commentator.

30 Tocqueville, *Democracy in America*, tr. Arthur Goldhammer, 722–24.

31 Tocqueville, *The Ancien Régime and the Revolution*, tr. Gerald Bevan, 85–89.

32 Notes cited by Lamberti, *Tocqueville and the Two Democracies*, tr. Arthur Goldhammer, 200.

33 Tocqueville, "Why Great Revolutions Will Become Rare," *Democracy in America*, tr. Arthur Goldhammer, 747–60.

34 Tocqueville, "What Kind of Despotism Democratic Nations Have to Fear," *Democracy in America*, tr. Arthur Goldhammer, 816–21.

35 Tocqueville, "Continuation of Preceding Chapters," *Democracy in America*, tr. Arthur Goldhammer, 822, 829; and "General View of the Subject," 834.

36 Mill to Aristide Guilbert, May 8, 1835, cited in Iris Wessel Mueller, *John Stuart Mill and French Thought* (Urbana, IL: University of Illinois Press, 1956), 134.

37 Cited in and see Byung-Hoon Suh, "Mill and Tocqueville: A Friendship Bruised," *History of European Ideas*, Vol. 42 No. 1 (2016), 55–72. The other careful look at their relationship is H.O. Pappe, "Mill and Tocqueville," *Journal of the History of Ideas*, Vol. 25 No. 2 (April–June 1964), 217–34.

38 Cited in André Jardin, *Tocqueville: A Biography*, trs. Lydia Davis and Robert Hemenway (New York: Farrar, Straus and Giroux, 1988), 275.

39 J.S. Mill, "Civilization," *Essays on Politics and Culture*, ed. Gertrude Himmelfarb (Garden City, NY: Doubleday, 1963), 56, 60–61.

40 John Stuart Mill, *London Review*, in Tocqueville, *Democracy in America*, tr. Henry Reeves, ed. Isaac Kramnick (New York: W.W. Norton & Company, 2007), 681.

41 Mill, "M. de Tocqueville on Democracy in America," in *The Philosophy of John Stuart Mill*, ed. Marshall Cohen (New York: Modern Library, 1961), 136.

42 Ibid., 169. The passage quoted is from Volume 2, Book 4, Chapter VII of *Democracy in America*, but Mills altered the translation.

43 Ibid., 172–77.

44 Michael Levin, who bucks the trend, makes this same point in his *J.S. Mill on Civilization and Barbarism* (London: Routledge, 2004), 125.

45 John Collwyn Rees, *John Stuart Mill's* On Liberty (Oxford: Clarendon Press, 1985), 148.

46 Alan Ryan, *The Philosophy of John Stuart Mill* (London: Macmillan, 1987), 234, 240.

47 *The Cambridge Companion to Mill*, ed. John Skorupski (Cambridge: Cambridge University Press, 1998). In the *Companion*'s 600 pages Humboldt appears twice in passing. A more recent anthology has no mention of Humboldt. See *J.S. Mill's Political Thought: A Bicentennial Reassessment*, eds. Nadia Urbinati and Alex Zakaras (New York: Cambridge University Press, 2007). Conversely, scholars of Humboldt pay close attention to Mill and his relationship to Humboldt. See, for instance, John Roberts, *Wilhelm von Humboldt and German Liberalism: A Reassessment* (Oakville, Ontario: Mosaic Press, 2015), 91–115.

48 R.H. Hutton in *The National Review* (1859), p. 81, as reprinted along with other reviews in *Liberty: Contemporary Responses to John Stuart Mill*, ed. Andrew Pyle (Bristol: Thoemmes Press, 1994).

49 J.S. Mill, *Autobiography*, in *Collected Works of John Stuart Mill*, Vol. 1, eds. John M Robson and Jack Stillinger (Indianapolis, IN: Liberty Fund, 2006), 259.

50 Richard Reeves, "John Stuart Mill," *Salmagundi*, No. 153–54 (Winter–Spring 2007), 48; and see his *John Stuart Mill: Victorian Firebrand* (London: Atlantic Books, 2007).

51 David Stack, "The Death of John Stuart Mill," *The Historical Journal*, Vol. 54 No. 1 (March 2011), 169.

52 John Stuart Mill, *On Liberty*, ed. Gertrude Himmelfarb (Middlesex: Penguin Books, 1985), 120–21.

53 For a discussion of Mill's use of China, see Robert Kurfirst, "John Stuart Mill's Asian Parable," *Canadian Journal of Political Science / Revue canadienne de science politique*, Vol. 34 No. 3 (September 2001), 601–619.

54 Mill, *On Liberty*, ed. Gertrude Himmelfarb, Chap. III, 119–40.

55 Anon., *Saturday Review* (February 19, 1859), in *Liberty: Contemporary Responses to John Stuart Mill*, ed. Andrew Pyle, 20.

56 Cited from his journal in G. Otto Trevelyan, *The Life and Letters of Lord Macaulay*, Vol. 2 (New York: Harper & Brothers, 1875), 385–86. See Robert E. Sullivan, *Macaulay: The Tragedy of Power* (Cambridge: Harvard University Press, 2009), 461–62.

57 Anon., *British Quarterly Review* (1860), reprinted in Mill, *On Liberty*, ed. Edward Alexander (Peterborough, Canada: Broadview Press, 1999), 218.

58 James Fitzjames Stephen, *Liberty, Equality, Fraternity* [first edition: 1873] (Chicago: University of Chicago Press, 1991), 83–84.

59 L.S. [Leslie Stephen], "Social Macadamisation," *Fraser's Magazine*, Vol. 86 (1872), 150–68.

60 For a discussion of character in mid-Victorian thought, see Stefan Collini, *Public Moralists: Political Thought and Intellectual Life in Britain, 1850–1930* (Oxford: Clarendon Press, 1991), 91–118.

61 J.S. Mill, *Autobiography*, in *Collected Works of John Stuart Mill*, Vol. 1, eds. John M. Robson and Jack Stillinger, 259–60.

62 I'm combining texts from two translations: Constantine Leontyev, "The Average European as an Ideal and Instrument of Universal Destruction," in *Russian Philosophy*, Vol. 2, trs. George Kline and William Shafer, eds. James M. Edie et al. (Chicago: Quadrangle Books, 1965), 272–73; and a different version in *Against the Current: Selections from the Novels, Essays, Notes, and Letters of Konstantin Leontiev*, tr. George Reavey, ed. George Ivask (New York: Weybright and Talley, 1969), 173.

63 Leontyev, "The Average European," trs. George Kline and William Shafer, eds. Edie et al., in *Russian Philosophy*, Vol. 2, 270.

64 Nicolas Berdyaev, *Leontiev*, tr. George Reavey (Orono, ME: Academic International, 1968), 86.

65 Leontiev, cited in Stephen Lukashevich, *Konstantin Leontev (1831–1891): A Study in 'Heroic Vitalism'* (New York: Pageant Press, 1967), 124.

66 Leontiev, cited in Ibid., 110. For a good overview of Leontiev, see Sidney Monas, "Leontiev: A Meditation," *Journal of Modern History*, Vol. 43 No. 3 (September 1971), 483–94.

67 Alexander Herzen, *From the Other Shore and The Russian People and Socialism*, trs. Moura Budberg and Richard Wollheim (New York: Meridian Books, 1963), 6.

68 Ibid., 93–95.

69 Herzen, "The Provisional Government and the Revolution," in Herzen, *Letters from France and Italy, 1847–1851*, tr. and ed. Judith E. Zimmermann (Pittsburgh, PA: University of Pittsburgh Press, 1995), 262–63.

70 Herzen, cited in E.H. Carr, *The Romantic Exiles* (London: Serif Publishing, 2007), 119.

71 All of this is recounted with admirable insight and subtlety in Carr's *Romantic Exiles*, first published in 1933.

72 Martin Malia, *Alexander Herzen and the Birth of Russian Socialism* (New York: Grosset & Dunlap, 1965), 14.

73 Jane Caryle, cited from the Carlyle Papers in Monica Partridge, *Alexander Herzen: Collected Studies* (Nottingham: Astra Press, 1993), 105. This is written to Jane's brother, not her husband, to whom she wrote a tamer version.

74 Herzen, *My Past and Thoughts: The Memoirs of Alexander Herzen*, Vol. 3, tr. Constance Garnett (London: Chatto & Windus, 1968), 1076–1077.

75 Mill, *On Liberty*, ed. Gertrude Himmelfarb, 136–37.

76 Herzen, cited in Aileen M. Kelly, *The Discovery of Chance: The Life and Thought of Alexander Herzen* (Cambridge, MA: Harvard University Press, 2016), 429.

77 Herzen, *My Past and Thoughts*, Vol. 3, tr. Constance Garnett, 1085.

78 Ibid., 1082.

79 Cited in Lukashevich, *Konstantin Leontev*, 49–51.

80 Hans Baron, "Burckhardt's 'Civilization of the Renaissance' a Century after Its Publication," *Renaissance News*, Vol. 13 No. 3 (Autumn 1960), 207.

81 Jonathan Jones, "Jacob Burckhardt: The Renaissance Revisited," *The Guardian*, July 9, 2010.

82 J.P. Mayer, "Jakob Burckhardt, or The Flight from Politics," *Dublin Review*, Vol. 105 No. 418 (July–September 1941), 42.

83 Albert Salomon, "Crisis, History and the Image of Man," *Review of Politics*, Vol. 2 No. 4 (October 1940), 417.

84 Jacob Burckhardt, *The Civilization of the Renaissance in Italy*, tr. S.G.C. Middlemore (London: Penguin Books, 2004), 99.

85 Lionel Gossman, *Basel in the Age of Burckhardt: A Study in Unseasonable Ideas* (Chicago: University of Chicago Press, 2000), 243. This is an exemplary study.

86 *Jacob Burckhardts Briefe an seinen Freund Friedrich von Preen, 1864–1893* (Stuttgart: Deutsche Verlags-Anstalt, 1922), 24 (July 20, 1870).

87 Burckhardt, cited in Mayer, "Jakob Burckhardt," 40.

88 Burckhardt, cited in Gossman, "Jacob Burckhardt: Cold War Liberal?" *Journal of Modern History*, Vol. 74 No. 3 (September 2002), 548, 552.

89 Burckhardt, cited in Gossman, *Basel in the Age of Burckhardt*, 246. For two recent studies that deal with these issues, see Richard Sigurdson, *Jacob Burckhardt's Social and Political Thought* (Toronto: University of Toronto Press, 2004), esp. 136–44; and John R. Hinde, *Jacob Burckhardt and the Crisis of Modernity* (Montreal: McGill-Queen's University Press, 2000).

90 Oliver Zimmer, *A Contested Nation: History, Memory and Nationalism in Switzerland, 1761–1891* (Cambridge: Cambridge University Press, 2003), 89.

91 Jacob Burckhardt, *On History and Historians*, tr. Harry Zohn (New York: Harper & Row, 1965), 266. The German phrase for "everything varied and different" was "alles Vielartige und Verschiedene." J. Burckhardt, *Historische Fragmente*, ed. by Emil Dürr (Stuttgart: K.F. Koehler Verlag, 1957), 318. Kahan emphasizes the role of diversity in Burckhardt's thought; see Kahan, *Aristocratic Liberalism*, 104–105.

92 For a thorough appraisal, see Niall Bond, "'Gemeinschaft und Gesellschaft': The Reception of a Conceptual Dichotomy," *Contributions to the History of Concepts*, Vol. 5 No. 2 (2009), 162–86.

93 For his politics and plans for a community of scholars, see Arthur Mitzman, *Sociology and Estrangement: Three Sociologists of Imperial Germany* (New York: Knopf, 1973), 84–94.

94 Friedrich Paulsen, *An Autobiography*, tr. Theodor Lorenz (New York: Columbia University Press, 1938), 329–30.

95 Adam Smith, *An Inquiry into the Nature and Causes of the Wealth of Nations*, Vol. I (London: W. Strahan and T. Cadell, 1776), 27.

96 Ferdinand Tönnies, *Community and Society (Gemeinschaft und Gesellschaft)*, tr. and ed. Charles P. Loomis (New York: Harper & Row, 1963), 76–81. See David Inglis, "Tönnies and Globalization," in *The Anthem Companion to Ferdinand Tönnies*, ed. Christopher Adair-Toteff (London: Anthem Press, 2016), 79–98.

97 Tarde, cited in and see René Worms, "La Philosophie sociale de G. Tarde," *Revue Philosophique de la France et de l'Étranger*, Vol. 60 (July–December 1905), 136.

98 Tönnies to Friedrich Paulsen, as cited in Rudolph Binion, *Frau Lou: Nietzsche's Wayward Disciple* (Princeton, NJ: Princeton University Press, 1968), 116.

99 Gabriel Tarde, *The Laws of Imitation*, tr. Elsie Clews Parsons (Gloucester, MA: Peter Smith, 1962), 383–93. Tarde apparently had hopes for this transformation, since he later wrote a utopian novel that develops these ideas. The last two chapters of his utopian novel, *Underground Man*, are titled "Love" and "The Aesthetic Life." Both love and aesthetics flourish in Tarde's utopia, which exists underground after the sun has burnt out. His new society rests on "our devotion to beauty and our faith in the divine omnipotence of love . . . the starting point of our enthusiasms." In the "glittering and superficial epochs" that preceded ours, the "age of paper and electro-plating" and of a "contagious monomania" of luxury and globetrotting, "love was held in check." Now, he writes, love is liberated. Tarde, *Underground Man*, tr. Cloudesley Brereton (London: Duckworth & Co., 1905), 144–45, 172.

100 Émile Durkheim, *The Division of Labor in Society*, tr. George Simpson (New York: Free Press, 1964), 142.

101 Ibid., 136.

102 Ibid., 136–39.

103 Tyler Cowen, *Creative Destruction: How Globalization is Changing the World's Cultures* (Princeton, NJ: Princeton University Press, 2002), 14–16, 128.104 Adam Smith, *The Wealth of Nations*, ed. Alan B. Krueger (New York: Bantam Dell, 2003), 987–88 (Book V, Chapter 1, Article 2d).

105 Émile Durkheim, *Suicide: A Study in Sociology*, trs. John A. Spaulding and George Simpson (Glencoe, IL: The Free Press, 1951).

106 Henry [Enrico] Morselli, *Suicide: An Essay on Comparative Moral Statistics*, tr. and abridged by the author (London: C. Kegan Paul, 1881). Thomas [Tomá š] G. Masaryk, *Suicide as a Social Mass Phenomenon of Modern Civilization*, trs. William B. Weist and Robert G. Batson (Chicago: University of Chicago Press, 1970).

107 See Howard I. Kushner, "Suicide, Gender, and the Fear of Modernity in Nineteenth-Century Medical and Social Thought," *Journal of Social History*, Vol. 26 No. 3 (Spring 1993), 461–90.

108 See, in general, Charles E. Marske, "Durkheim's 'Cult of the Individual' and the Moral Reconstitution of Society," *Sociological Theory*, Vol. 5 No. 1 (Spring 1987), 1–14. The last part of *The Division of Labor* takes up "abnormal forms" that lead to social breakdown, but Durkheim's whole point is that these forms are "exceptional," that is, deviation from the normal solidarity.

109 See W.S.F. Pickering, "The Enigma of Durkheim's Jewishness," in *Debating Durkheim*, eds. W.S.F. Pickering and H. Martins (Abingdon, Oxon: Routledge, 1994), 37.

110 Émile Durkheim, "Anti-Semitism and Social Crisis" [1899], tr. and ed. Chad Alan Goldberg, *Sociological Theory*, Vol. 26 No. 4 (December 2008), 299–323.

111 Ibid., 322.

112 Durkheim to Bouglé, cited in Pierre Birnbaum, "French Jewish Sociologists between Reason and Faith: The Impact of the Dreyfus Affair," *Jewish Social Studies*, New Series, Vol. 2 No. 1 (Autumn 1995), 7. For a careful discussion of Durkheim, his Judaism, and his role in the Dreyfus Affair, see this piece as well as Pickering's "The Enigma of Durkheim's Jewishness," 10–39.

113 Steven Lukes, "Durkheim's 'Individualism and the Intellectuals,'" *Political Studies*, Vol. 17 No. 1 (March 1969), 25. This article includes the text of Durkheim's essay.
114 Durkheim to Paul Lapie and Durkheim to Bouglé, both cited in Birnbaum, "French Jewish Sociologists between Reason and Faith," 17, 7.
115 J.S. McClelland, *The Crowd and the Mob: From Plato to Canetti* (London: Unwin Hyman, 1989), 138.
116 Gustave Le Bon, *The Crowd: A Study of the Popular Mind*, tr. uncredited (Mineola, NY: Dover Publications, 2002), xii–xiv.
117 See Robert A. Nye, *The Origins of Crowd Psychology: Gustave Le Bon and the Crisis of Mass Democracy in the Third Republic* (London: SAGE Publications, 1975), 177–79.
118 Hans Joas, Introduction to Emil Lederer, "On the Sociology of World War" [1915], tr. Austin Harrington, ed. Hans Joas, *European Journal of Sociology / Archives Européennes de Sociologie / Europäisches Archiv für Soziologie*, Vol. 47 No. 2 (2006), 241.
119 Hans Speier, Foreword to Emil Lederer, *State of the Masses: The Threat of a Classless Society* (New York: W.W. Norton and Company, 1940), 15.
120 Lederer, *State of the Masses*, 153–55, 72–73.
121 Lederer, "On the Sociology of World War" [1915], tr. Austin Harrington, ed. Hans Joas, 266, 247, 249. For a recent appreciation of Lederer, see Daniel R. Huebner, "Toward a Sociology of the State and War: Emil Lederer's Political Sociology," *European Journal of Sociology / Archives Européennes de Sociologie*, Vol. 49 No. 1 (April 2008), 65–90; and the introduction by Claus-Dieter Krohn to the German translation of the *State of the Masses, Der Massenstaat. Gefahren der klassenlosen Gesellschaft*, tr. Angela Kornberger (Graz-Vienna: Nausner & Nausner, 1995), 9–44.
122 Bourne, cited in Louis Filler, *Randolph Bourne* (New York: Citadel Press, 1966), 53.
123 Christopher McKnight Nichols, "Rethinking Randolph Bourne's Trans-National America: How World War I Created an Isolationist Antiwar Pluralism," *Journal of the Gilded Age and Progressive Era*, Vol. 8 No. 2 (April 2009), 218.
124 Philip Gleason remains a good guide to these debates. See his *Speaking of Diversity: Language and Ethnicity in Twentieth-Century America* (Baltimore, MD: Johns Hopkins University Press, 1992).
125 Randolph Bourne, "Trans-National America," *War and the Intellectuals: Collected Essays, 1915–1919*, ed. Carl Resek (New York: Harper & Row, 1964), 107–108.
126 Randolph Bourne, "The Handicapped," *The Radical Will: Selected Writings, 1911–1918*, ed. Olaf Hansen (New York: Urizen Books, 1977), 73–74.
127 Kallen, quoted in Daniel Greene, "A Chosen People in a Pluralist Nation: Horace Kallen and the Jewish-American Experience," *Religion and American Culture: A Journal of Interpretation*, Vol. 16 No. 2 (Summer 2006), 165.
128 Leonard Harris and Charles Molesworth, *Alain L. Locke: Biography of a Philosopher* (Chicago: University of Chicago Press, 2008), 5.
129 Alain Locke, "Pluralism and Ideological Peace," *The Works of Alain Locke*, ed. Charles Molesworth , Forward by Henry Louis Gates Jr.(New York: Oxford University Press, 2012), 567. It is a bit extraordinary that this volume, which Gates

calls in his forward "the definitive collection of Alain Locke's work," offers virtually no information as to where and when these various pieces were written. Locke died in 1954, and his writings span decades. In this regard, an earlier collection is superior: *The Philosophy of Alain Locke: Harlem Renaissance and Beyond*, ed. Leonard Harris (Philadelphia, PA: Temple University Press, 1989).

130 This phrase comes from an autobiographical note cited by Kallen in "Alain Locke and Cultural Pluralism," *Journal of Philosophy*, Vol. 54 No. 5 (February 28, 1957), 121.

131 William James, *The Will to Believe and Other Essays*, in *Pragmatism and Other Essays*, ed. Joseph L. Blau (New York: Washington Square Press, 1963), 187–88.

132 James, "On a Certain Blindness in Human Beings," *Pragmatism and Other Essays*, ed. Joseph L. Blau, 269.

133 James, *The Varieties of Religious Experience* (New York: Longmans, Green, and Co., 1902).

134 James, "A Pluralistic Mystic," in James, *Writings 1902–1910* (New York: Library of America, 1987), 1310.

135 Ibid., 1295. Kallen later edited a book by Blood and cited this same passage in his introduction. See Benjamin Paul Blood, *Pluriverse: An Essay in the Philosophy of Pluralism*, Introduction by Horace Meyer Kallen (London: Kegan Paul, Trench, Trubner and Co., 1920), xix. On James's politics and anti-imperialism, see Jonathan M. Hansen, *The Lost Promise of Patriotism: Debating American Identity, 1890–1920* (Chicago: University of Chicago Press, 2003), 29–38.

136 *The Philosophy of William James: Drawn from His Own Works*, ed. Horace M. Kallen (New York: Modern Library, 1925), 310–11.

137 James, *A Pluralistic Universe*, in James, *Writings 1902–1910*, 776.

138 "Cultural pluralism is an analogue of political pluralism, and the American idea of political pluralism was also inspired by James." Louis Menand, *The Metaphysical Club: A Story of Ideas in America* (New York: Farrar, Straus and Giroux, 2001), 379. "The metaphysical pluralism that was James's became the cultural pluralism of Kallen." Milton R. Konvitz, "Horace Meyer Kallen (1882–1974): Philosopher of the Hebraic-American Idea," *American Jewish Year Book*, Vol. 75 (1974–75), 63.

139 Bourne, "Trans-National America," *War and the Intellectuals*, ed. Carl Resek, 117.

140 Kallen, "Alain Locke and Cultural Pluralism," 119.

141 Horace Kallen, "Democracy versus Melting-Pot," *Culture and Democracy in the United States* (New York: Boni and Liveright, 1924), 115–24.

142 Kallen, *Culture and Democracy in the United States,* 61.

143 Ibid., 41–43.

144 Henry Louis Gates Jr., Foreword to *The Works of Alain Locke*, ed. Charles Molesworth, viii.

145 For a discussion of the tombstone and Locke's relations to Baha'i, see David Weinfeld, "Isolated Believer: Alain Locke, Baha'i Secularist," in *New Perspectives on the Black Intellectual Tradition,* eds. Keisha N. Blain, Christopher Cameron, and Ashley D. Farmer (Evanston, IL: Northwestern University Press, 2018), esp. 95–96.

146 These quotations are from two manuscripts unpublished during Bourne's lifetime, "The State" and "Disillusionment," included in *The Radical Will*, ed. Olaf Hansen, 356, 360, 366, 405.

147 Everett Helmut Akam, *Transnational America: Cultural Pluralistic Thought in the Twentieth Century* (Lanham, MD: Rowman & Littlefield Publishers, 2002), 102.

148 For a recent appraisal of Kallen, see Werner Sollors, *Challenges of Diversity: Essays on America* (New Brunswick, NJ: Rutgers University Press, 2017), 121–43. See also David Weinfeld, "What Difference Does Difference Make? Horace Kallen, Alain Locke, and the Birth of Cultural Pluralism," which responds to criticism of Kallen by Sollors and others [in *Philosophic Values and World Citizenship : Locke to Obama and Beyond*, eds. Jacoby Adeshei Carter and Leonard Harris (Lanham, MD: Lexington Books, 2010), 165–88].

149 John Higham, *Strangers in the Land: Patterns of American Nativism, 1860–1925* (New York: Atheneum, 1963), 329–30. This is the second edition; the first was published in 1955.

150 Stephen J. Whitfield, "The Mystique of Multiculturalism," *Virginian Quarterly Review*, Vol. 72 No. 3 (Summer 1996), 429.

151 Kallen, *Culture and Democracy in the United States*, 122–23.

152 Kallen, cited in and see the discussion in Greene, "A Chosen People in a Pluralist Nation," 178. Also see Greene's book, which notes that Kallen later departed from the biological interpretation of pluralism: Daniel Greene, *The Jewish Origins of Cultural Pluralism: The Menorah Association and American Diversity* (Bloomington, IN: Indiana University Press, 2011), 183; and Noam Pianko's piece which challenges the biological reading of Kallen: "'The True Liberalism of Zionism': Horace Kallen, Jewish Nationalism, and the Limits of American Pluralism," *American Jewish History*, Vol. 94 No. 4 (December 2008), 299–329.

153 "It was not his father or grandfather who informed Kallen's Jewish identity, but his adopted (and non-Jewish) ancestors Barrett Wendell [a Harvard professor] and William James." Greene, *The Jewish Origins of Cultural Pluralism*, 78. Nor did Kallen's own children and grandchildren stick to the Jewish faith. The memorial for his son, David J. Kallen, a sociologist who died in 2009, was held in an Episcopalian Church. [https://www.legacy.com/obituaries/lsj/obituary.aspx?page=lifestory&pid=126492704] One of David J. Kallen's sons, Hugh Kallen, has served as a pastor in a Protestant church; videos of his sermons at Bluffton Church in Michigan can be found on YouTube.

EPILOGUE

1 Constant, *Political Writings*, tr. and ed. Biancamaria Fontana (Cambridge: Cambridge University Press, 1988), 76–77.

2 Alejandro Páez Varela, cited in Jon Lee Anderson, "Boundary Issues," *New Yorker*, October 9, 2017, 28. See also Andrew Jacobs and Matt Richtel, "A Nasty, Nafta-Related Surprise: Mexico's Soaring Obesity," *New York Times*, December 12, 2017, https://www.nytimes.com/2017/12/11/health/obesity-mexico-nafta.html.

3 UCLA College of Letters and Science, "Report from the Diversity Initiative Implementation Committee," September 19, 2014, http://www.uei.ucla.edu/wp-content/uploads/2018/02/3-implementation-committee-report.pdf.

4 Thomas Carlyle, "Signs of the Times," *Selected Writings*, ed. Alan Shelston (Middlesex: Penguin Books, 1971), 59–86.

5 Irving Kristol, *Two Cheers for Capitalism* (New York: Basic Books, 1978). For a survey of American conservative anti-capitalist thought, see Peter Kolozi, *Conservatives Against Capitalism* (New York: Columbia University Press, 2017). Kolozi considers Kristol to be among such critics.

6 Robert Lindner, *Must You Conform?* (New York: Grove Press, 1956).

7 T. W. Adorno, "Cultural Criticism and Society," *Prisms*, trs. Samuel and Shierry Weber (London: Neville Spearman, 1967), 19.

8 Kraus, cited in Harry Zohn, *Karl Kraus and the Critics* (Columbia, SC: Camden House, 1997), 19. Translation slightly altered—the original German quote is from *Die Fackel*, No. 315–16 (January 26, 1911), 13 (Web); and Karl Kraus, "Nestroy and Posterity," *The Kraus Project*, tr. and ed. Jonathan Franzen (New York: Farrar, Straus & Giroux, 2013), 251.

9 Alexander Mitscherlich, *Massenpsychologie ohne Ressentiment* (Frankfurt: Suhrkamp, 1972), 44. Translation from Frankfurt Institute for Social Research, *Aspects of Sociology*, tr. John Viertel (Boston: Beacon Press, 1972), 72.

10 Gilles Lipovetsky, *The Empire of Fashion: Dressing Modern Democracy*, tr. Catherine Porter (Princeton, NJ: Princeton University Press, 1994), 123–24.

11 Tocqueville's career as a politico included some unsavory chapters in which he supported censorship and suppression of the Left. He partially redeemed himself in his arrest protesting the coup of Louis Napoleon. For a careful accounting, see Sharon B. Watkins, *Alexis de Tocqueville and the Second Republic, 1848–1852: A Study in Political Practice and Principles* (Lanham, MD: University Press of America, 2003).

12 Cited in Alfred Werner, "Romain Rolland's Letters to Elie Walach," *Jewish Quarterly*, Vol. 3 No. 1 (1955), 7. Walach, a young Polish-French Jew, was captured and executed by the Nazis in 1942. The phrase "optimism of the will, pessimism of the intellect" is often attributed to Antonio Gramsci, but derives from Rolland—specifically, from Rolland's review of Raymond-Louis Lefebvre's *The Sacrifice of Abraham*, published in *L'Humanité*, March 19, 1920, 1. See David James Fisher, "Conclusion: Pessimism of the Intelligence, Optimism of the Will" in his study *Romain Rolland and the Politics of Intellectual Engagement* (Berkeley, CA: University of California Press, 1988), 292–303.

Index

ABOUT THE AUTHOR

Russell Jacoby's books range in topic from the place of psychology in American society (*Social Amnesia: A Critique of Conformist Psychology*) to the role of utopian thought (*The End of Utopia: Politics and Culture in the Age of Apathy*) and the origins of violence (*Bloodlust: On the Roots of Violence from Cain and Abel to the Present*). His *The Last Intellectuals: American Culture in the Age of Academe* introduced a term that has been picked up everywhere—"public intellectual"—and is considered an essential text in American letters. Originally from New York, he has a Ph.D. in history from the University of Rochester, where he worked with Christopher Lasch. He lives in Los Angeles and teaches history at UCLA. In 2017 Jacoby was short-listed for the *Times Literary Supplement*'s All Authors Must Have Prizes Prize.